WITNESSES TO FAITH?

11 September 2001 in New York; 11 March 2004 in Madrid; 7 July 2005 in London: these dates remind us that suicide bombings, or 'martyrdom operations', have become the common coin of international politics in the West.

What exactly is meant by 'martyrdom' today, whether in Islam or Christianity? This book tries to give an answer. Muslim and Christian scholars come together to find a common understanding, based on the scriptures and traditions of each faith, of martyrdom in today's violent world. Part One presents the historical background and contemporary relevance of each tradition. Part Two asks whether martyrs from one tradition could be recognized as such by the other, as well as discussing the practice of 'venerating' martyrs and examining two dramas of martyrdom by twentieth century writers. Part Three includes a study of martyrdom in Shia Islam and some short studies of past and present suicidal operations. Three appendices reproduce some classic discussions of martyrdom frequently referred to in the book, plus a plea for non-violent options within the Muslim tradition.

This book is dedicated to the memory of Sir Arthur Hockaday, who died while it was in preparation. He was second permanent under-secretary of state in the British Ministry of Defence from 1976 to 1982, and director-general of the Commonwealth War Graves Commission from 1982 to 1989. Arthur served with great distinction as chairman of the Council on Christian Approaches to Defence and Disarmament from 1989 to 1999, and made many contributions to its research and publications, especially on the ethical difficulties of defence policy and the conduct of war in the nuclear age. The authors of this book remember him with much respect and affection, and wish to remind their readers of his work for justice and peace.

Witnesses to Faith?

Martyrdom in Christianity and Islam

Edited by

BRIAN WICKER
*Chairman of the Council on Christian Approaches to Defence
and Disarmament (CCADD), UK*

ASHGATE

Published by
Ashgate Publishing Limited
Gower House
Croft Road
Aldershot
Hampshire GU11 3HR
England

Ashgate Publishing Company
Suite 420
101 Cherry Street
Burlington, VT 05401-4405
USA

Ashgate website: http://www.ashgate.com

British Library Cataloguing in Publication Data
Witnesses to faith? : martyrdom in Christianity and Islam
   1. Martyrdom – Christianity 2. Martyrdom – Islam 3. Martyrdom
   I. Wicker, Brian, 1929–
   272

Library of Congress Cataloging-in-Publication Data
Witnesses to faith? : the concept of martyrdom in Christianity and Islam / edited by Brian Wicker for the Council on Christian Approaches to Defence and disarmament.
       p. cm.
  Includes bibliographical references and index.
  ISBN 0-7546-5667-5 (hardcover : alk. paper)
  1. Martyrdom. 2. Martyrdom—Christianity. 3. Martyrdom—Islam. I. Wicker, Brian, 1929– II. Council on Christian Approaches to Defence and Disarmament.

  BL626.5.W58 2006
  272—dc22

2005026509

ISBN-10: 0-7546-5667-5

Typeset in Times by J.L. & G.A. Wheatley Design, Aldershot, Hampshire.
Printed and bound in Great Britain by TJ International Ltd, Padstow, Cornwall.

Contents

PART THREE

APPENDICES

List of Contributors

Dr Asma Afsaruddin, Associate Professor of Arabic and Islamic Studies, University of Notre Dame, is the author and editor of three books, and has written numerous articles on various aspects of Islamic thought. Currently she is investigating competing perspectives on *jihad* and martyrdom, with a Harry Frank Guggenheim grant.

Dr Maha Azzam is Associate Fellow at the Royal Institute of International Affairs, London, and formerly Associate Fellow of the Royal United Services Institute.

Dr Peter Bishop, a Methodist minister and a specialist in the history of religions, was formerly head of the Department of Humanities at the University of Brighton. A former presbyter of the Church of South India, he worked in Tamilnadu for seven years.

Abolfazl Ezzati has taught at the University of Tehran and is the author of *The Spread of Islam* (1976).

Dr Richard Finn OP is a Dominican friar and Regent of Blackfriars Hall, Oxford, where he teaches Church History. He is a member of the Theology Faculty at the University of Oxford.

Harfiyah Haleem gained an MA in English from Oxford University and another in Islamic Studies from the School of Oriental and African Studies (SOAS), University of London. She is a freelance writer, editor and broadcaster on Islam. Formerly she worked for 14 years with the IQRA Trust (a UK educational charity) on Islam and, before that, at the Centre for Islamic Studies in Oxford.

Dr Anthony Harvey was formerly Canon of Westminster Abbey and Lecturer in Theology in the University of Oxford.

Michael Smart, a former senior civil servant, was International Affairs Secretary of the British Council of Churches from 1986 to 1990. He is an Anglican layman who is also an attender at a local Society of Friends meeting.

Brian Wicker holds masters degrees in English (Oxford), Philosophy (Birmingham) and War Studies (King's College, London). He is Chairman of CCADD and was formerly a senior lecturer at Birmingham University and, latterly, Principal of Fircroft College of Adult Education, Selly Oak.

Foreword

In the Christian tradition the word 'martyr' is integrally related to the Greek word for 'witness'. Martyrs are those who witness not just by their lives, but by their deaths, to the truth in which they believe. Within the early Church, martyrs were the great heroes of the faith, and significant shrines and churches were built in their honour.

In the modern world, the concept of martyrdom has once again come to the fore through suicide bombers who have been exhorted to act in this way on behalf of their faith. These bombers have raised questions in many people's minds about the validity of the whole concept of martyrdom. Indeed, it has been suggested that many of the early Christians were too eager, almost clamouring, to go to their deaths.

In a world where there is so much misunderstanding and where misunderstanding between religions is particularly dangerous, it's very good to have this serious and scholarly study of martyrdom in both Christianity and Islam. It will help all of us to be better informed and be less at the mercy of our prejudices and stereotypes.

Richard Harries
Bishop of Oxford
President of the Council on Christian Approaches to
Defence and Disarmament (CCADD)

Preface

This book was in the final stages of preparation when the London bombs went off on 7 July 2005. While it was too late to discuss those particular atrocities and the ideological motivations behind them within the main body of our text, we hope that our work will be of some use in helping people to understand the genuine Muslim tradition of martyrdom, and how it has been perverted under the slogan of 'martyrdom operations' in the context of actions such as those of Madrid, Bali and 11 September, as well as of the appalling atrocities being committed almost daily in Iraq, Israel and many other places.

It seems clear that the London explosions were the work of suicide bombers whose 'rationale' (if we can dignify their acts by the use of this term) was in some sense 'Islamic', despite such self-justification being dismissed with disgust by the vast majority of Muslims in Britain. Yet one commentator, Donald Macintyre (in *The Independent*, 13 July 2005), has already quoted Abdul Rahman Makdad, a notorious organizer of earlier bombings in Jerusalem, in these terms: 'The easiest thing is to find a martyr. In our nation we have thousands of people who want to be martyrs.' On the other hand, in a statement issued by a group of senior Muslim leaders in Britain, from the Central Mosque in London, on 15 July, it was affirmed unanimously that 'those who carried out the bombings in London should in no sense be regarded as martyrs'. As this is being written, a group of Sunni Muslims is set to issue a *fatwa* outlawing suicide bombing as a 'crime against humanity'. The secretary-general of the British Muslim Forum, Gul Mohammed, says this *fatwa* will proclaim that 'those who die in such acts do not die a death of martyrdom'.[1]

Part of the purpose of this book is to counteract a false ideology of martyrdom wherever it rears its head. Millions of words are certain to be written in commentary on, and analysis of, the latest atrocities in London and their antecedents, if only because they happened in a large Western city in which people have not (yet!) got used to such things. Many commentators will dwell on the role of an 'Islamic' allegiance to explain or even excuse such acts. We hope that our discussion of the true history and theology of martyrdom in Islam and Christianity will help readers deepen their understanding of what is at stake in today's world, and thus perhaps lessen the chances of such atrocities being repeated in the future. Anyhow, we hope that our book will be understood in some small way as a memorial to all the victims of suicide attacks, and as an expression of solidarity with their families and friends.

This book is the product of discussion between a group of Muslim and Christian scholars over a period of several years. As a group, we wish to acknowledge joint 'ownership' of Parts One and Two of the book. The chapters alternate between Muslim and Christian approaches. After an introduction which discusses the ideas raised on both sides, Part One contains substantial studies of the concept of martyrdom in the early phase of each tradition, by Dr Asma Afsaruddin (for Islam) and Dr Anthony Harvey, Dr Richard Finn and Michael Smart (for Christianity). These chapters lead to a more philosophical/ theological consideration of martyrdom in Islam by Harfiyah Haleem. Part Two, which is concerned with a further exploration of the principles raised in Part One, begins by envisaging a widening of the concept of martyrdom, in the light of twenty-first-century experience, to permit the possibility by each faith of acknowledging martyrs from the other (Brian Wicker). (This theme is explored further in Appendix 2.) A 'dialogue' representing the two approaches to the subject of the 'veneration' of martyrs then follows (Harfiyah Haleem and Brian Wicker), leading to a study of two twentieth-century dramas of martyrdom: T.S. Eliot's *Murder in the Cathedral* (1935) and al-Sabur's *Murder in Baghdad* (1965) (Brian Wicker). Part Three begins with a reprinted essay on a distinctive approach to martyrdom from a Shia perspective, and is followed by three short studies of suicidal terrorist activities, respectively those by the Japanese kamikaze, the Tamil Tigers and Palestinian militants. Finally there are three useful appendices:

1   the treatment of martyrdom (in English) by St Thomas Aquinas from the *Summa Theologiae* (a classic text referred to by several of the authors quoted);
2   a reprint of an important article by a modern Christian theologian, Karl Rahner, 'The Broadening of a Classical Concept';
3   a discussion by Harfiyah Haleem of 'Non-Violent Options for Resolution of Conflict in Islam'.

Note

1   *The Guardian*, 16 and 17 July 2005.

Brian Wicker

Acknowledgements

The Editor wishes to thank all those who have helped with the compilation of this book, in particular:

- The Council on Christian Approaches to Defence and Disarmament for unfailing support and encouragement throughout the project.
- All of the scholars who have contributed chapters to the text, for their unstinting readiness to participate in the work and to engage in a common endeavour of mutual understanding between faiths.
- Takako Mendl for help with translation from the Japanese of some broadcast material on the kamikaze suicides, and Professor Ian Nish of STICERD, London School of Economics, for comments on the latter.
- Revd Dr Patrick Sookhdeo for some general comments on the draft.
- Professor Kenneth Cragg for taking part in the discussion, and for suggesting the comparison made in Chapter Six.
- The Dominicans at Blackfriars, Oxford, for providing congenial surroundings in which to conduct our various meetings.
- Sarah Lloyd, Anne Keirby, Sarah Charters, Linda Cayford and all those associated with Ashgate Publishing, who have encouraged us to keep going and who made possible the speedy production of the book.
- Professor M.A.S. Abdel Haleem, of the School of Oriental and African Studies, for the meticulousness of his translation of the Qur'an and for the valuable guidance provided by his notes to the Qur'anic text.
- Teresa Wicker for invaluable assistance in the compilation of the index.
- Liza and Clive Hamilton for help with computing and editorial assistance.

Grateful thanks are due to the following for permission to reproduce material included in this book:

- The Editor of *Theology* (SPCK) for the use, in Chapter Four, of material published in Vol. CVI, No. 831 (May–June 2003), pp. 159–67, under the title *Conflict and Martyrdom after 11 September 2001*.
- Faber and Faber Ltd (London) for the use, in Chapter Six, of material from *Murder in the Cathedral* by T.S. Eliot.

- E.J. Brill (Leiden) for the use, in Chapter Six, of material from the translation by Khalil I. Semaan of 'Abd al-Sabur's play *Murder in Baghdad.*
- The Muhammad Trust of Great Britain and Northern Ireland for the reprinting, in Chapter Seven, of Dr Ali Ezzati's article on 'The Concept of Martyrdom: A Shia Perspective', from *Al-Serat*, Vol. XII (1986).
- The English Province of the Dominican Order for reprinting, in Appendix 1, the English translation of the *Summa Theologiae*, Iia IIae Q. 124 (Volume 42) on martyrdom, published by Eyre and Spottiswode (London) and McGraw-Hill (New York).
- The Director of Secretariat of *Stichtung Concilium* for permission to reprint, in Appendix 2, Karl Rahner's article, 'Dimensions of Martyrdom: A Plea for the Broadening of a Classical Concept', from *Concilium*, No. 163 (March 1983) on 'Martyrdom Today'.

Quotations from the Qur'an are taken throughout from the translation by M.A.S. Haleem (Oxford University Press, 2004), except in Chapter One where the author has used her own translations from the Arabic.

Following the spelling used in Chapter 1 we have throughout referred to 'Medina' and 'Mecca' rather than Madinah and Makkah. Also, where we have used masculine pronouns for the sake of simplicity this does not imply that only men are, or have become martyrs, or indeed terrorists.

Authorship for the appendices and permission to reprint material already published elsewhere is acknowledged in a note in each case.

Introduction

Brian Wicker

This book took shape in response to the widespread use of the word 'martyrdom' in contemporary discussions of terrorism, and especially of suicidal bombings carried out in the wake of '9/11'. The Council on Christian Approaches to Defence and Disarmament (CCADD) had earlier produced *The Crescent and the Cross: Muslim and Christian Approaches to War and Peace* (Macmillan, 1998), which was a product of consultation, between scholars of both faiths, about the ethics of modern warfare. The present study follows this work by deploying a similar group of scholars in an attempt to reveal similarities and differences in the interpretation of the concept of martyrdom in the two religions. It is hoped that our study will encourage greater understanding of this subject, as well as probing the deeper theological and ideological implications of the concept itself. It is also hoped that it will discourage the misuse of the word 'martyr' as a tool of misunderstanding or fanaticism on either side of the debate.

From the following chapters, a striking similarity may be detected in the history of the concept of martyrdom within each tradition. For Islam and Christianity are both religions 'of the book', with deep roots in the Abrahamic world. Both inevitably begin, therefore, from the concept of a martyr as a 'witness' within an ancient legal framework.

Asma Afsaruddin's study of early Islam (Chapter One) emphasizes that in the Qur'an the Arabic term *shahīd* refers only to a witness, more specifically a legal or 'eye-witness'. Similarly, as Anthony Harvey, Richard Finn and Michael Smart make plain, a *martys* was a simply 'witness' in the Greek, Roman or Jewish legal tradition. But in that framework a witness was valued not so much for his (and it nearly always was *his*) account of facts as for a certain reliability of character. The key question was: can we trust this man's word? Is he the kind of person who can be relied upon to tell the truth? In the early stages of Christianity, as is pointed out, being a witness to God – that is, a 'martyr' – did not necessarily involve dying, or being killed, for the faith. You could witness to it simply by the way in which you lived. It was some time before the term 'martyr' involved the question 'Can we trust this person's claim to be a witness to God's truth – that is, to things which cannot be verified by visible or tangible evidence?' so that the witness's whole manner of life and death became the primary 'evidence' of the truth of what he was claiming. Hence the development of the specialized meaning of the word 'martyr' to refer to someone willing to be *killed* for the faith. But it was not until the death of St Polycarp in 155 CE that this specialized meaning of martyrdom began to take hold. By the time of St Augustine, in the late fourth century CE, after the Diocletian persecutions, it had become the norm. Eventually, in the thirteenth century, in discussing martyrdom St Thomas Aquinas concluded, with some qualifications, that 'the perfect idea of martyrdom requires one to endure death for Christ's sake'.[1]

Similarly, in the first Meccan phase of Islam, the Qur'an permitted only non-violent resistance to persecution by the pagan Meccans. It was not until the Medinan phase that permission was given to fight, but even then only after other, peaceful, means had been exhausted. But in both the Meccan and Medinan periods, Muslims continued to engage in their daily struggle (*jihad*) to uphold what was right and forbid wrongdoing in myriad ways, as an important part of affirming their faith and service to God. But in Medina the faithful were also exhorted to resort to armed defence of their community and of their faith against those who wished to cause them harm. Thus *jihad* acquired a new, military dimension in the Medinan period. Yet the term *shahīd* itself would not acquire the primary meaning of 'martyr' until some time in the second century of Islam (eighth century CE), possibly under the influence of Christian terminology, as Dr Afsaruddin suggests. In the early period, martyrdom could be won in multiple ways, as attested in early hadith literature. Thus, an individual who met his or her death while living and behaving in a suitably devout manner could be regarded as a martyr, as could the valiant warrior who fell on the battlefield in defence of Islam. Unfortunately, some modern translators have muddied the waters by consistently translating the Qur'anic term *shahīd* as 'martyr', thus imparting to it a certain colouring which it did not have to begin with.[2] And now, of course, the *recent* use of the term 'martyr' (in English or other Western languages) by Islamic militants themselves, to promote their campaigns, has been fed back into Muslim discourse itself.

In both traditions, then, the concept of witnessing to the faith originated in a non-violent context, but later, as a result of persecution of the faithful, became specialized into *dying* for it. One can conceive of circumstances in which this development need not have happened. If Christians had been recognized earlier as full, reliable citizens of the Roman Empire, and thus as reliable witnesses, and if Muslims had not been attacked so soon by enemies who threatened to destroy their community, things could have turned out differently. Of course, given the nature of each faith in its early stages, and the context in which each emerged, it would have needed a miracle for these persecutions not to have taken place. But the point remains: witnessing and dying are two different things, and it is only human oppression that makes them so difficult to keep apart in practice.

A further point, related to what I have just said, is worth noting. Dr Afsaruddin mentions the role of the theory of 'abrogation' (*naskh*), as articulated by some exegetes, in developing the specialized meaning of *shahīd* in the later practice of Islam. According to this theory, where there is a potential difference in meaning between two Qur'anic verses on some point, the later verse is assumed in some cases to have superseded, or 'abrogated', the earlier verse. Hence, according to Dr Afsaruddin, the exaggerated importance, in certain historical circumstances, or even misinterpretation in much of post-Qur'anic discourse, given to the so-called 'sword' verses (9:5, 9:29), which are dated to the Medinan period.[3]

This theory made it possible for the concept of fighting for Islam to emerge as the dominant meaning of the term *jihad*. Accordingly, as a subsequent development, *shahīd* also acquired the primary meaning of dying for the faith, usually on the battlefield. The earlier, non-violent meanings of both *jihad* and *shahīd* tended to be buried (but not completely erased) under the weight of the later usages of these terms, particularly in juristic literature. But other types of literature, such as the ethical and mystical, continued to valorize the non-violent dimensions of these terms. The narrowing of the general Qur'anic concept of *jihad* ('struggle') into armed combat has been the focus of much attention in recent times. Many scholars, whether Muslim or not, tend to dwell on this point.[4] Patrick Sookhdeo[5] in his recent book *Understanding Islamic Terrorism* makes much of it, and suggests that until the doctrine of 'abrogation' (*naskh*) is modified by Muslims themselves, there is little hope of overcoming the terrorist threat. Alas, there seems little hope of this as long as the West persists with policies which are profoundly resented by the Muslim world, and which seem to Muslims to be intrinsically unjust. But Dr Afsaruddin circumvents this difficulty by showing that there was (and indeed still is) a living alternative tradition of non-violent witness to the faith within Islam (a tradition not confined to Sufis). The problem is how to reassert the authority of this older tradition against the later 'hardline' position to which many Islamic militant groups adhere, given that Islam has no central focus of authority in the teaching of the faith.

In any case, the theory of 'abrogation' is itself the subject of scholarly debate. As was pointed out in *The Crescent and the Cross*, the great Muslim scholar Mahmud Shaltut, the shaikh of Al-Azhar University from 1958 to 1963, condemned some theorists for excessive use of it. And al-Ghunaimi, in his *The Muslim Conception of International Law and the Western Approach* (1968), went on to maintain that the scope of the doctrine of 'abrogation' is far narrower than many of the theorists of violent *jihad* suppose. It was designed originally only to apply to the replacement of earlier religions and their scriptures by the Qur'an, not to the cancellation of the significance of the early verses of the Qur'an itself by later ones.[6] As Professor Haleem pointed out,[7] the term 'abrogation' is anyhow not an accurate rendering of the Arabic *naskh*, which, properly speaking, means 'supersede', as in the Qur'anic verse 2:106: 'any revelation We cause to be superseded or forgotten, We replace with something better or similar'.[8] It was the jurist al-Shafi'i (768–820 CE) who developed the concept of *naskh* in such a way that the verse prescribing fighting (2:216) came to cancel out the significance of earlier, non-violent interpretations of *jihad*. Putting the verse into its historical and textual context shows not only that the 'prescription to fight' refers at most only to self-defence, but that it may even be about a requirement to *endure* attack rather than to inflict it. For the verb in Arabic (*qital*) means both fighting and being fought. Because of this misunderstanding about both the scope of 'abrogation' and the failure to recognize the two meanings of *qital*, since al-Shafi'i's time *jihad* as an obligatory duty to engage in warfare 'subtly became an institution in Islamic law, and was even included by some as a sixth "pillar" of Islam'.[9] Hence the assumption by many writers today, such as Firestone and Sookhdeo, that the violent meaning of *jihad* is the one classic, or orthodox, Muslim doctrine, with its alternative as no more than a faint remnant of a past era. So the problem now is not so much to change the meaning of *naskh* as to restore its original sense: that is, to get the alternative, non-violent message heard amidst the cacophony of violent discourse which has dominated discussion on both sides in the twenty-first century CE. It is one purpose of this study of martyrdom to rescue this alternative tradition from the oblivion into which it has sunk in recent decades.

A further related point concerns the possibility of men engaged in armed conflict being recognized as martyrs. Here a clear difference between the traditions seems to emerge. Christian teaching is quite emphatic: you cannot be recognized as a martyr if your death comes about simply as the result of participation in war, even in a just war.[10] Thomas Aquinas takes this point for granted in his discussion of martyrdom[11] and does not see any need to argue for it: he simply assumes that it is an established tradition for which there is no need, at least at this stage of the argument, to offer reasons.[12] This teaching continues to this day. Even though there must be many cases of soldiers doing heroic things in war, out of truly charitable motives, with little or no intention of committing violence – say, rescuing wounded comrades under fire[13] – even the Roman Catholic Church, which of all the Christian traditions represents that which is most willing to canonize martyrs, has never thought fit to consider such military actions as material for the award of the martyr status. Even less plausible is the case for soldiers heroically killing others, even in self-defence, in actual combat in a just war. As Harfiyah Haleem points out, the award of the Victoria Cross 'for valour' could well point to behaviour which in other circumstances would be recognized as fit for the martyr's crown,[14] but such recognition has never been granted by the Church. Presumably this is because it is not valour, but charity (including love of the enemy) which has to be the directing virtue of the martyr.[15]

On the other hand, for Muslims dying in the course of armed conflict 'in the way of God' (with all the restrictions this imposes[16]) in defence of Islam against its enemies can well count as martyrdom. A person who dies in such circumstances is often recognized as a *shahīd*, or witness to the faith, as the discussion of suicide below shows.[17] Some Islamists even suggest that the supreme martyrdom in its purest sense actually consists in dying while fighting. For example, Hasan al-Banna of the Muslim Brotherhood remarks:

'The supreme martyrdom is only conferred on those who slay or are slain in the way of God.'[18]

The gap between these opposed positions is striking. Presumably the reason for the Christian refusal to recognize soldiers as martyrs has to do, as Harvey, Finn and Smart point out in this book, with the early days of Christianity when martyrdom was understood as an imitation of, even indeed a kind of participation in, the crucifixion of Jesus.[19] Solidarity with Christ, as a member of his body, was often the primary motive of the first Christian martyrs. Martyrdom is a freely chosen gift of one's life and, as such, is a gift from God: a vocation. Anyhow, until the end of the second century CE there were hardly any Christians in the Roman army: military service and the ritual observances acknowledging the worship due to the Roman gods were regarded as a kind of idolatry.[20] However, as A. Ezzati points out, there is a certain parallelism with this belief in the Shia tradition, where the *shahīd* is both a model and a martyr and thus a paradigm in both senses.[21] But martyrdom can also be a calling from God in the Sunni tradition, despite the current emphasis, especially among 'militants' who advocate suicide operations, on the martyr's own personal decision to die in the struggle for Islam.[22]

Be that as it may, dying for the faith is a matter of free choice. The martyr, in the Christian scheme of things, is one who *chooses* to die rather than to do something contrary to the faith. But in war, the free choice of the soldier is severely circumscribed, sometimes by conscription into the army. And soldiers often have little choice but to do what they are told, even under extreme pressure, not only where killing is concerned, but even where there is a willingness to be killed rather than (say) allowing comrades to be overrun. And even when the war itself, and also the specific operation being undertaken, is rightly seen as 'just', the taint of violence and of compulsion in it renders the crown of martyrdom inappropriate. The award of medals by the state, and even veneration by the Church, is not the same thing as being recognized, let alone canonized, as a martyr.

Here, perhaps, the divergence from the Muslim tradition seems to be at its starkest. Yet the difference can be exaggerated. For so-called 'martyrdom operations', such as suicide bombings, are not really acts of war at all, *pace* George W. Bush's talk of a 'war on terror'. They are better understood as criminal, rather than military, actions,[23] which are freely undertaken by individual members of small inchoate groups of militants, who cannot rightly be regarded as constituting an army, and are not fighting in defence of a legally constituted state. This is certainly not legitimate warfare as understood by modern international law, or by classical Islamic law.[24] Sincere believers who are members of such groups doubtless think of themselves as chosen by God for their task. But equally clearly, both the mainstream Christian and Muslim traditions say that they are mistaken about this. Suicidal behaviour is forbidden, not permitted, let alone encouraged, either by the Christian gospel or by the Qur'an. This is something that all the authors of this book agree upon. Furthermore, there may be discerned a steady coming-together of the traditions,[25] in so far as it is being increasingly acknowledged that martyrdom can be recognized purely in a struggle for justice, even in the absence of the *odium fidei* which was once regarded by the Church as a necessary component of any cause for recognizing somebody as a martyr. How far this convergence may go, in the future, it is impossible at this stage to tell.

The veneration of martyrs is another aspect of our subject that requires further comment. There is a difference of view about this between the Sunni and the Shia traditions. Shia Islam is happy with the presence of shrines to those who have died for the faith, in line with the veneration given to the first Shia martyrs, Hassan and Husayn.[26] Even popular Sunni Muslim practice can verge on such veneration. The teachings of the eighteenth-century founder of Wahhabism in Saudi Arabia, Muhammed 'Abdul Wahhab, originated in response to a growing appeal of saint adulation and excessive visitations to shrines in that country.[27] In Palestine today it is possible to encounter quasi-shrines to the martyred, and many Palestinians express great pride in their martyrs and have their pictures posted on walls. Indeed, such veneration of those who have given their lives in a popular cause is virtually impossible to avoid, whatever official teaching may say. The memories, and the stories by which they are remembered, are bound to be etched deeply into any persecuted community's understanding of itself. But what this veneration of the dead amounts to, beyond simply remembering and commemorating, is not always clear. After all, a difficulty was recognized by Protestant Christians over the cult of saints and martyrs, and this entailed its abolition in many countries after the Reformation. Where this was not sheer vandalism, much of the physical destruction was supposedly directed to the extirpation of superstition and corruption. But there was always the danger of throwing the baby out with the bathwater.

Be that as it may, the Qur'an forbids praying to martyrs, or to anyone other than God (10:105–6 is commonly cited here), on the grounds that it constitutes *shirk*, often translated as 'attributing partners to God'. As the Introduction to the Haleem translation of the Qur'an makes clear,[28] use of the term *shirk* was aimed in the first place at polytheists who believed in 'the sharing of several gods in the creation and government of the universe'. It would seem therefore to be a mistake to use it equally against Christians, for no Christian of any theological sophistication would dream of supposing that the martyrs to whom he prays are 'partners of God'. For Christians, prayer for, and to, the dead (including the Blessed Virgin, Mother of God) is an act of solidarity in Christ amongst the members of the one human family.[29] No Christian supposes the dead to be 'gods', or somehow sharers in divinity, let alone to threaten the unity of the Godhead. Indeed, philosophical reflection indicates that the notion of God the Creator having 'partners' is not so much false as senseless. Since God is the Creator of all the kinds of things that there are, as both religions agree, He cannot Himself be countable as a member of any of these 'kinds'. For only members of the same kind, or *genus*, are

countable, and God is not in any *genus*.[30] He is not even a member of a
kind that can have only one member, like 'Living Queen of England' (a term
which refers to a certain kind of person, even though only one person can be
a member of it). Admittedly, the logic of the word 'God' is difficult, indeed
deeply mysterious. But it is not made any clearer by supposing that God could
share His divinity with a 'partner'. This is certainly not what the Christian
doctrine of the Trinity is about. ('I believe in one God' is the first sentence of
the Nicene Creed, and the Trinitarian sentences which follow do not contradict
this.) So no Christian would entertain, for a moment, the notion of a plurality
of gods, any more than a Muslim would.

Of course, veneration of martyrs is bound up with what Richard Finn calls
'cult and discourse'. He shows how deeply, in the Christian tradition, the
concept of martyrdom has been bound up with the narratives which have
shaped, and been shaped by, people's memories, and the cults in which
they have been told and retold. Similarly, Asma Afsaruddin writes of the
'literature' of martyrdom, quoting many stories and reports of the sayings
(though fewer of the alleged deeds) of those who have died in defence
of the Muslim faith. In the tradition of Sufism, martyrdom literature has
proliferated, just as the cult of martyrs has thrived. In his massive four-
volume study of the great one-time-Sufi martyr Mansur al-Hallaj (d. 922 CE)
Louis Massignon devotes almost one entire volume to the martyr's legacy,
consisting of accounts of the popular narratives and celebrations of his life
and death which have taken hold all over the Muslim world, and indeed
well beyond it, in the centuries since he was barbarically crucified.[31]
Another martyr who has long been venerated is al-Suhrawardi (d. 1191 CE),
a mystic Muslim follower of Plotinus, who was executed under Salah-ad-Din
and whose memory has been used 'to endow the mystic with an almost
Hallajian charisma'.[32] A modern example of such 'veneration' is to be found
in the drama on the life and death of al-Hallaj by 'Abd al-Sabur, which is
discussed below.[33] Doubtless, studies of the legacies left by other Muslim
martyrs have been, or could be, undertaken.[34] Yet, in the Sunni tradition, a
certain reticence reveals itself about the popular pursuit of such cults. This
tradition seems to share some of the misgivings of Christian Protestants
about encouraging any *cult* of martyrdom, possibly for parallel reasons:
namely horror of the popular superstitions which almost inevitably tend
to circulate around stories and shrines dedicated to the dead, who after all
are no longer with us to discourage our excesses. Much the same reticence
can understandably be expressed about the modern Catholic requirement
that, before a person can be canonized as a martyr, a credible miracle has
to be attested to, as having been brought about through prayer to her or
him. Nevertheless, the point of insisting on this condition is clear enough:
the witness needs to be able to produce 'evidence' that is visible within the
material world.[35] So the point remains: veneration of the martyrs rests upon
the solidarity which human beings share not only with the living but with the
dead who have gone before them. For it is this solidarity which is at the root

of any genuine, as distinct from superstitious, cult of those who have died so that we may have life more abundantly.

Suicide is clearly forbidden in both traditions.[36] Yet in both, as several chapters of this book attest, there are or have been attempts to justify martyrdoms achieved by suicide. Thomas Aquinas considers the suicide of acknowledged martyrs as an objection to the thesis that martyrdom is an act of virtue. He notes that St Augustine had quoted several cases of women, such as Pelagia and her sisters, who 'hurled themselves into a river to avoid those who attacked their chastity' and yet have been acknowledged as martyrs. But, given the long-standing prohibition of suicide by the Church, praise of such suicide seems misplaced. How can these opposed viewpoints be squared? Aquinas' reply to the objection (or rather Augustine's reply quoted by Aquinas at this point) may perhaps seem rather lame: 'divine authority has persuaded the Church, by manifestations worthy of credence, to honour the memory of these holy women'.[37] For this answer does not easily dispose of the objection that, as suicides, these women had acted in a manner contrary to the Christian teaching. Indeed, the reply seems to suggest that God may be contradicting his own commandment. Yet even in his fuller discussion of suicide, in IIa IIae Q. 64, Art. 5, Aquinas offers the same, seemingly lame, excuse. Would it not have been better to show that somehow the women's actions did not constitute suicide at all? But Aquinas will have none of this. He clearly accepts that these holy women did indeed commit suicide, just as Samson did.[38] So the seemingly lame excuse is all that can be offered.

Because suicide is forbidden in both traditions, people have sometimes resorted to arguing that those tempted along this path were not actually committing suicide at all. For example, as Harfiyah Haleem points out, Shaikh Yusuf al-Qaradawi[39] argues that some suicide bombings 'are not suicide operations [because] these are heroic operations, and the heroes who carry them out don't embark on this action out of hopelessness and despair but are driven by an overwhelming desire to cast terror and fear into the hearts of the oppressors'.[40] The implication here seems to be that the self-killing is not really suicide, since the bomber's objective is not to kill himself, but to inflict fear on the enemy. On this basis, the death of the (suicidal) 'martyr' is only a foreseen but unintended consequence of an action undertaken for a different purpose. The martyr's own death is a case merely of 'collateral damage'. So it is not really deliberate suicide. This seems to be a desperate rhetorical manoeuvre to avoid the Qur'anic prohibition. For if we are asking whether a particular *action* is a case of suicide, then what counts is what the alleged suicide does, not what his motives or his purposes are. The question is: has this person killed himself or herself? If the answer is yes, then it is suicide. Of course, suicide committed out of hopelessness or desperation, or when the balance of the mind is disturbed, is often excusable, indeed forgivable; but forgiveness depends on the action itself being admitted as suicidal and not evaded under the rubric of being something else. This is a conclusion that clear-headed Muslims and Christians can surely agree on.

Another argument in justification of suicide operations is offered by Ayman al-Zawahiri, the leader of the Jihad Movement, a prominent theorist of al-Qa'ida as well as someone who claims to follow the fourteenth-century scholar Ibn Taymiyya. Maha Azzam, of the Royal Institute of International Affairs, quotes al-Zawahiri as approving of some early Muslims, who were captured by 'idolaters', refused to recant their faith and were duly killed.[41] Al-Zawahiri admits that their deaths were suicidal. (This seems, on the face of it, to be a mistake, for presumably they were killed by their persecutors, not by themselves.) Yet they were acting for the glory of God, as contemporary Muslims scholars have tacitly admitted by refusing to condemn them. Hence, al-Zawahiri concludes, it is licit after all for a Muslim to commit suicide, despite the Qur'anic prohibition, provided that it is done for a greater good. In effect, this is an argument that it is licit to do evil that good may come. Here, a solid ethical barrier, which both religions have accepted, is being flatly undermined. Aquinas, for one, clearly rejects any such argument.[42] Presumably he would have said that the Muslim captives killed by 'idolaters' cannot be compared to Pelagia and her sisters, who clearly drowned themselves, whereas the Muslims were killed by other people. It therefore seems bizarre, as well as mistaken, to call their deaths suicidal. The same point is made by Maha Azzam: 'This [argument] provides the movement with the legitimacy for suicide attacks, which 1500 years of Islamic theology would view as heretical.'[43]

It has already been pointed out that, for the Muslim tradition, a key virtue of the martyr is courage. As is quoted below in Chapter Four, Muslim beliefs give their fighters 'a courage which Western writers and journalists marvel at'.[44] But, despite what some militant Islamist literature proclaims today about martyrdom and the centrality of *martial* courage in its construction, perusal of early Islamic sources suggests, rather, that the key, bottom-line virtue of the martyr was and is patience and fortitude, or steadfastness. This perspective allowed the application of the term 'martyr', therefore, to a woman who dies during labour, to an individual who dies from the plague or while engaged in the pursuit of education or in earning a livelihood, in addition to the one who dies defending the faith on the battlefield. Thus not all martyrs need to be physically courageous but they must all be patient and forbearing. Patience clearly has to be displayed during the commission of virtuous and charitable acts, doing good 'in the way of God'; patience manifested during an immoral act obviously has no redeeming value. The basic definition of *jihad*, after all, is the struggle to uphold what is good and prevent what is wrong. This is the motivational force behind virtue in the Islamic tradition, while patience always, and courage sometimes, are components of overall virtue. As Asma Afsaruddin mentions below,[45] a virtuous person who dies peacefully in his or her bed could be regarded as a martyr. Such a perspective on martyrdom reveals commonalities with the Christian one. Perhaps the obvious difference between the two is a matter of degree rather than of principle. Christianity has traditionally distinguished martyrs, who die steadfastly in defence of their faith against manifest persecution, from other saints whose virtues are rooted in a wider variety of circumstances, whereas in Islam the two categories are less clearly distinguished. This difference may be somewhat lessened when the Christian concept of martyrdom is broadened along lines suggested in Appendix 2 below.

When Aquinas – here representing, I think, the central Christian teaching – says that courage is the 'directly engaged moving force' which 'brings out the act' in martyrdom, while it is charity which is the 'directing virtue', he seems to be echoing what this book understands as the central Islamic teaching, as also when he writes that courage 'gets its meritorious nature from charity . . . without charity it is of no value'.[46] And it is agreed on both sides in this book that modern suicide attacks do not stem from charity at all. Trying to instil fear in an enemy, out of desperation and military weakness, could be seen as an act of deterrence against an enemy harming the people the suicidal person loves, or as retribution for the death of a loved one at the hands of the enemy. But in practice it does not deter; it only provokes. It certainly does not imply love of the enemy.

Perhaps the deepest question, which we have no room to explore in this book, is exactly what is meant by the 'theological virtue' of charity, and its pre-eminence among the virtues. How far, in its true colours, does charity underpin the thinking both of Muslims and of Christians, not only in the context of martyrdom but in many other areas of human life? Perhaps this is a question best left to both sides to consider on another occasion.

These observations arise from a scrutiny of the chapters which follow, and from thinking about some of their implications. All the authors of this study of martyrdom in two traditions share the hope that our work will help to purify some otherwise dangerously muddy waters, as well as stimulating readers into further study of a thorny subject.

Notes

1 *Summa Theologiae*, IIa IIae Q. 124, Art. 4.
2 The first English translation directly from the Arabic, by George Sale (1734) used the term 'martyr' for *shahīd*. Not all of his successors did so, however, preferring 'witness' instead.
3 See Chapter One below, pp. 20–21. See also *The Qur'an: A New Translation* by M.A.S. Haleem (Oxford, Oxford University Press, 2004), p. 116 and notes.
4 For example, Reuven Firestone, *Jihad: The Origins of Holy War in Islam* (New York, Oxford University Press, 1999); Patrick Sookhdeo, *Understanding Islamic Terrorism* (Pewsey, Isaac Publishing, 2004), pp. 20–21, 28–29, 214–17. But see also Chapter One below, pp. 15ff and Harfiyah Haleem *et al.*, *The Crescent and the Cross* (Basingstoke, Macmillan, 1998), pp. 63–64, 75.
5 A member of CCADD.
6 Haleem *et al.*, *The Crescent and the Cross*, p. 64.
7 Ibid., p. 75. See also Chapter One below, 'Competing Perspectives on *Jihad* . . .'.
8 It is worth noting that here the doctrine of 'abrogation' comes close to some of the arguments put forward by John Henry Newman in his classic book *The Development*

of Christian Doctrine (1845). I think this parallel between the faiths is worth exploring further at a future date.

9   Haleem *et al.*, *The Crescent and the Cross*, p. 76.

10   True, Paul Johnson claims that Pope John VIII (872–882 CE) 'thought that such a person would even rank as a martyr', but he gives no evidence for this apparently eccentric papal opinion. See Johnson, *A History of Christianity* (London, Penguin Books, 1976), p. 242.

11   *Summa Theologiae*, IIa IIae Q. 124, Art 5:3. See also Appendix 1 below.

12   However, as Harfiyah Haleem points out, he does admit of the possibility of members of the crusading 'military orders' becoming martyrs, even though such men aim more at shedding the blood of enemies, rather than giving up their own as other martyrs typically do. His reasoning has to do with the status of these religious orders as dedicated directly to God's service, unlike ordinary soldiers whose task is to serve the prince in a secular capacity. (See *Summa Theologiae*, IIa IIae Q. 188, Art. 6 ad 2.) Some Muslim arguments in defence of 'martyrdom operations' seem to echo this sort of reasoning.

13   For example, Captain Richard Annand VC, who won his award for rescuing his own wounded batman on 16 May 1940. See his obituary in *The Guardian*, 17 January 2005.

14   See Chapter Three below, p. 67.

15   *Summa Theologiae*, IIa IIae Q. 124, Art. 2 ad 2.

16   See Haleem *et al.*, *The Crescent and the Cross*, pp. 65ff.

17   See Chapter Four below, p. 87 (and note 49).

18   Hasan al-Banna, *Five Tracts of Hasan al-Banna* (Berkeley, University of California Press, 1978), pp. 155–56, quoted by Sookhdeo, *Understanding Islamic Terrorism*, p. 133.

19   See Chapter Two below, p. 37.

20   See David G. Hunter, 'A Decade of Research on Early Christians and Military Service', *Religious Studies Review*, Vol. 18, No. 2 (April 1992), pp. 87–93 for a balanced assessment of the historical evidence for Christian participation in military service before Constantine.

21   See Chapter Seven below, p. 118.

22   Qur'an 3:140 (see p. 44, note b in Haleem translation).

23   Cf. Philippe Sands, *Lawless World* (London, Allen Lane, 2005), pp. 207–8. See also Shirley Williams, *God and Caesar* (London, Continuum, 2003), p. 115: 'Treating the attacks as crimes rather than acts of war mobilizes all those who believe in justice, human rights and the rule of law on the same side.'

24   Sands, *Lawless World*, Chapter 9 *passim*. Dr Afsaruddin points out that classical Islamic law says that a legitimate war can only be declared by a head of state. In modern terms this would translate as a president, prime minister or king. She adds that, according to this strict requirement and other rules that govern conduct during a legitimate war, al-Qa'ida and others are clearly terrorists because they have stepped outside the boundaries of *jihad* as just war. The reason why this sounds so much like modern international law is because it has been suggested that Hugo Grotius was influenced by the Islamic principles of just conduct during war. See below, Chapter One, pp. 25–6.

25   As argued below in Chapters Four and Six, and Chapter Three, pp. 70–72.

26   See Chapter Three below p. 52, and the discussion of the al-Hallaj example in Chapter Six.

27   See John L. Esposito, *Islam: The Straight Path*, expanded edn (Oxford, Oxford University Press, 1994), p. 117.

28   Qur'an, p. xvii.

29   For a sound and wholly orthodox account of prayer among Christians, see Herbert McCabe OP, *God Matters* (London, Geoffrey Chapman, 1987), Chapter 18: 'Prayer'.

30   *Summa Theologiae*, Ia Q. 3, Art. 5. See also Rowan Williams, 'Analysing Atheism: Unbelief and the World of Faiths', paper presented at Georgetown University, Washington, DC, 29 March 2004.

31   Louis Massignon, *Hallaj, Mystic and Martyr* (originally published in French in 1922),

trans. Herbert Mason (Princeton, Princeton University Press, 1982), Vol. 2, pp. 337–436: 'The Hallajian Legend, Its Origins, Its Literary Flowering'.

32   I.R. Netton, 'Suhrawardi's Philosophy of Illumination' in L. Lewisohn (ed.), *The Legacy of Mediaeval Persian Sufism* (New York, 1992, in association with the London SOAS Centre of Near and Middle Eastern Studies), p. 249. Netton writes at some length of the Islamic '"myth" of martyrdom . . . which stretches from the age of the great martyr of Karbala, Husayn, through Hallaj . . . and (perhaps) al-Farabi, up to our own subject Suhrawardi – and, of course, beyond into the present. It is an ineluctable reality that the tragic ends of each of these figures enhance, if only unconsciously, the message which they bore during their lifetimes, in the mind of the reader.'

33   See Chapter Six below.

34   On this see Sookhdeo, *Understanding Islamic Terrorism*, pp. 159–60.

35   However, Pope John Paul II is reported to have considered a proposal to abolish miracles as requirements for sainthood. See *The Tablet*, 1 January 2005, p. 24.

36   Qur'an 2:195 is generally understood as forbidding suicide. See Haleem translation, p. 22, note b.

37   *Summa Theologiae*, IIa IIae Q. 124, Art. 1:2 and ad 2; Art. 4. Quoted from translation.

38   For a discussion of the Samson case, see 'Samson Terroristes: A Theological Reflection on Suicidal Terrorism', *New Blackfriars*, Vol. 84, No. 983 (January 2003), pp. 42–60.

39   Al-Qaradawi is banned from the USA, but visited the UK in July 2004, where his views about suicide bombings caused considerable political controversy in the media.

40   See below, Chapter Three, p. 59. See also *The Guardian*, 9 July 2004, p. 3 for a summary of al-Qaradawi's views on suicide bombing. Of course, the spread of opinions by Islamic scholars on this question is very wide, and many of them repudiate al-Qaradawi's view as contrary to the teaching of the Qur'an.

41   Maha Azzam, *Al-Qaeda: The Misunderstood Wahhabi Connection and the Ideology of Violence*, RUSI Middle East Programme, Briefing Paper No. 1 (February 2003), p. 4.

42   *Summa Theologiae*, IIa IIae Q. 64, Art. 5 ad 3.

43   See above, note 41.

44   See below Chapter Four, p. 88 and note 53.

45   See below, Chapter One, p. 28.

46   See Appendix 1: IIa IIae Q. 124, Art. 2 ad 2.

PART ONE

Chapter One

Competing Perspectives on *Jihad* and 'Martyrdom' in Early Islamic Sources

Asma Afsaruddin

Introduction

Jihad and martyrdom have arguably become the most common words associated with Islam and Muslims in the post-September 11 period. More misconceptions than historically accurate perspectives abound in regard to these two emotive issues, among both Muslims and non-Muslims. Ideological assertions and political claims have muddied the waters considerably in discussions of these topics in the contemporary period. The main purpose of this chapter is to outline broadly the historical trajectory of the meanings ascribed to *jihad* in early Islamic sources, starting with the Qur'an followed by hadith works containing statements attributed to the Prophet Muhammad and his Companions, and thus to offset them against later, post-classical meanings to indicate the semantic transformations that occurred over time. It will be argued that the Arabic terms for 'martyr' and 'martyrdom' also evince a similar evolution in their spectrum of meanings, which were tied to a considerable degree to the particular inflections of the term *jihad* in varying historical circumstances. This study is far from being an exhaustive treatment of this subject.[1] Other important perspectives such as the Sufi and the Shia are not part of our discussion, primarily due to constraints on length and also because they fall somewhat beyond the temporal purview of this essay. More modestly, I seek to establish the wider range of meanings associated with these terms in the early period when these groups, which were themselves influenced by these early trends in their subsequent development, had not fully emerged.

By the early third century of the Islamic era – that is, in the ninth century CE – *jihad* as primarily 'armed combat' had become the accepted meaning in influential circles, particularly in the administrative and juridical ones. This occurred despite the fact that the term *jihad* in Qur'anic usage is clearly a polyvalent word and, as even a cursory reading of some of the related literature reveals, was understood as such by several early religious authorities and scholars. Exegetical glosses on the full Qur'anic phrase '*al-jihad fi sabil Allah*' (translated as 'striving or struggling in the path of God') explain it as referring to a wide array of activities: embarking on pursuit of knowledge, earning a licit livelihood and engaging in charitable works, in addition to military defence of Islam. Concomitantly, extra-Qur'anic literature (primarily exegesis and hadith) records various perspectives on martyrdom (Ar. *shahada*, a term which does not occur in the Qur'an in this sense) that reflect the polyvalence of the term *jihad*. As we shall see later, a believer who met with death while struggling in any licit and noble pursuit during his mundane existence on earth could be called a martyr (Ar. *shahīd*, pl. *shuhada'*).

The different legal and ethical articulations of war and peace that have emerged in Islamic thought testify to the different – and conflicting – ways of reading and interpreting some of the key Qur'anic verses dealing with this topic. Some of these variant ways of understanding the text will be outlined below. A comprehensive understanding of the Qur'anic treatment of the term *jihad* and other related terms is a necessary prelude to our discussion of the concept of martyrdom which appears to be a later, extra-Qur'anic, development.

The Qur'anic Discourse

The specific Qur'anic terms that have a bearing on our topic are *jihad*, *qital*, and *harb*. *Jihad* is a much broader term and its basic Qur'anic signification is 'struggle', 'striving', 'exertion'. The lexeme *jihad* is frequently conjoined to the phrase *fi sabil Allah* (lit. 'in the path of God'). The full locution in Arabic, *al-jihad fi sabil Allah*, consequently means 'struggling/striving for the sake of God'. This translation points to the polyvalence of the term *jihad* and the potentially different meanings that may be ascribed to it in different contexts, since the phrase 'in the path of/for the sake of God' allows for human striving to be accomplished in multiple ways. *Qital* is the term which specifically refers to 'fighting' or 'armed combat' and is a component of *jihad* in specific situations. *Harb* is the Arabic word for war in general. The Qur'an employs this last term to refer to illegitimate wars fought by those who wish to spread corruption on earth (5:64); to the thick of battle between believers and non-believers (8:57; 47:4); and, in one instance, to the possibility of war waged by God and His Prophet against those who would continue to practise usury (2:279). This term is never conjoined to the phrase 'in the path of God'.

At the semantic level, the simplistic translation of *jihad* into English as 'holy war', as is common in some scholarly and non-scholarly discourses, constitutes a severe misrepresentation and misunderstanding of its Qur'anic usage. According to the Qur'anic world-view, human beings should be constantly engaged in the basic endeavour of enjoining what is right and forbidding what is wrong. The struggle implicit in the application of this precept is *jihad*, properly and plainly speaking, and the endeavour refers to both an individual and a collective one. The means for carrying out this struggle may vary, depending on individual and collective circumstances, and the Qur'an often refers to those who 'strive with their wealth and their selves' (*jahadu bi-amwalihim wa-anfusihim*; for example, 8:72).

Many of the Qur'anic strictures pertaining to both non-violent and armed struggle against evil and to uphold good cannot be properly understood without relating them to specific events in the life of the Prophet. A significant number of Qur'anic verses are traditionally understood to have been revealed in connection with certain episodes in the Prophet Muhammad's life. Knowledge of the 'occasions of revelation' (Ar. *asbab al-nuzul*), as obtained from the biography of the Prophet and the exegetical literature, is indispensable for contextualizing key verses that may at first sight appear to be at odds with one another.[2] A specific chronology of events needs to be mapped out so that the progression in the Qur'anic ethics of warfare and the taking of human life may be understood against its historical backdrop, to which we proceed next.

The Meccan Period

According to our sources, from the onset of the revelations to the Prophet Muhammad in c. 610 CE until his emigration to Medina from Mecca in 622 CE, which marks the end of the Meccan period and the onset of the Medinan, the Muslims were not given permission by the Qur'an to physically retaliate against their persecutors, the pagan Meccans. Verses revealed in this period counsel the Muslims rather to steadfastly endure the hostility of the Meccans. While recognizing the right to self-defence for those who are wronged, the Qur'an maintains in this early period that to bear patiently the wrongdoing of others and to forgive those who cause them harm is the superior course of action. Three significant verses (42:40–43) reveal this highly significant, non-militant dimension of *jihad* in this early phase of the Prophet's career:

> The requital of evil is an evil similar to it: hence, whoever pardons and makes peace, his reward rests with God – for indeed, He does not love evil-doers. Yet surely, as for those who defend themselves after having been wronged – no blame whatever attaches to them: blame attaches but to those who oppress people and behave outrageously on earth, offending against all right; for them is grievous suffering in store!
> But if one is patient in adversity and forgives, this is indeed the best resolution of affairs.

Further,

> Pardon and forgive them until God gives His command. (2:109; cf. 29:59; 16:42)

Sabr ('patience'; 'forbearance') is thus an important component of *jihad* as well. The verses quoted above underscore the non-violent dimension of *jihad* during the Meccan period, which lasted 13 years compared to the Medinan period of ten years. The Qur'anic verses which were revealed during this period and dictated the conduct of the Prophet and his Companions are thus of extremely important consideration in any discussion on the permissibility of engaging in armed combat within the Islamic context. As these early verses show, the Muslims were allowed to engage in self-defence but without resorting to fighting in the early period. For the most part, this meant resisting the Meccan establishment by first secret and then active public propagation of the faith, through manumission of slaves who had converted to Islam, and, for some, by emigration to Abyssinia/Ethiopia, whose Christian king was sympathetic to the early Muslims, and later to Medina.

Both Muslim and non-Muslim scholars, medieval and modern, however, have tended to downplay the critical Meccan phase in the development of the Qur'anic doctrine of *jihad*. It is, however, practically impossible to contextualize the Qur'anic discourse on the various meanings of *jihad* without taking the Meccan phase into consideration. The introduction of the military aspect of *jihad* in the Medinan period can then be appropriately and better understood as a 'last resort' option, resorted to when attempts at negotiations and peaceful proselytization among the Meccans had failed during the first 13 years of the propagation of Islam.

The Medinan Period

In 622 CE, which corresponds to the first year of the Islamic calendar, the Prophet received divine permission to emigrate to Medina, along with his loyal followers. There he set up the first Muslim polity, combining the functions of prophecy and temporal rule in one office. The Medinan verses, accordingly, now have increasingly more to do with organization of the polity, communitarian issues and ethics, and defence of the Muslims against Meccan hostilities. A specific Qur'anic verse (22:39–40) permitting fighting was revealed in Medina, although its precise date cannot be determined. The verse states:

> Permission [to fight] is given to those against whom war is being wrongfully waged, and indeed, God has the power to help them: those who have been driven from their homes against all right for no other reason than their saying, 'Our Provider is God!'
>
> For, if God had not enabled people to defend themselves against one another, monasteries, churches, synagogues, and mosques – in all of which God's name is abundantly glorified – would surely have been destroyed.

Another verse states:

> They ask you concerning fighting in the prohibited months. Answer them: 'To fight therein is a serious offence. But to restrain men from following the cause of

God, to deny God, to violate the sanctity of the sacred mosque, to expel its people from its environs is with God a greater wrong than fighting in the forbidden months. [For] disorder and oppression are worse than killing. (2:217)

Until the outbreak of full-fledged war a little later in the same year, the Qur'an, in this and other verses previously cited, refers to the reasons – *jus ad bellum* – that justify recourse to fighting. In verses 42:40–43, where self-defence is allowed but not through violent means, the reasons are the wrongful conduct of the enemy and their oppressive and immoral behaviour on earth. In verses 22:39–40 quoted above, a more explicit reason is given: wrongful expulsion of the Muslims from their homes for no other reason than their avowal of belief in one God. Furthermore, the Qur'an asserts, if people were not allowed to defend themselves against aggressive wrongdoers, all the houses of worship – it is worthy of note here that Islam is not the only religion indicated – would be destroyed and thus the Word of God extinguished. In the final verse cited (2:217), the Qur'an acknowledges the enormity of fighting during the prohibited months[3] but at the same time asserts the higher moral imperative of maintaining order and challenging wrongdoing. Therefore, when both just cause and righteous intention exist, war in self-defence becomes obligatory:

Fighting is prescribed for you, while you dislike it. But it is possible that you dislike a thing which is good for you, and that you love a thing which is bad for you. But God knows and you know not. (2:216)

The Qur'an further asserts that it is the duty of Muslims to defend those who are oppressed and cry out to them for help (4:75), except against a people with whom the Muslims have concluded a treaty (8:72).

With regard to initiation of hostilities and conduct during war (*jus in bello*), the Qur'an has specific injunctions. Qur'an 2:190, which reads 'Fight in the cause of God those who fight you, but do not commit aggression, for God loves not aggressors', forbids Muslims from initiating hostilities. Recourse to armed combat must be in response to a prior act of aggression by the opposite side. The Qur'an further counsels, 'Let not rancor towards others cause you to incline to wrong and depart from justice. Be just; that is closer to piety' (5:8). This verse may be understood to complement 2:190 in spirit and intent, warning against excesses that may result from an unprincipled desire to punish and exact revenge.

It is relevant to mention here that this Qur'anic concern for establishing legitimate reasons for waging war and mandating just conduct during such wars resulted in the emergence of a specific body of laws within classical Islamic jurisprudence called *siyar*, referring to 'the law of nations', or what we would roughly call international relations today.[4] *Siyar* regulations require that a call to war may only be proclaimed by the publicly recognized caliph or imam and proscribes wanton destruction of property or attacks upon non-combatants. According to these legal standards, those who unilaterally and thus illegally declare a call to war, attack unarmed civilians and recklessly destroy property are in flagrant violation of the Islamic juristic conception of *bellum justum*. Islamic law has a name for such rogue militants, *muharibun*, which may be rendered in modern parlance as 'terrorists', and their acts are to be branded as *hiraba* ('terrorism'), the very antithesis of *jihad* waged as legitimate armed combat against aggressors and oppressors. *Hiraba* is strictly proscribed in Islamic law and those who perpetrate it are subject to a severe penalty, usually capital punishment.[5] In the aftermath of September 11, it was this body of laws which was invoked by Muslim jurists worldwide to establish a legal consensus on the criminality of the attacks launched by al-Qa'ida and to brand Usama bin Laden and his cohorts as terrorists.

The Outbreak of War

In the month of Ramadan in the third year of the Islamic calendar (624 CE), full-fledged hostilities broke out between the Muslims and the pagan Meccans in what became known as the battle of Badr. In this battle, the small army of Muslims decisively trounced a much larger and more experienced Meccan army. Two years later, the battle of Uhud was fought, in which the Muslims suffered severe reverses, followed by the battle of Khandaq in 627. Apart from these three major battles, a number of other minor campaigns were fought until the Prophet's death in 632. Some of the most trenchant verses exhorting the Muslims to fight were revealed on the occasions of these military campaigns. One such verse, which has been termed the 'sword verse' (Ar. *ayat al-sayf*), states:

> And when the sacred months are over, slay the polytheists wherever you find them, and take them captive, and besiege them, and lie in wait for them at every conceivable place. (9:5)

Another verse, often conjoined to the above, runs:

> Fight against those who – despite having been given revelation before – do not believe in God nor in the Last Day, and do not consider forbidden that which God and His messenger have forbidden, and do not follow the religion of the truth, until they pay the *jizya* with willing hand, having been subdued. (9:29)

The first of the 'sword verses' (9:5), with its internal reference to the polytheists who may be fought after the end of the sacred months, would circumscribe its applicability to the pagan Arabs of Muhammad's time; this is how, in fact, many medieval scholars, such as al-Shafi'i (d. 820) and al-Tabari (d. 923), understood the verse. The second of the 'sword verses' is seemingly directed at the People of the Book, that is, Jews and Christians but, again, a careful reading of the verse clearly indicates that it does not intend all the People of the Book but only those from among them who do not, in contravention of their own laws, believe in God and the Last Day and, in a hostile manner, impede the propagation of Islam. This understanding is borne out by comparing verse 9:29 to verses 3:113–15, which state:

> They are not all the same. Among the People of the Book are a contingent who stand [in prayer] reciting the verses of God at all times of the night while they prostrate. These are they who believe in God and the Last Day and enjoin what is right and forbid what is wrong. They hasten to [perform] good deeds and they are among the righteous. And whatever they do of good will not be rejected [by God] and God knows best the God-fearing. (3:113–15)

The Qur'an, in another verse, makes it unambiguously clear that, should hostile behaviour on the part of the foes of Islam cease, then the reason for engaging them in war also lapses. This verse states:

> And fight them on until there is no chaos (*fitna*) and religion is only for God, but if they cease, let there be no hostility except to those who practice oppression. (2:193)

The harshness of the two 'sword verses' is thus considerably mitigated and their general applicability significantly restricted by juxtaposing them to conciliatory verses, such as the one cited immediately above, and other such verses. Among other such verses is the one that has been characterized as the 'peace verse':

> If they incline toward peace, incline you toward it, and trust in God. Indeed, He alone is all-hearing, all-knowing. (8:61)

And

> Slay them wherever you catch them, and turn them out from where they have turned you out; for persecution is worse than slaughter. But if they cease, God is Oft-forgiving, Most Merciful (2:191–92)

> God does not forbid you from being kind and equitable to those who have neither made war on you on account of your religion nor driven you from your homes. God loves those who are equitable. (60:8)

These verses make warring against those who oppose the propagation of the message of Islam and consequently resort to the persecution of Muslims contingent upon their continuing hostility. Should they desist from such hostile persecution and sue for peace instead, the Muslims are commanded to accede to their request. Qur'an 60:8 further makes clear that non-Muslims of goodwill and peaceableness cannot be the targets of war simply on account of their different religious background.[6]

Competing Perspectives on *Jihad*

By the early Abbasid period, roughly mid to late second/eighth century, the military aspect of *jihad* would receive greater emphasis in the opinions of some jurists and would be understood by them to override the other spiritual and non-militant significations of this term. As the jurists and religious scholars of all stripes became consolidated as a scholarly class and accrued to themselves commensurate religious and political authority by the fourth/tenth century, they arrogated to themselves the right to authoritatively define *jihad* and circumscribe the range of activities prescribed by it. With the powerful theory of 'abrogation' (*naskh*)[7] at their disposal, some of these jurists – certainly not all – effectively rendered null and void the positive injunctions contained in the Qur'anic verses that explicitly permitted the conclusion of truces with foes and counselled peaceful coexistence with the People of the Book in particular. Instead, these scholars privileged the so-called 'verse of the sword' (Qur'an 9:5, to which was sometimes added a second verse, 9:29), which they understood to sanction ideological, even offensive, warfare against non-Muslims. From now on, a monovalent understanding of *jihad* would be promoted by a number of these scholars, undermining the rich diversity of meanings associated with the term in Qur'anic and early hadith discourse. Accordingly, martyrdom also progressively came to be understood almost exclusively in a military sense and a hortatory genre developed around the merits, often greatly exaggerated, of falling on the battlefield in defending and advancing the cause of Islam.[8]

The jurist Muhammad b. Idris al-Shafi'i (d. 820 CE) is said to have been the first to permit *jihad* to be launched against non-Muslims as offensive warfare, although he is believed to have qualified non-Muslims as referring only to pagan Arabs and not to non-Arab non-Muslims. He also divided the world into *dar al-islam* ('the abode of Islam') and *dar al-harb* ('the abode of war', referring to non-Muslim territories), while recognizing a third possibility, *dar al-'ahd* ('the abode of treaty'), referring to non-Islamic states that may enter into a peace treaty with the Islamic state by rendering the *jizya*, an annual tribute.[9] None of these categories is referred to in the Qur'an and the Sunna; their invention rather reflected ad hoc juristic and political responses to the realpolitik of the early Abbasid period. These legal postulations are therefore not doctrinally binding in any way. And, in fact, by the fourth century of Islam (tenth century CE), these terms had fallen into desuetude because they no longer accurately described contemporary historical and political reality. Accordingly, juristic thinking in this period, in accommodation of these changed realities, came to consider *jihad* as a caliphal duty that was basically in abeyance but which could be revived in times of crisis. The famous philosopher Ibn Khaldun (d. 1406) would characterize this change in the juristic conception of *jihad* as reflective of a 'change in the character of the nation from the warlike to the civilized stage'.[10]

It should be stressed that not all scholars subscribed to the view that the Qur'anic verse 9:5 had abrogated earlier conciliatory verses and had overridden particularly the critical verse 2:256 which specifically prohibited forcible conversion. Two celebrated Qur'an commentators, Muhammad Jarir al-Tabari (d. 923)[11] and Ibn Kathir (d. 1373),[12] for example, resolutely maintained that 2:256 had not been abrogated and that its injunction remained valid for all time. Ibn Kathir stressed that an individual retained the God-given right to choose his or her religion free from coercion by stating: 'God, the Exalted, said, "There is no compulsion in religion"; that is to say, you cannot compel anyone to enter the religion of Islam. Truly that is made clearly evident.'[13] Ibn Kathir's famous teacher and mentor, Ibn Taymiyya (d. 1328), subscribed to the view that *jihad* was a defensive war and could be waged only against those unbelievers who were guilty of hostility towards Muslims.[14] Through the classical and post-classical periods, there was no consensus among scholars regarding the number and status of abrogating and abrogated verses, or even regarding the legitimacy of the concept itself.[15] The legal purview of *jihad* as military activity continued to be actively debated and questioned throughout the pre-modern period and, indeed, continues to this day.

Alternative Views on Jihad

To recover, therefore, the full semantic and historical trajectory of the term *jihad* and the duties understood to be inherent in it in the formative period of Islam, and thereby the multiple significations of martyrdom, we have to go back to the sources that record early, variegated points of view. The usual, conventional accounts lead one to the belief that by the ninth century CE (that is, the third century of Islam), the 'hawks' (to use present-day jargon) had basically won and the 'doves' had receded to the sidelines at best, or at worst been completely superseded. Yet a careful scrutiny of alternative sources at our disposal – alternative, that is, to standard juristic, exegetical and hadith literature – establishes that the supposedly superseded views of the doves continued to be preserved and disseminated in works that emanated from dissenting, pietistic circles.[16] This trend would become even more strongly manifested in Sufism in later centuries, but one of my purposes in this chapter is to show that these alternative opinions are not to be merely dismissed or marginalized as Sufi for they pre-date the rise of institutionalized Sufism.

The 'protest literature', if I may call it that, left behind by the 'doves' constitutes in part a genre called in Arabic *fada'il al-sabr*, which means 'the excellences or virtues of patience'. It is a genre that is meant to be in competition with the well-known genre of *fada'il al-jihad*, which praises the excellences or merits of armed combat. In almost a conscious, vaunting fashion, the *fada'il al-sabr* serves as a genre that extols a very important Qur'anic virtue having a crucial bearing on the discussion of *jihad*. This virtue is patience or forbearance, the active inculcation of which is frequently insisted upon in the Qur'an and for which generous posthumous rewards are promised. For instance, Qur'an 39:10 states that 'those who are patient will be given their reward without measure' and Qur'an 25:75 states that 'They will be awarded the high place [in heaven] for what they bore in patience . . . abiding there forever.' This high Qur'anic estimation of the moral attribute of patience is reflected in a statement attributed to the Prophet Muhammad found in the *Sahihayn* (the two 'sound' hadith compilations) of al-Bukhari (d. 870) and Muslim b. al-Hajjaj (d. 875), which states that humans have not been given anything better or more abundant than patience.[17]

It should further be stressed here that in Qur'anic discourse, patience *is* a component and a manifestation of the *jihad* of the righteous; quietist and activist resistance to wrongdoing are equally valorized. For example, one Qur'anic verse states: 'As for those who after persecution fled their homes and strove actively (*jahadu*) and were patient (*sabaru*) to the last, your Lord will be forgiving and merciful to them on the day when every soul will come pleading for itself' (16:110). Another states: 'We shall put you to the test until We know the active strivers (*al-mujahidin*) and the quietly forbearing (*al-sabirin*) among you' (47:31). However, quietist, non-violent struggle is not the same as passivity which, when displayed in the face of grave oppression and injustice, is clearly earmarked as immoral in the Qur'anic view; '[t]hose who are passive', in this sense, referred to as *al-Qa'idun* in Arabic, earn divine rebuke in the Qur'an, as in verse 4:95.

Patience as quietist struggle in contrast to activist struggle is thus amply vouched for in Qur'anic verses and in the reports contained in the hadith literature that praise the attribute of *sabr*. Together they represent countervailing and competing definitions of how best to struggle for the sake of God. A third/ninth-century work, for instance, on the merits of patience by Ibn Abi al-Dunya (d. 894), called *al-Sabr wa-'l-thawab 'alayhi* ('Patience and the Rewards for it'), records the following report on the authority of 'Isma Abi Hukayma, who related:

> The Messenger of God, peace and blessings be upon him, wept and we asked him, 'What has caused you to weep, O Messenger of God?' He replied, 'I reflected on the last of my community and the tribulations they will face. But the patient from among them who arrives will be given the reward of two martyrs (*shahidayn*).'[18]

This report clearly contests those reports that assign the highest merit to military martyrs and trumps them by allocating the reward of two such martyrs to the patient individual. Reports such as this challenge Reuven Firestone's statement in his monograph on *jihad* to the effect that there is little evidence of dissenting traditions challenging the militaristic concept of *jihad* in the medieval period.[19] Careful scrutiny of these *fada'il al-sabr* reports has the potential to yield invaluable insights which would considerably nuance and transform our current state of knowledge concerning early, multiple perspectives on how best to strive in the way of God. The two genres of literature – *fada'il al-jihad* ('excellences of armed struggle') and its mirror equivalent, *fada'il al-sabr* ('excellences of patience') – may together be adduced as evidence of early and competing definitions of 'striving in the path of God' and of the relatively late development of the notion of *jihad* as *primarily* armed combat. As my preliminary survey suggests, a close and systematic study of these two literatures, read as hortatory narratives composed during specific socio-political circumstances, reveals much about the historical and political consciousness of the early Islamic community and the multiple understandings and functions of *jihad*, and thus also of martyrdom, in it.

Conceptualizing Martyrdom

The reasons for proposing this thesis are as follows. The Qur'an, the earliest document we possess for the Muslim community, attests to multiple meanings of the locution *al-jihad fi sabil Allah* ('striving/struggling in the path of God'). Furthermore, the Qur'an does not have a single word for martyr or martyrdom, two concepts that are intrinsically linked to the concept of *jihad* as armed combat against the enemies of Islam. The Qur'anic verse that has been construed to refer to the special status of the military martyr runs thus: 'Do not think that those who were slain in the path of God are dead. They are alive and well provided for by their Lord' (3:169). Some of the exegetical and hadith works, however, make clear that the phrase 'slain in the path of God' was not understood to be restricted to those fallen in battle, but could be glossed in several ways, as discussed below.

The non-Qur'anic provenance of the concept of martyrdom may come as a surprise to us today, confronted as we are by the spectre of self-confessed Muslims who blow themselves up, apparently courting religious martyrdom and thus the attendant heavenly rewards promised in the *fada'il al-jihad* literature. One may be inclined to think that only the most explicit and trenchant scriptural imperative would be capable of eliciting this kind of proclivity for self-immolation, but this is not the case. The common Arabic word for martyr is *shahīd*. It is telling that nowhere in the Qur'an is this word used for a martyr; rather it is only used, interchangeably with *shāhid*, to refer to a legal or eye witness. Only in later extra-Qur'anic tradition does this word acquire the meaning of 'one who bears witness for the faith', particularly by laying down his life.

Extraneous, particularly Christian, influence may be suspected in this development since this secondary meaning clearly overlaps with the signification of the Greek term *martys*, rendered as 'martyr' in English, and since self-sacrifice for the sake of religion in the Christian tradition very early became a laudable and sought-after end. This influence very likely emanated via the Levantine Christians whom the Muslims encountered in the late seventh and eighth centuries, after the Prophet's death. Scholars have remarked on the highly probable influence of the cognate Syriac word for martyr-witness *sahedo* on the Arabic *shahīd*.[20] The fact that we encounter the term *shahīd* as martyr only in the hadith literature already implies the later development of this strand of meaning.

Many of the *fada'il al-sabr* reports contained in Ibn Abi al-Dunya's work referred to above testify in fact to a competitive discourse on piety that emphasizes the primacy of patience and forbearance over other traits and activities, including *jihad*, understood as armed combat. One such laudatory report is attributed to Qatada b. Di'ama, the Basran *tabi'i* or successor (that is, from the second generation of Muslims following the Companions of the Prophet), who is quoted as saying, 'Patience in relation to faith is like the hands in relation to the body. Whoever is not patient in the face of misfortune is not grateful for his blessings (*shakir al-ni'ma*). If patience were a man, he would be generous and handsome (*kariman, jamilan*).'[21] Two important ethical and Qur'anic references resonate in this report: the concept of *shukr al-ni'ma*, which refers to the gratitude of the believer for God's bounties conferred on him or her, which is the polar opposite of the concept of *kufr al-ni'ma*, which refers to the ingratitude of human beings for such bounties and, therefore, is the quintessential trait of the unbeliever. The second reference is to the Qur'anic description of patience as beautiful (*sabr jamil*) in verses 12:18 and 12:83.

Another report attributed to a certain Abu 'Imran al-Juni states, 'After faith, the believer (*'abd*) has not been given anything more meritorious (*afdal*) than patience with the exception of gratitude, but it [sc. patience] is more meritorious of the two and the fastest of the two to reap recompense (*thawab*) [for the believer].'[22] A similar report attributed to Sufyan b. 'Uyayna says, 'The believers (*al-'ibad*) have not been given anything better or more meritorious than patience, by means of which they enter heaven.'[23]

These reports are clearly at loggerheads with other, probably more frequently quoted reports which claim that falling on the battlefield brings swift and immeasurable heavenly rewards to the martyr. One of the best-known reports on the issue of compensation for the *shahīd* is the one recorded by Muslim b. al-Hajjaj and Ibn Maja (d. 887) in their authoritative collections of Hadith which declares that God forgives all the sins of the martyr except for his debt.[24] Another report in an early collection of Hadith by 'Abd al-Razzaq al-San'ani (d. 826) is attributed to the early authority al-Hasan al-Basri (d. 728), in which he relates that the Prophet had stated, 'Embarking upon the path of God or returning from it is better than all the world and what it contains. Indeed, when one of you stands within the battle ranks, then that is better than the worship of a man for sixty years.'[25] 'Abd al-Razzaq records another report in which a certain Abu Mujliz relates that he was passing by a Qur'an reciter, who was reciting 'God has favored those who strive with their wealth and their selves by conferring on them a rank above those who are sedentary' (4:95). At this point Abu Mujliz interrupted the reciter by saying, 'Stop. It has reached me that it is seventy ranks, and between each two levels, [a distance of] 70 years is reserved for the emaciated charge horse.' Abu Mujliz's impromptu exegesis is, first of all, evidence that *jihad* has come to be understood in certain circles by at least the late eighth century to primarily indicate armed combat even though the Qur'anic locution here, *al-mujahidin bi-amwalihim wa-anfusihim* ('those who strive with their wealth and their selves'), admits of a wider range of interpretative possibilities. It is also indicative of how high *jihad* in the sense of armed combat had risen as a religiously mandated activity in the estimation of a number of influential people, expressed in terms of generous recompense in the hereafter.

Interestingly, a report found in praise of patience invokes the language of this report in praise of *jihad*, establishing that there were efforts made to counter this kind of excessive glorification of the merits of military activity. This hadith is recorded by Ibn Abi al-Dunya in his work on *sabr* and is attributed to 'Ali b. Abi Talib. 'Ali relates:

> The Messenger of God, peace and blessings be upon him, said, 'Patience is of three kinds: patience during tribulations; patience in obedience to God, and patience in avoiding sin. Whoever has patience during a tribulation until he averts it by the seemliness of his forbearance, God will ordain for him three hundred levels [of recompense]; the distance between each level would equal that between the sky and the earth. And whoever has patience in obedience to God, God writes down for him six hundred levels; the distance between each level would equal that between the boundaries of the earth till the edge of the divine throne. And whoever has patience in avoiding sin, God prescribes for him nine hundred levels; the distance between each level is twice the distance between the boundaries of the earth up to the edge of the divine throne.'[26]

The shared idiom of these two reports in terms of how many levels or ranks the armed combatant and the patient quietist would earn or rise to in the hereafter suggests the vaunting nature of these reports and their conscious positing of opposed hierarchies of moral excellence.

A report recorded by Ibn Abi al-Dunya challenges the monovalent understanding of *jihad* as armed combat. The report emanates from 'Abd al-'Aziz b. Abi Rawwad, a pious *mawla* (a non-Arab Muslim convert) of Khurasanian descent who died in Mecca in 159/775, who states, 'A statement affirming the truth (*al-qawl bi'l-haqq*) and patience in abiding by it is equivalent to the deeds of the martyrs.'[27] Another report is attributed to al-Hasan al-Basri and is recorded by 'Abd al-Razzaq in his *Musannaf*. In this report al-Hasan says, 'There is nothing more arduous or exacting (*ajhad*) for a man than the money which he spends honestly or for a right cause and the prayer that he says deep in the middle of the night.'[28] Al-Hasan's use of the Arabic superlative *ajhad*, related etymologically to the term *jihad*, stresses the greater moral excellence of basic, non-militant personal acts of piety. Reports such as these highlight the general signification of *jihad* as striving to better oneself and one's social environment. Therefore, the emphasis is on non-military actions of courage: for example, speaking the truth even at the cost of imperilling one's life or facing other negative consequences, and on charity and prayer. Of course, this meaning is consistent with the famous prophetic hadith which describes the various means of resisting wrongdoing: by the hand, by the tongue, and by intent (that is, silently with the heart).[29]

These verbal jousts over which specific actions are to be considered the most morally excellent remains a predominant theme throughout this kind of literature and reflects the medieval Muslim's concern to identify and rank the moral valences of specific deeds. That there was a sizeable contingent of people who challenged the growing prevalence of the idea of *jihad* as primarily armed combat and the consequent romanticization of the concept of military martyrdom is often clear from the content of many of the early *akhbar* or reports that are labelled *mawquf* traditions: that is, they go back only to a Companion of the Prophet. For instance, the *Musannaf* of 'Abd al-Razzaq, which was compiled earlier than al-Bukhari's authoritative collection of hadith, contains a number of Companion reports that relate competing definitions of *shahīd*. A few examples will suffice. One report attributed to the Companion Abu Hurayra states that the *shahīd* is one who, were he to die in his bed, would enter heaven.[30] The explanatory note that follows states that it refers to someone who dies in his bed and is without sin (*la dhanb lahu*). Another report is related by Masruq b. al-Ajda', who states: 'there are four types of *shahada* or martyrdom for Muslims: the plague, parturition or delivery of a child, drowning, and a stomach ailment'.[31] Significantly, there is no mention of martyrdom being earned on account of dying on the battlefield in this early report. An expanded version of this report, however, originating with Abu Hurayra, quotes the Prophet as adding to this list of those who achieve martyrdom, 'one who is killed in the way of God (*man qutila fi sabil Allah*)'.[32] It is this expanded version containing the full five definitions of a *shahīd* that is recorded later in the authoritative hadith work of al-Bukhari.[33]

Another early, eighth-century hadith work records multiple significations of the term *shahīd*. The work, called *al-Muwatta'* ('The Well-Trodden [Path]') of Malik b. Anas (d. 795), states:

> The martyrs are seven, apart from death in God's way. He who dies as a victim of an epidemic is a martyr; he who dies from drowning is a martyr; he who dies from pleurisy is a martyr; he who dies from diarrhoea is a martyr; he who dies by [being burned in] fire is a martyr; he who dies by being struck by a dilapidated wall falling is a martyr; and the woman who dies in childbed is a martyr.[34]

This report and the one cited above assign martyrdom to the believer who suffers a painful death from a variety of debilitating illnesses, or a difficult labour for women in particular, or being victim to an unfortunate accident such as being crushed to death by a falling wall, in addition to falling on the battlefield.

The multiple, non-militant significations of the phrase *fi sabil Allah*, particularly in the early period, is further clear from a noteworthy hadith recorded in 'Abd al-Razzaq's *Musannaf*, which relates that a number of the Companions were sitting with the Prophet when a man from the tribe of Quraysh, apparently a pagan and of muscular build, came into view. Some of those gathered exclaimed, 'How strong this man looks! If only he would expend his strength in the way of God!' The Prophet asked, 'Do you think only someone who is killed [sc. in battle] is engaged in the way of God?' He continued, 'Whoever goes out in the world seeking licit work to support his family he is on the path of God; whoever goes out in the world seeking licit work to support himself, he is on the path of God. Whoever goes out seeking worldly increase has embarked, however, on the way of the devil.'[35] Another report praises the commission of charitable deeds as a commendable act of *jihad*, as recorded by three of the most authoritative Sunni hadith compilers, al-Bukhari, Muslim and al-Tirmidhi (d. 892). In this hadith, the Prophet declared, 'the one who helps widows and the poor are like the fighters in the path of God'.[35] Yet another prophetic statement found in the relatively early hadith works of Ahmad ibn Hanbal (d. 855) and al-Tirmidhi testifies to the inner, spiritual aspect of *jihad*. It states, 'One who strives against his own self is a *mujahid*, that is, carries out *jihad*.'[37] The range of meanings documented in these statements is to be expected since the quotidian struggle of the individual to live his or her life 'in the way of God' (*fi sabil Allah*) infuses even the most ordinary activities with moral and spiritual significance and thus meets with divine approbation.

Lastly, it should be mentioned that there are hadiths found in authoritative ninth-century compilations which counsel against military zeal and the courting of martyrdom. Al-Bukhari records reports in which the Prophet counsels that it is forbidden for an individual, first, to wish for death and, second, to wish for an encounter with the enemy.[38] Saving one's life and the lives of others is a high ethical priority in the Qur'an (5:32), even to the extent that the Qur'an expressly permits the believer to abjure his or her faith publicly under duress, as long as one's heart remains firm in belief (16:106). The wilful seeking of martyrdom is not at all condoned in Islam's normative texts and is regarded as a form of suicide or self-destruction, categorically proscribed in the Qur'an (2:195; 4:29) and in hadith.[39]

Conclusion

As the preceding survey will have made clear, consulting a wide variety of sources is particularly fruitful for uncovering a wider range of meanings assigned to both *jihad* and *shahīd* in the formative period of Islam. The retrieval of this semantic spectrum challenges the notion increasingly peddled today that these are monovalent terms and that they were, and are, intrinsically connected with armed combat and violence. Needless to say, those who make such assertions often have no scholarly training and are unable to access the primary sources. Alternatively, there are those who are able to consult such

works but still wilfully misrepresent them or only selectively quote from
them. They include both Muslim and non-Muslim extremists, who thereby
do great intellectual violence to the ethical precepts of classical Islam on the
critical issues of war and peace.

Notes

1   This chapter arises out of my monograph-length work now in progress, *Striving in the
    Path of God: Discursive Traditions on Jihad and the Cult of Martyrdom*.
2   These traditional sources were used by the editors of the standard 1924 Cairo edition
    of the Qur'an to determine a chronology of Qur'anic verses and chapters that is
    widely accepted. The two German scholars Nöldeke and Schwally also came up with a
    chronology popular among Orientalists. For a useful discussion of these two systems, see
    Hanna Kassis, *A Concordance of the Qur'an* (Berkeley, University of California Press,
    1983), pp. xxxv–xxxix.
3   These were the four months deemed sacred in the pre-Islamic period during which
    fighting was prohibited.
4   One of the most extensive discussions in English on this topic remains Majid Khadduri's
    The Islamic Law of Nations: Shaybani's Siyar (Baltimore, Johns Hopkins University
    Press, 1966), especially pp. 4–70.
5   For an extensive discussion of these issues, see the recent monograph by Khaled Abou
    el Fadl, *Rebellion and Violence in Islamic Law* (Cambridge, Cambridge University
    Press, 2001). On the issue of legitimate war, the parallels between the Islamic law of
    nations and modern international law are obvious. Islamic influence on the development
    of modern international law has long been suggested by scholars. Hugo Grotius, the
    'father' of European international law, was believed to have learnt of Islamic legal tenets
    from two contemporary Spanish sources, which in turn had been inspired by the Islamic
    legal tradition that had held sway in medieval Spain under its Muslim rulers. For this
    intriguing discussion, see, for example, J.B. Scott, *Classics of International Law* (New
    York, Columbia University Press, 1939), pp. 17–21; Marcel Boisard, 'On the Probable
    Influence of Islam on Western Public and International Law', *International Journal of
    Middle East Studies*, Vol. 2 (1980), p. 445.
6   Many of these points are further discussed by Sohail Hashmi, 'Interpreting the Islamic
    Ethics of War and Peace', in Terry Nardin (ed.), *The Ethics of War and Peace* (Princeton,
    Princeton University Press, 1996), pp. 146–66.
7   For a brief and accessible introduction to this concept, see the article 'naskh', *Encyclopedia
    of Islam*, new edition, ed. C.E. Bosworth *et al.* (Leiden, E.J. Brill, 1993), 7: 1009–12.
    The Arabic term *naskh* is often translated as 'abrogation' but may also be rendered as
    'supersession', 'change' or even the 'privileging' of some thing over another.
8   See, for example, Ibn al-Mubarak, *Kitab al-Jihad*, ed. N. Hammad (Beirut, 1977).
9   Al-Shafi'i, *al-Risala*, ed. Ahmad Shakir (1891), pp. 430–32.
10 Cited by Majid Khadduri, *War and Peace in the Law of Islam* (Baltimore, Johns Hopkins
    University Press, 1955), pp. 65–66.
11 Al-Tabari, *Jami' al-bayan 'an ta'wil ay al-Qur'an* (Beirut, 1995), 3:25.
12 Ibn Kathir, *Tafsir al-Qur'an al-'azim* (Riad, Maktabat Dar al-Salam, 1998), 1:416–17.
13 Ibid., 1:416. See also David Dakake, 'The Myth of a Militant Islam', in Joseph E.B.
    Lumbard (ed.), *Islam, Fundamentalism, and the Betrayal of Tradition* (Bloomington,
    University of Indiana Press, 2004), p. 15.
14 See Ibn Taymiyya, *al-Siyasa al-Shar'iya*, ed. 'Ali al-Nashshar and A.Z. 'Atiya (Cairo,
    1951), pp. 126–53.
15 Thus the medieval scholar al-Suyuti (d. 1505) cites 21 instances of 'abrogation' while

the eighteenth-century scholar Shah Waliullah records only five. The Ahmadi scholar Maulana Muhammad 'Ali in the twentieth century, however, questioned the validity of the concept itself by arguing that there were no unassailably reliable reports to support *naskh*.

16 See, for example, Muhammad al-Qurtubi, *Jami Ahkam al-Qur'an* (Cairo, 1935), 2:348.
17 See A.J. Wensinck, *Concordance et indices de la tradition musulmane* (Leiden, E.J. Brill, 1936–69), 3:242.
18 See Ibn Abi al-Dunya, *Al-Sabr wa-'l-thawab 'alayhi* (Beirut, 1997), p. 85.
19 See his *Jihad: The Origin of Holy War in Islam* (Oxford, Oxford University Press, 1999), p. 100.
20 See the previously cited useful article by A.J. Wensinck, 'The Oriental Doctrine of the Martyrs', in his *Semietische Studiën uit de nalatenschap* (Leiden, 1941), pp. 91–113, which establishes striking parallels between Christian and post-Qur'anic Muslim concepts of martyrdom; and the article by Etan Kohlberg, 'Shahid', in the *Encyclopaedia of Islam*, 9:104.
21 Ibn Abi al-Dunya, *al-Sabr wa'-l-thawab*, p. 112.
22 Ibid.
23 Ibid., p. 51.
24 Wensinck, *Concordance*, 3:200.
25 'Abd al-Razzaq al-San'ani, *Al-Musannaf*, ed. Habib al-Rahman al-A'zami (Beirut, 1970–72), 5:259, #9543.
26 Ibn Abi al-Dunya, *al-Sabr wa-'l-thawab*, p. 31.
27 Ibid., p. 116.
28 'Abd al-Razzaq, *Musannaf*, 11:105.
29 This is a hadith reported by Muslim; see al-Nawawi's *Forty Hadith*, trans. Ezzeddin Ibrahim and Denys Johnson-Davies (Salimiah, Kuwait, International Islamic Federation of Student Organizations, 1993), p. 110.
30 Ibid., 5:268.
31 Ibid., 5:271.
32 Ibid., 5:270–71.
33 Al-Bukhari, *Sahih*, ed. Qasim al-Shamma'i al Rifa'i (Beirut, n.d.), 2:420–21.
34 Malik b. Anas, *al-Muwatta*, ed. Bashshar 'Awad Ma'rut and Mahmud Muhammad Khalil (Beirut, 1994), 1:366–67.
35 *Musannaf*, 5:272.
36 Wensinck, *Concordance*, 1:389.
37 Ibid.
38 Cited by A.J. Wensinck, 'The Oriental Doctrine of the Martyrs', in his *Semietische Studiën uit de nalatenschap* (Leiden, A.W. Sitjhoff, 1941), p. 95.
39 Al-Bukhari records a hadith in which the Prophet relates that God forbade Paradise to a man who took his own life after being badly wounded in a battle; see the *Sahih of Imam al-Bukhari*, trans. Muhammad Muhsin Khan (Medina, 1971), Vol. 4, Book 56, #669.

Chapter Two

Christian Martyrdom: History and Interpretation

Anthony Harvey, Richard Finn and Michael Smart

The Word *Martys*

The origin and the principal use of the Greek word *martys*, 'witness', is found in the law-court, or at least in business with legal implications (such as 'witnessing' a will or a contract). This is easily said, but it is important not to project modern legal conceptions on to institutions of the ancient world. One significant difference is that for Greeks, Romans and Jews, physical or circumstantial evidence played a much smaller part in legal proceedings than it does today. The question was not so much 'Does this witness's account square with all the facts we know?' as 'Can we rely on this witness's word and is he the sort of man we can trust?'. Various factors might complicate this question. In a Greek or Roman court a witness might resort to rhetorical skills to persuade the judge, and this would have to be allowed for. In Jewish procedure the witness might also be involved in both the arrest and the prosecution of the defendant. True, his testimony would be subject to the scrutiny of the court.[1] But the paramount question was always whether the witnesses were persons of known[2] credibility. Were they of a reputation and a standing which would command respect? As a last resort, in default of such a witness, the defendant could swear an oath – 'call God to witness'. This settled the matter: God was a 'witness' whom the court could hardly challenge; if the oath-taker was not telling the truth he ran the risk of a heavy punishment from God.

This reliance on the personal credibility of witnesses for the effective functioning of the legal system explains the high social and moral esteem awarded to people who commanded respect for their testimony. Citizens who would be fair and truthful witnesses were highly valued. A false witness in a Jewish court would be liable to severe punishment – the equivalent of that which the defendant would have received if found guilty (Deut. 19:16–21); one proved unreliable could not testify again. A deceitful witness was also subject to moral censure: 'A truthful witness saves lives, but one who utters lies is a betrayer' (Prov. 14:25). This also helps to explain the primary metaphorical use of the word as 'witness', not to an objective fact, but to an opinion or a philosophy of life. The Stoic philosopher

Epictetus described the man whose character was formed to practise Stoic or Cynic virtues even when under conditions of extreme poverty, misfortune or persecution as a 'witness' to his philosophy:[3] it was a man of observable character – self-sufficient, unaffected by physical adversity and so forth – whose 'witness' to the viability of Stoicism or Cynicism could be most trusted.

Witnessing to God

This question of the reliability of witnesses has an important application in the religious sphere. How do we know that God exists? If he does exist, what is he like? No one has seen God at any time – there is no direct evidence of his existence and his character. There are of course 'signs' – answers to prayer, significant weather phenomena, unexpected military victories – but these tend to be ambivalent, and moreover God has an awkward tendency not to do in any easily observable way what his justice seems to demand: the flourishing of the ungodly is a challenge to belief. Consequently, to be accepted and believed in, God requires 'witnesses';[4] and for these to be effective they must be people who, for one reason or another, are known to be deserving of trust.

Christianity was born in a culture where the existence of God was not seriously doubted. No witnesses were needed to attest to it. If anything, it was God's justice, or his faithfulness in the protection of his own people, which might require the testimony of persons believed to have privileged access to him and to be worthy of respect in such matters, such as the prophets. But with Christianity a new case for God had to be presented – the case that God had 'sent' Jesus, anointed him with the Holy Spirit, acknowledged him as his Son, inspired his mighty works, destined him for death and (above all) raised him from the dead. How was all this to be believed? To a certain extent, God had furthered his own case with signs and miracles (for example, Acts 2:22); but the crucial weight of proof rested on the 'witnesses', whose task was to persuade others of the truth of these claims. The authentication of these witnesses derived in the first instance from the fact that they had personally 'witnessed' the resurrection – this became the principal qualification for being an 'apostle' (Acts 1:8). But witnessing to Christ in a wider sense required establishing that the witness was trustworthy – a problem for the early Christians, since their leaders were not of a social class or distinction to command immediate respect (1 Cor. 1:26–28). It was soon seen that the only way for these 'witnesses' to persuade others of the truth was to live by the same truth themselves and show by their life and conduct that they were totally committed to the testimony they gave. In the same sense as the followers of Epictetus, they were 'witnesses' to the religious philosophy they preached in so far as their lives were impressive demonstrations of the life which that philosophy recommended.

This kind of witness might, of course, involve suffering or even death, and their manner of bearing these things would be a significant part of their testimony. Socrates was by no means the last of the pagan philosophers to have paid the ultimate penalty for his convictions;[5] and the bearing of such men remained an example to their followers. But it was only in the Judaic tradition that this suffering had come to take on a positive significance in itself. The story begins already in Deutero-Isaiah, where the 'suffering servant' goes to his death bearing the transgressions of others (Isa. 53:11). It continues in Daniel and subsequent apocalyptic literature, where the sufferings of the righteous are a necessary stage in the drama leading to their ultimate vindication and the establishment of God's kingdom. And it finds its classic expression in the saga of the Maccabean heroes, whose exemplary faithfulness in the face of ruthless torture and execution is alluded to in the New Testament (Heb. 11:35; cf. 2 Macc. 7:9, 29) and was kept fresh in the memory by the large number of those who bore their forenames (Simon, Judas and so on) in the time of Christ.

Purpose and Motive

What was the purpose of their sufferings? The account in 2 Maccabees (written some time between the mid-second and mid-first century BCE) suggests a number of explanations. One is the widely shared view that suffering is a necessary discipline imposed on the righteous for their own good: 'he disciplines us with calamities' (2 Macc. 6:16). Another is the strength of example: those who submit to this discipline will 'leave to the young a noble example of how to die a good death willingly and nobly for the revered and holy laws' (2 Macc. 6:28). Again, by submitting to death at the hands of a pagan ruler they could be assured that the perpetrator would receive exceptional punishment by God (2 Macc. 7:30–38). But also (and most significantly, in view of future Christian reflection on the death of Christ and of his followers), their suffering was understood to effect atonement, not only for their own sins (2 Macc. 7:32), but for those of their nation (2 Macc. 7:38); and this thought is further developed in 4 Maccabees (written early in the first century CE), where the deaths of the noble victims are called a 'purification' (2 Macc. 6:29), a 'ransom' (2 Macc. 17:21) and an 'atoning sacrifice' (2 Macc. 17:22) for their sinful nation.

Throughout this literature the motivation of the Maccabean sufferers themselves is described more simply. Challenged by their pagan oppressors to renounce their allegiance to their ancestral laws and (for example) to accept a dish of pork, they chose death rather than commit such flagrant apostasy. This in itself marks them out as something virtually unique in the ancient world. The Jewish historian Josephus draws the attention of his Roman readers to this remarkable national characteristic: 'it becomes natural to all Jews immediately and from their very birth to esteem those books [that is, the Law of Moses] above all else to contain divine precepts, and to persist in them, and if occasion be, to die for them' (*Contra Apionem* 1.8). Philo, similarly, writing in Alexandria a bare generation earlier, noted that the Jews living in Judea 'were men, physically strong, of great courage and spirit, who are willing to die in defence of their national customs and laws in a spirit which some opponents might call barbaric and which in reality is free and noble' (*Legatio* 215). This is not to say, of course, that pagans were unwilling to die for the philosophical or political principles that they held dear; and, although the motivation of these pagan 'martyrs' was often as much political as religious, there were occasions on which they could be regarded as 'God's witnesses' against tyranny.[6] Yet Jewish history showed astonishing examples of national willingness to die for their customs and beliefs (notably the mass resistance, which could have been suicidal, to attempts to paganize the Jerusalem temple in 40 CE), for which there is virtually no parallel in the ancient world.[7] And the Jewish culture is certainly unique in ascribing positive and expiatory value to the sufferings of the righteous.

But nowhere in the literature are these sufferers described as 'martyrs' or 'witnesses'. The Jewish Law, after all, did not need individual witnesses to its existence in the way that a belief in God or in exalted moral principles might have done. Its observance by the Jewish nation was an observable fact, and men were prepared to die, not so much to give testimony to its existence as to offer a supreme example of piety and obedience to the commandments of God, setting a standard for others to follow and atoning for the lesser faith shown by the nation as a whole.

That 'witnessing' to the Christian faith could lead to suffering and even death was, of course, understood right from the outset. The vocabulary of 'witnessing' is prominent in John's Gospel, where Jesus's disciples are explicitly described as 'witnessing' to Jesus (John 15:27 and elsewhere); and in the Lukan writings the apostles are regularly called 'witnesses' (Luke 24:48; Acts 1:8 and frequently).

The suffering involved in this witnessing was accepted as a necessary phase of history before the end of the present age, and one which would test and purify the early Church: the Book of Acts records the violent death of several of the Church's leaders at the hands of their fellow Jews, and, in the case of Stephen (Acts 22:20), his death is described as that of a 'witness' (*martys*), perhaps because at his death he had a vision of the risen Christ at the right hand of God. Christians became the object of sporadic persecution also by the Romans from the time of Nero onwards; and the author of Revelation (doubtless with some hyperbole) describes Rome (under the figure of Babylon) as a woman 'drunk on the blood of the saints and on the blood of the witnesses' (*martyres*) of Jesus – the two categories may be the same, for it was of the essence of Christian 'saints' that they were 'witnesses' to Christ, and no one doubted that this witness might incur suffering and even death.

Witnessing by Dying

Yet for at least a hundred years this ultimate 'witnessing' by death was not distinguished from lesser hardships endured for the sake of Christ. The technical sense of 'martyrdom' appears first in *The Martyrdom of Polycarp*, which was written in Asia Minor shortly after Bishop Polycarp's death in 155 CE. Thereafter the words *martys* and *martyria* became technical terms for the witness which is given by the martyr in death and was distinguished from merely 'confessing' the faith under conditions of persecution. Why this linguistic development took place is a matter of scholarly debate, and no explanation has found general favour.[8] But the change in the meaning of the word was accompanied by a rapid development in the understanding of martyrdom itself.

The first explicit theology of martyrdom is found in the letters of St Ignatius, particularly those to the Romans, Smyrnaeans and Ephesians. Ignatius was a bishop (though not exactly what we mean by a bishop today) in the Christian community at Antioch, where his leadership had sparked controversy and opposition. He was arrested for his beliefs and, in 113 CE or thereabouts, wrote a series of letters to various churches while he was being sent under armed escort to Rome.[9]

Ignatius does not talk about his death as an act of witness or martyrdom.[10] It looks as though Ignatius talks of those whom we would term 'martyrs' only as those 'slain for God'.[11] However, Ignatius repeatedly presents himself in self-deprecating terms, whether as an off-cast or humble offering (*peripsema*)[12] or as a dedication: he tells the Ephesians that he 'dedicates himself' to them (*hagnizomoi*)[13] and is their 'expiation' (*antipsychon*).[14] The *Letter to the Romans* suggests that he, in fact, sees his death as a self-sacrifice, for he writes in Pauline terms: 'Grant me nothing more than that I be poured out as a libation for God, while an altar is still ready . . .'.[15] That altar is the arena. Ignatius presents himself to the church at Smyrna as empowered by Christ to undergo and endure suffering.[16] He sees himself as drawing close to God by means of his death, and, in the *Letter to the Romans*, sees that death as a matter of imitating Christ in his Passion: 'allow me to be an imitator of the suffering of my God'.[17] Philip Rousseau has rightly emphasized the way in which Ignatius' theology of martyrdom develops out of his attack on docetism, his defence of Christ as true man and true God: 'martyrdom was a proof of the Incarnation, a living formula of Christology, a symbol of humanity and divinity conjoined. It made present in the community . . . the saving effect of Christ.'[18] Thus, Ignatius uses his letters to make his approaching death a testimony to the Catholic faith that he has defended at Antioch. That death will, in turn, set the seal of authenticity to his letters and the teaching they contain. Act and text together define as they pass on the faith within the Christian churches.

Language and Theology

The Martyrdom of Polycarp has a strong claim to open the second period
in which a developed language and theology of martyrdom determine the
Christian experience of persecution. The author weaves together a theme
found in Ignatius, namely the imitation of Christ, with the language of
scripture, and, as will become apparent later, a discourse of virtuous suffering
already found in Polycarp's own writing. Let us look first at the language of
martyrdom itself. In the opening chapters the author develops a threefold
account of what it might be to be a witness or martyr. On the one hand, we
find an adaptation of the older concept of being an eye-witness of Christ:
the conduct of the martyrs under torture is to be explained by their vision of
Christ; yet this is also a fixing of their attention on the grace or goodness
of Christ and a keeping before their eyes of their escape from eternal fire,
a revelation to the 'eyes of the heart' of those good things which St Paul in
1 Corinthians writes as 'what no eye has seen, nor ear heard, nor the heart of
man conceived, what God has prepared for those who love him' (2:9). The
sight of Christ, the Divine Word, is here extended to our hold on revelation by
faith. The literal and miraculous shade into the metaphorical. Furthermore,
Polycarp is presented as witnessing to Christ by the Christ-like manner and
pattern of his death, a claim to be borne out in the narrative which follows.
The bishop knows of his approaching betrayal and execution: he will be
arrested on a Friday night when he has been lying in an upper room; the
eirenarch or justice of the peace who arrests him is one Herod, who comes
with an armed guard 'as though for a robber' – Christ's words in Gethsemane;
the bishop will enter the city on a donkey; his death is desired by the Jews
of the city, who add their cries to those of the pagans; he will make of his
death a sacrificial offering; and his body will be pierced, not by a lance but
a dagger. To a much lesser extent, the other martyrs also share in this form
of witness by their silence under torture. At his death Polycarp thanks God
for 'numbering him among the martyrs in the cup of your Christ', and it is
this novel form of witness – the imitation of Christ's suffering understood as
participation in that mystery – which defines martyrdom: the author presents
the 'martyrs' as 'disciples and imitators of the Lord'.[19]

Texts written about the martyrs before the advent of Christian emperors
in the fourth century repeatedly celebrate the virtue of patient courage or
'endurance' – the Greek *hypomone*. In this they follow *The Martydom of
Polycarp*, where the young martyr Germanicus is praised at the beginning
of the story for his 'endurance' in the arena;[20] on entering the amphitheatre a
voice from heaven calls on Polycarp to 'be strong and act like a man' and he is
said to show that courage during his interrogation.[21] The bishop's 'endurance'
is praised at the story's end.[22] In the *Acta* of Justin and his companions, when
Rusticus asks Justin during his interrogation whether he hopes to rise from
the dead, the teacher likewise replies that he hopes to do so on account of his
'endurance'.[23]

We can now see how *The Martyrdom of Polycarp* is extensively shaped by what Polycarp himself had written in a letter to the church at Philippi many years earlier, when he urged the faithful to practise this same virtue which they have witnessed in Ignatius and his companions; they are to imitate Christ's 'endurance' and 'if we suffer for his name, let us glorify him. For he has given us this example himself and we have believed it . . . So I urge you all to obey the word of righteousness and to endure with all forbearance, which you saw with your own eyes not only in the holy ones, Ignatius, Zosimos and Rufus . . .'[24] It looks as though this passage is the hermeneutic key taken by the author of *The Martyrdom* to guide his portrayal of Polycarp's death. It was to be highly influential beyond the Greek churches. The Latin equivalents for *hypomone* are *sufferentia* and *tolerantia*. In the *Passio of Perpetua and Felicity* Perpetua relates how, at her baptism shortly after her arrest, the Spirit inspired her to pray for '*sufferentiam carnis*' – endurance in the flesh.[25] It is a late Latin word and is not found, therefore, in the Oxford Latin Dictionary, although it is used four times by Tertullian, three in the context of possible martyrdom.[26]

The Letter of the Churches of Lyons and Vienne elaborates what we may think of as a theatre of opposing extremes. We find the language of 'nobility' in 'endurance': on their arrest the Christians 'nobly endured what the crowd together rained down on them'.[27] It is a theatre of extremes because, on the one hand, the martyrs 'endured punishments which beggar all description'.[28] The slave-girl Blandina is said to exhaust her torturers. She survives torments any one of which should have killed her.[29] She is sent into the arena not once, but twice. On the other hand, the author repeatedly draws attention to the power of God to give the essential virtue of endurance to notably weak protagonists: God's grace 'shielded the weak, and set up in defence secure pillars capable by their endurance of drawing to themselves the whole onslaught of the evil one'.[30] Blandina's sex and social status already mark out her vulnerability. Her mistress is described as being fearful for Blandina, because of her 'physical weakness'.[31] After her first appearance in the arena we are told that 'small, weak and easily despised, she would convince her brothers, for she had put on the great and unbeatable athlete, Christ'.[32] In a very similar way, the elderly bishop Pothinus is described as 'physically very weak'.[33]

This theatre of extremes displays Christ's power to triumph over evil, and the martyrs' endurance is presented as the privileged locus where that power is seen at work. Christ is said to conquer over the tortures 'through the endurance of the blessed'.[34] Much is made of how a group of Christians who had earlier apostatized are persuaded by the martyrs' example finally to confess their faith. Christ's mercy towards them is said to reveal itself 'through the endurance' of the martyrs.[35] So, what *The Martyrdom of Polycarp* presents largely in terms of an imitation of Christ has become an arena in which Christ himself is active in turning apparent weakness to strength. The same shift is also seen in the Carthaginian *Passio of Perpetua and Felicity*, which dates at least in part from the early third century. When Felicity is questioned by a prison flunkey as to how she will bear the pains of martyrdom if she suffers so much in giving birth, the slave-girl replies that while 'now I am the one who suffers what I suffer, but then another will be within me who will suffer for me, because I shall be suffering for him'.[36] This response is echoed elsewhere – *The Martyrdom of Montanus and Lucius* tells of a vision by a deacon, Flavian, not long after the execution of Cyprian at Carthage. He asks Cyprian how painful the blow of execution will be, only to be told that 'another flesh suffers when the mind is in heaven'.[37]

The Message of the Texts

What are we to make of all this? May we presume that these texts were written, but also copied and disseminated, in large part to strengthen the resolve of Christians at risk of persecution and so of apostasy? There is certainly evidence to support this rather obvious approach. *The Letter of Phileas*, the early fourth-century bishop of Thumis in the Egyptian Thebaid, says that the Alexandrian martyrs of his day were prepared for death through 'all the examples available to us, the models and noble tokens set out in the sacred and divinely-inspired scriptures'.[38] He has in mind, first, the biblical texts: the word for 'model' here (*hypogrammos*) is that found in 1 Peter 2:21 (Christ suffered for you, leaving you an example). But we need to recognize the wider hagiographical literature in which the early Christians were immersed and by which they were influenced. What may be the paraenetic intent of these works is sometimes given visible form within them. In *The Passio of Perpetua and Felicity* the martyr Saturus, moments before his death and drenched in his own blood after being mauled by a leopard, exhorts the soldier Pudens with the words 'Farewell – remember the faith and me; do not let these things confound you, but let them embolden you.'[39] This type of exhortation is found within a number of *acta* from this middle period. In another North African text, *The Martyrdom of Marian and James*, two bishops on their way to execution encounter at Mugae, near Cirta, a group of Christians including Marian and James whom they are said to exhort to share their fate:

> So strong was the life-giving and gracious spirit within them that for such holy and famous witnesses of God it was but little for them to devote their own precious blood to a glorious martyrdom, if they did not also create other martyrs by inspiring them with their own faith. So great was their love, their affection, for the brethren that, although they could have built up the faith of their brothers without a word by the example of their firm courage and dedication, they watered our breasts with the dew of a salutary sermon in the hope of further strengthening our perseverance.[40]

In like fashion, *The Martyrdom of Montanus and Lucius* has a group of martyrs who, on arrival at their place of execution, exhort the people by 'a generous flow of speech'.[41]

We may take all this as modelling within the text a central call to perseverance which the texts themselves are meant to communicate. But we should not see this primarily in terms of training the individual for his or her own martyrdom: after all, persecution was sporadic until the Decian and Valerian persecutions of the mid-third century. These texts, read out in churches on the martyrs' feast days and also read in private, structure the moral imagination of early Christians, shaping and interpreting the ecclesial experience of persecution so that it became bearable for the community. The *acta* relate these particular evils to faith in God's victory over evil in Christ. Dogma has not only to be formulated; it has to be imaginatively received and handed on. Indeed, this artful and liturgical literature runs ahead of any dogmatic formulation. Christian teachings that matter are here passed on in a narrative key. The texts also determine how Christians see their past – as marked by heroic success rather than the often tawdry reality in which a great many Christians kept their heads down, sacrificed or bought fake certificates of sacrifice.

Paese and Thecla

We can also look at the changing role of martyrs' *acta* and the cult of the martyrs once persecution was over. A Coptic codex from the ninth century includes a tale of a prosperous and charitable bachelor, Paese, and his widowed sister, Thecla, from a village in the Hermopolite nome of Roman Egypt, who were reportedly martyred during the persecution unleashed by Diocletian in the opening years of the fourth century.[42] The story may have some historical kernel (the village's existence is now known from papyri fragments of the mid-fourth century), but contains much stock and legendary material. It purports to tell how a Christian landowner, Paese, was inspired by the Holy Spirit to seek his own death on watching the courageous martyrdom at Alexandria of a young aristocrat, Victor, whose name is surely no accident.[43] Repeatedly tortured and repeatedly saved from his torments by the archangel Raphael, Paese's sufferings are in turn witnessed by 'the multitude' and, as a result of what they see, 'the number of people who believed on that day was twenty-four souls'.[44] Then, as one miraculous escape from death follows another, so prison guards and torturers come to confess Christ. What matters for the authors of the text is, first, these martyrs' ability to cheat death through their prayers and, second, the intervention of the archangel Raphael. For Paese and Thecla came to be patrons of an important shrine where the sick came to find healing and which the *acta* serve to promote. The story presents Jesus as promising our hero and heroine, shortly before their execution, that:

I will set My blessing and My peace in the place where your bodies shall be laid. And behold, I have set the angel Raphael to minister to your shrine; and great numbers of sick people suffering from divers diseases shall come to your shrine, and obtain healing, and go home in peace.[45]

In addition to promoting the cult and shrine of its protagonists, the tale of Paese and Thecla gives shape to ethical ideals in the lives of the characters. We are told not only that Paese is unmarried, but that he has resisted his parents' encouragement to marry: we are presented therefore with an exemplary asceticism in renouncing marriage. Though a wealthy landowner, he is said to perform 'great acts of charity', setting aside a certain number of fleeces and a certain amount of his crops to aid widows, orphans and others among the poor.[46] He makes provision shortly before his death for his remaining wealth to be distributed as charity by his former business partner and fellow Christian, Paul.[47] Thecla likewise refuses offers of a second marriage and distributes clothing and bedding to the destitute in the city of Antinoou, taking the naked into her house to clothe and feed. When persecution breaks out, both prepare food for those held in prison.[48] Shortly before her death she instructs her son to distribute her clothing 'to the naked'.[49] The value attaching to these various forms of almsgiving and asceticism is made explicit by the praise heaped on our protagonists: prisoners tell Paese that he has acted as Christ had spoken in Matthew 25:36 and 10:42; an angel promises Thecla that her gifts of clothing will be matched by God's gift to her of 'garments of light'.

Ideals of Christian virtue are here shaped and held up for admiration. Scriptural verses are mapped on to specific charitable practices, so that the former authorize the latter while being in turn interpreted by them. Few readers of these stories, or listeners to them, would have shared such wealth and only some would have practised the same forms of sexual asceticism, but the story advocates the value of these practices within Christian communities, together with the recognition that some in those communities, the widows and orphans, and the destitute, had a privileged claim to the charity shown by their fellow Christians. Another legend from a ninth-century codex, concerning the martyrdom of Shenoufe and his 11 brothers, places a similar emphasis on the almsgiving practised by the future martyrs.[50] Paese receives a vision in which he sees the rewards awaiting those on earth who 'glorify a saint'. In heaven the martyr intercedes for those who have built a shrine in his or her honour, who have buried a poor person, made an offering or given alms on the saint's day, or given a gospel book to the shrine.[51] Here, an ethic of generous giving is an important element in the cult of the martyrs, which patterns and motivates that giving.

Martyrs' Cults

Local cults to the martyrs spread like wildfire in the late fourth and fifth centuries. Not only did they provide a focus of unity after the disarray caused by persecution, but they also offered local heroes to cities whose civic pride and identity had been closely bound to specific temple cults. In some cases, a martyr could be used to challenge the supposed power of a pagan deity. At Antioch it was apparently the Caesar Gallus who, with the support of the local bishop, interred the relics of St Babylas, a former bishop and martyr who had died in prison during the Decian persecution, in a new martyrium or shrine at Daphne, deliberately polluting the shrine there of Apollo and so silencing the oracle. It was a highly contentious move. When the pagan emperor, Julian, removed the martyr's relics a mysterious fire swept through the pagan temple complex, which pagans attributed to Christian arsonists but which Christians presented as the martyr's verdict on his eviction.[52] The pagan teacher of rhetoric, Libanius, addressed the gods in his oration for Julian on the emperor's death: 'A creed which we had until then laughed to scorn, which had declared such violent, unceasing war against you, has won the day, after all.'[53] The reports of miracles worked by the martyrs at their shrines were important to bishops in particular, to 'demonstrate' to pagans the truth of the faith, its power and thus the folly of paganism. Hilary, late fourth-century bishop of Poitiers, wrote how the tombs of the apostles and martyrs proclaimed the Christ by the miracles which were performed at them.[54]

Through their healing miracles, recalled and celebrated in Christian discourse, martyrs' shrines supplanted the role of pagan temples as places where the sick travelled in search of a cure. The tomb of St Felix at Nola was constructed in such a way that perfumed oil could be poured in and extracted from the tomb, a practice known to have been taking place by 406, but which was probably much older.[55] The extracted oil was considered to have healing properties. How such holy oil might be kept and used can be seen from the fifth-century *Religious History* by Theodoret of Cyrrhus. Theodoret recounted for his readers how he had been protected during the night from demonic attack by a flask of oil containing the blessing received from many martyrs hung up near his bed, as well as by the blanket or cloak under his head which came from the famous ascetic, James.[56]

Bishops were not slow to realize the value of martyrs' relics in dealing with Christian dissidents. Ambrose made good use of the timely 'discovery' at Milan of the supposed relics of the martyrs Gervasius and Protasius in his conflict with Arian Christians in the imperial capital. He moved their relics from the church in which they were found into the basilica which came to bear his name, and their miracles testified to his orthodoxy. Ambrose's biographer related how one of the demoniacs whom Late Antique men and women expected to find at such a shrine 'suddenly possessed by an unclean spirit, began to cry out that those were tortured as he himself was tortured who denied the martyrs or did not believe the unity of the trinity as Ambrose was teaching'.[57] The bishop made the most of his find: he sent further relics of the saints to bishops who shared his defence of Nicene Christianity. Through the stories which were told of the martyrs, but also the practices which took place around their shrines, Christians passed on the faith to new converts and determined the form of Christianity passed to a new generation of Christians who had no experience of persecution.

The North African theologian Tertullian closed his *Apology* with the triumphant and paradoxical claim that the blood of the martyrs is the seed of Christians: 'we grow in number the more often you mow us down: Christians' blood is seed'. The pagan philosophers had taught the proper endurance of suffering and death, but their eloquent arguments, Tertullian claimed, won fewer disciples than Christian conduct under persecution; the steadfast refusal to sacrifice which pagan magistrates condemned as obstinacy spoke with authority to those who beheld it.[58]

Martyrdom was, indeed, highly important to the transmission of the faith in the early Church, as the texts we have studied show, but not as the raw experience of persecution, if such a thing exists; persecution was creatively interpreted by the discourse and cult which grew up around it. And only in the final phase, after the end of persecution, was martyrdom at all important in the conversion of pagans to Christianity; it mattered far more as a means to the preservation of faith within the Christian community, and that faith was shaped in the process. So, Christians' blood is indeed seed – but only by the transforming power of imagination and ink.

Later Martyrdoms

The Roman persecutions of the Church during the first three centuries of its existence formed the classic and defining period of Christian martyrdom. This is not to say that persecution ceased after the conversion of Constantine or that martyrdom became a rare event: a major persecution of Christians was initiated by Shapur II, emperor of Persia (309–379 CE), mainly for political reasons (he suspected them of being sympathetic to his enemy, Rome), and it is estimated that within half a century many thousands of Christians were martyred in the Middle East.[59] Nevertheless, at least in the Western Church, a change took place in the sense that, apart from the persecutions inflicted by Christians on one another at the Reformation, martyrdom ceased to be the probable fate of those who dedicated their lives most wholeheartedly to Christ. Yet it remained the highest grade of sanctity: the martyr was revered more intensely than other saints, and it became necessary to define the circumstances under which the death of a Christian should be considered as a genuine martyrdom in order to discourage Christians from actively seeking the prestige of having apparently given up their lives for the faith. These conditions were eventually codified by Pope Benedict XIV in the early eighteenth century: to be recognized as a martyr it was necessary not only to have shown constancy and courage in the face of persecution, but there also must have been a specific *odium fidei* prompting the attack; there must be no deliberate seeking of death; if death occurred on the battlefield the engagement must have been in a war waged specifically on religious grounds; and so forth. Given these conditions, and given the holiness of life presupposed in the ability to suffer such a fate, the martyr remained the highest example of Christian discipleship. However, the canonical definitions involved prevented other forms of self-sacrifice by Christians, even if they resulted in death, from being recognized as martyrdom, and sought to ensure that the purity of the martyr's motive should be guaranteed by proofs of a virtuous life.

The Example of the Quakers[60]

There has fortunately been no significant occurrence in Britain of men or women being put to death for their faith for 400 years, and, to that extent, experience of martyrdom in the strict sense is remote. However, dissenters were fiercely persecuted for nearly 30 years after the Restoration of the Stuarts in 1660, and many deaths resulted, notably among the recently formed Society of Friends. It is estimated that some 12000 were imprisoned up to 1688 and that, of these, over 300 died in the generally appalling prison conditions at the time.[61] Their sufferings were often exacerbated by a principled refusal to bribe their gaolers in order to obtain better treatment.

Quakers are not, in general, given to systematic theology but there is intensive contemporary testimony to their experience and how it was to be understood and borne. Imprisonment and other penalties were seen as unavoidable consequences of obedience to Christ, who 'hath given us faithfully to suffer for his Name without shrinking or fleeing the Cross'.[62] The main lesson was steadfastness in the faith so as to continue the meetings for worship in the face of persecution. As Robert Barclay noted:

> . . . this patient but yet courageous way of Suffering made the Persecutors' work very heavy and wearisome unto them, so the Courage and Patience of the Sufferers, using no Resistance, nor bringing any Weapons to defend themselves, nor seeking any way of Revenge upon such Occasions, did secretly smite the Hearts of the Persecutors.[63]

A further characteristically businesslike piece of advice was given by George Fox: that cases of persecution should be carefully recorded and made known.

> Let a true and plain copy of such sufferings be sent up to London . . . that the sufferings may be laid on the heads of them that cause the sufferings. And if any be beaten or wounded in going to Meetings, or struck or bruised in Meetings, or

taken out of Meetings and imprisoned, let copies of such things be taken, and sent as aforesaid, under the hands of two or three witnesses, that the Truth may be exalted, and the power and life of God lived in.[64]

These experiences were to leave a distinctive and lasting stamp on the Society of Friends in its formative years, both in upholding and proclaiming often unpopular protests against abuses, firmly but without violence, and in impressive mutual support and solidarity. The faithfulness of the Society in its work and witness over the succeeding centuries, bringing death in extreme cases, has given its members a place in the great company of Christian martyrs.

Recent Perceptions

Today Benedict XIV's conditions are being modified, both in official Roman Catholic thinking and in popular perception. In particular, the necessity of an explicit *odium fidei* as the cause of martyrdom has been called into question. There is support even in Aquinas[65] for a definition that includes death suffered for Christian principles if undergone out of love for Christ. Given this wider definition, it may be said that it was not the first three centuries of the Church's existence, but the twentieth, which saw by far the greatest number of those who met their death as Christian martyrs – both those who were murdered specifically because they were Christians (such as the countless victims of Stalin) and those who, from love of Christ, devoted their lives to the cause of justice and peace and paid the ultimate penalty at the hands of tyrannical regimes. A study of those recognized as martyrs today (of many Christian denominations) may not necessarily reveal sanctity of life (in the traditional sense), but tends to show a consistency of character and will[66] which makes it inappropriate to question their motivation; and the cause for which the martyr dies may be the pursuit of justice for the poor and oppressed (motivated by Christian faith),[67] rather than the explicit profession of the name of Christ in the face of religious persecution. The tomb of one of the Jesuits martyred in El Salvador 30 years ago has the inscription: '*por justicia y fe*' ('for justice and faith') – in that order. To this extent, the original concept of witness, though still present, has tended to become secondary to that of a martyrdom which demonstrates the power of a willingly accepted death to validate the Christian faith and to advance the cause of justice and peace.

Notes

1   All these factors are present in the story of Susanna and Daniel (Sus. 28–55). For the judicial examination of witnesses, see Mishnah Sanhedrin, 3.6. The Pharisees actually gave greater weight to the word of a reliable witness than to apparently contradictory factual evidence. See Z.W. Falk, *Introduction to Jewish Law of the Second Commonwealth* (Leiden, E.J. Brill, 1972), pp. 121–22.

2   According to the Mishnah (Rosh Ha-shanah 2.1) the witnesses must always be persons known to the judges.

3   Epictetus, *Diss.* 3, 22.86; 24.112; 26.28.

4   Isa. 43:12: 'You are my witnesses, says the Lord. I am God; from everlasting I am he.' Cf. 44.8.

5   Seneca was one of the most notable Stoic 'saints' who was forced to take his own life by Nero.

6   Epictetus, *Diss.* 1, 29.47.

7   W.H.C. Frend, *Martyrdom and Persecution in the Early Church* (Oxford, Blackwell, 1965), p. 66 suggests that the nearest parallel is perhaps 'the suicidal madness of the Carthaginians after their defeat at Himera in 480 BC or at the tragic close of the Third Punic War'.

8   See the account of this debate by H. Lietzmann in Pauly-Wissowa, *Realencyclopaedie der classischen Alterumswissenschaft*, XIV.2 (Stuttgart, 1927) s.v.: Was it because the martyrs 'saw' Jesus in their last moments, and so became a special kind of 'witness'? (K. Holl); was it the influence of the Stoic idea of 'witness' to the truth confirmed by deeds, which for a Christian meant suffering and death? (R. Reitzenstein); or was it the influence of apocalyptic, suggesting that the ultimate Christian 'witness' was in confrontation with God at the Judgment? (E. Günther).

9   R.A. Norris, 'The Apostolic and Sub-apostolic Writings: The New Testament and the Apostolic Fathers', in F. Young, L. Ayres and A. Louth (eds), *The Cambridge History of Early Christian Literature* (Cambridge University Press, 2004), p. 14.

10   To be precise, Ignatius does so only at one point in the eleventh-century codex, which furnishes us with what scholars call the Middle Recension, the text taken by most scholars as the oldest version of the letters. In this version, at *Ephesians* 1.2, we hear of his 'martyrdom', but most scholars since Lightfoot have taken this as a much later interpolation. The principal modern scholar to argue for its retention, Robert Joly, believes the letters themselves to be forgeries produced in the 160s.

11   Likewise, when Justin in his *Second Apology* (2.2) describes the trial and execution of two Christians at Rome, Ptolemaeus and Lucius, he does not employ the language of martyrdom.

12   Ignatius, *Ep. ad Eph.*, 8.1.

13   Ibid.

14   Ibid., 21.1.

15   Ignatius, *Ep. ad Rom.*, 2.2.

16   Ignatius, *Ep. ad Smyr.*, 4.2.

17   Ignatius, *Ep. ad Rom.*, 6.3.

18   P. Rousseau, *The Early Christian Centuries* (London, Longman, 2002), p. 165.

19   *The Martyrdom of Polycarp*, 14 and 17; H. Musurillo, *The Acts of the Christian Martyrs* (Oxford, Clarendon Press, 1972), pp. 12 and 16.

20   *The Martyrdom of Polycarp*, 3; Musurillo, *Acts*, p. 4.

21   *The Martyrdom of Polycarp*, 9; Musurillo, *Acts*, p. 8.

22   *The Martyrdom of Polycarp*, 19; Musurillo, *Acts*, p. 16.

23   *The Martyrdom of Justin*, A.5.2 in Musurillo, *Acts*, p. 46.

24   Polycarp, *Letter to the Philippians*, 8.2–9.1.

25   *The Passio of Perpetua and Felicity*, 3.5; Musurillo, *Acts*, p. 108.

26   Tertullian, *Against Marcion*, 4.15.4; *On Prayer*, IV.5, CCSL I, 578 and 260.

27   *The Letter of the Churches of Lyons and Vienne*, 1.7; Musurillo, *Acts*, p. 62.

28   *The Letter of the Churches of Lyons and Vienne*, 1.16; Musurillo, *Acts*, p. 66.

29   *The Letter of the Churches of Lyons and Vienne*, 1.18.

30   *The Letter of the Churches of Lyons and Vienne*, 1.6.

31   *The Letter of the Churches of Lyons and Vienne*, 1.18; Musurillo, *Acts*, p. 66.

32   *The Letter of the Churches of Lyons and Vienne*, 1.42; Musurillo, *Acts*, p. 74.

33   *The Letter of the Churches of Lyons and Vienne*, 1.29; Musurillo, *Acts*, p. 70.

34   *The Letter of the Churches of Lyons and Vienne*, 1.27; Musurillo, *Acts*, p. 70.
35   Ibid., p. 45.
36   *Passio of Perpetua and Felicity*, 15.6; Musurillo, *Acts*, pp. 122 and 124.
37   *The Martyrdom of Montanus and Lucius*, 21.3–4, Musurillo, *Acts*, p. 234.
38   *The Letter of Phileas*, 2; Musurillo, *Acts*, p. 320.
39   *Passio of Perpetua and Felicity*, 21.3; Musurillo, *Acts*, p. 130.
40   *The Martyrdom of Marian and James*, 3.5–6; Musurillo, *Acts*, pp. 196 and 198.
41   *Martyrdom of Montanus and Lucius*, 13.3; Musurillo, *Acts*, p. 226.
42   E.A.E. Reymond and J.W.B. Barns (eds), *Four Martyrdoms from the Pierpoint Morgan Coptic Codices* (Oxford, Oxford University Press, 1973), pp. 33–79, trans. pp. 151–84.
43   Ibid., p. 157.
44   Ibid., p. 162.
45   Ibid., p. 182.
46   Ibid., p. 151.
47   Ibid., p. 179.
48   Ibid., pp. 152–53.
49   Ibid., p. 179.
50   Ibid., p. 189.
51   Ibid., p. 176.
52   Sozomen, *Ecclesiastical History*, 5.19.
53   Libanius, *Oration*, 17.7, *Libanius: Selected Works*, trans. A.F. Norman, 2 vols (Cambridge, MA and London, Harvard University Press, 1969–), Vol. I, p. 257.
54   Hilary, *On the Trinity*, 11.3, CCSL LXIIa, 531–32.
55   Paulinus of Nola, *Carmina* XVIII. 38–39 and XXI. 590–600 in A. Ruggiero, *Paolina di Nola, I Carmi*, 2 vols (Marigliano, 1996), 1.314 and 2.54.
56   Theodoret, *Religious History*, 21.16, SC 257.96.
57   Paulinus, *Life of Ambrose*, 16, trans. J.A. Lacy in R.J. Deferrari (ed.), *Early Christian Biographies* (New York, Fathers of the Church Inc., 1952), p. 42.
58   Tertullian, *Apology*, 50.13–15, CCSL I, 171.
59   Sozomen, *Ecclesiastical History* 2.14. For an account of this persecution, see S.H. Moffatt, *A History of Christianity in Asia*, Vol. 1 (San Francisco, Jossey Bass, 1992), ch. 7.
60   This section is contributed by Michael Smart.
61   Harold Loukes, *The Quaker Contribution* (London, SCM Press, 1965), p. 22.
62   J.P. Wragge, *The Faith of Robert Barclay* (London, Friends Home Service Committee, 1948), p. 128.
63   Ibid.
64   'No More But My Love', *Letters of George Fox* (London, Quaker Home Service, 1980), pp. 56–57.
65   For example, in *Ep. ad Rom.*, cap. 8 lectio 7: Patitur enim propter Christum non solum qui patitur propter fidem Christi sed etiam pro quocumque justitiae opere pro amore Christi. Cf. *Summa Theologiae*, IIa IIae Q. 124, Art. 5 ad 3. See also the article by Karl Rahner reprinted in this book as Appendix 2.
66   Andrew Chandler (ed.), *The Terrible Alternative* (London, Cassell, 1998), p. 8.
67   Cf. Jon Sobrino, *The True Church and the Poor* (New York, Maryknoll, 1981), p. 17: 'The Church is being persecuted because it defends the life of the poor, denounces the unjust destruction of life and promotes the historical practice of justice.'

Chapter Three

What is Martyrdom?

Harfiyah Haleem

The Christian Martyr

In order to define what is meant by martyrdom it is necessary to compare the
Christian concept(s) with the Islamic ones. St Thomas Aquinas, a controversial
writer in his time, and, as a Dominican friar, one who owed much to Muslim
thinkers, gives attention to this matter in his *Summa Theologiae*. Aquinas
considers martyrdom as an act of virtue:[1]

> Only virtuous action receives as its due the reward of blessedness. But according to
> Matthew (Mt. 5:10) martyrdom receives this reward: *Blessed are they who suffer
> persecution for justice's sake, for theirs is the kingdom of heaven.* So martyrdom
> is a virtuous act . . . it is essential to the nature of martyrdom that a man stands
> steadfastly in truth and justice against the assaults of persecutors. Clearly, then,
> martyrdom is an act of virtue.[2]

According to him, the true martyr holds cheap all the things of this world;
consequently, martyrdom normally implies losing one's life, thus showing
complete victory over worldly things:

> Now of all acts of virtue martyrdom exhibits most completely the perfection of
> charity. For a man's love for a thing is demonstrated by the degree to which, for
> its sake, he puts aside the more cherished object and chooses to suffer the more
> hateful. Now obviously, of all the blessings of life a man loves life itself most, and
> on the other hand hates death most, especially when accompanied by the pains
> of physical torture – from fear of these even brute animals *are deterred from the
> greatest pleasures*, as Augustine says. In this sense it is clear that of all human
> actions martyrdom is the most perfect in kind, being the mark of the greatest love.
> As St. John says (15:13), *Greater love has no man than this, that a man should lay
> down his life for his friends.*[3]

He considers that any human good directed to God may be the cause of
martyrdom:

> The good of the community is pre-eminent among human goods. But divine good,
> the proper reason for martyrdom, is superior to any human good. Yet since a
> human good can become divine, for instance when direct to God, any human good
> can become a reason for martyrdom, inasmuch as it is directed to God.[4]

I have not been able to find any mention of 'seeking martyrdom' in the *Summa Theologiae* but, according to St Gregory of Nazianzus, the true martyr does not seek martyrdom but is called to it:

> [He] sums up in a sentence the rule to be followed in such cases: it is mere rashness to seek death, but it is cowardly to refuse it. (Orat. xlii, 5, 6)[5]

Christians are aware of the words of Christ:

> Ye have heard that it hath been said, Thou shalt love thy neighbour, and hate thine enemy. But I say unto you, Love your enemies, bless them that curse you, do good to them that hate you, and pray for them which despitefully use you and persecute you . . . (Matt. 5:43–44)

and these words from the Epistle to the Romans:

> Do not be overcome by evil, but overcome evil with good. (Rom. 12:21)

In the light of these scriptures, a modern Christian Palestinian organization gives this statement about martyrdom:

> A Christian martyr totally trusts in the love of God, following the example of Jesus Christ. A Christian Martyr is prepared to be killed for the sake of truth and justice but he will not kill himself.[6]

However, according to St Thomas, even members of those orders established for military action could become martyrs:

> Those religious orders that are established for the purpose of military service aim more directly at shedding the enemy's blood than at the shedding of their own, which latter is more properly competent to martyrs. Yet there is no reason why religious of this description should not acquire the merit of martyrdom in certain cases, and in this respect stand higher than other religious; even as in some cases the works of the active life take precedence of contemplation.[7]

The Muslim *Shahīd*

The Qur'an consists of 114 sections (Suras), some much longer than others. All Muslims believe that it represents the words of God as received via the Angel Gabriel and delivered by the Prophet Muhammad to his people between 610 and 632 CE. It is the first and most important text on which Muslims base their understanding of life, themselves and the world around them, and which is the foundation and touchstone of Islamic law (*shari'ah*).

In addition to the Qur'an there is a large body of literature, known as Hadith, which consists of reports of the sayings and actions of the Prophet

Muhammad as written down by his followers, and transmitted faithfully, orally and in writing, to several generations after him. The main collections extant today date from the third Islamic century, and there exists a vast body of scholarship designed to sift, authenticate and dismiss individual hadiths and classes of hadiths. The hadith texts form the secondary source of *shari'ah* law, including moral guidance.

I shall base my discussion of the Islamic teachings about martyrdom on these two sources, as do all those who argue for and against current understandings of the term.

Bearing Witness to God – Devotion to God

The Arabic word normally used nowadays by Muslims and Arabs to mean 'martyr' is *shahīd* (pl. *shuhada*). In the Qur'an the word is not used in the singular to mean 'martyr', and even in the one instance (3:140–43), where the plural is used to refer to the dead in battle, it is arguable that it could be translated 'witnesses' as elsewhere in the Qur'an:

> ... if you have suffered a blow, they too have suffered one. We deal such days out in turn among people, for God to find out who truly believes, for Him to choose martyrs from among you – God does not love the evildoers – for Him to cleanse those who believe and for Him to destroy the disbelievers. Did you think you would enter the Garden without first God proving which of you would struggle for His cause and remain steadfast? Before you encountered it, you were hoping for death. Well, now you have seen it with your own eyes. (3:140–43)[8]

This brings to mind the sufferings of the Christian martyrs under the Romans and the way in which some Christians resorted to subterfuge and others succumbed to torture, while others remained strong in their witness to the Truth of Christ's teachings about the unity of God, refusing to worship Roman idols and emperors until they were killed.[9]

The noun *shahīd* (pronounced *shaheed*) is, in many ways, similar to the term 'martyr' (also meaning 'witness', in Greek) chosen to render it in this context. The root *sh-h-d* conveys 'to witness, to be present, to attend', but also 'to testify' or 'to give evidence'. Thus the martyrs here are chosen by God to witness Him in heaven, are given the opportunity to give evidence of the depth of their faith by sacrificing their worldly lives, and will testify with the prophets on the Day of Judgement.[10] In all other instances in the Qur'an, *shuhada'* means witnesses, and the verb *shahada* is used to refer to 'witnessing'. *Al-Shahīd* is one of the 'Names' of God, meaning that He witnesses all that we do (3:91), bears witness that there is no god but Him (3:18), that the Qur'an is true (4:166) and that Muhammad is a prophet (4:80).

Using almost the same words as Aquinas, the Qur'an urges believers, '*kunu qawamina bi'l-qisti, shuhada'a lillahi*':

. . . uphold justice and bear witness to God, even if it is against yourselves, your parents, or your close relatives. Whether the person is rich or poor, God can best take care of both. Refrain from following your own desire, so that you can act justly – if you distort or neglect justice, God is fully aware of what you do. (4:135)

The *Shahadah* is the word for the Muslim declaration of faith, the acceptance of which, even without stating it outwardly, entitles a person to be called a Muslim: 'There is no God but Allah, and Muhammad [is] His messenger.' This is repeated during each of the five daily prayers and is the last thing a Muslim should say before dying.

Shi'i Thought

In Chapter Seven of this book we print an article by A. Ezzati, who presents an account of martyrdom from the Shia perspective. According to Ezzati[11] *shahīd* also means 'model', the main example of which was the Prophet Muhammad's grandson, Hussein, who was killed at Karbala for being prepared to 'struggle and fight and give up his life for the truth . . .'. In this way he became 'a model, a paradigm, and an example for others, worthy of being copied, and worthy of being followed'. This explains why imams 'live a life of continuous struggle in the cause of Allah and of truth, and that is why they are all regarded as martyrs, whether they die on the battlefield or in bed' (for example, Imam Hussein, the grandson of the Prophet Muhammad).

> Nothing and nobody can intercede between the sinner and God. The concept of intercession in Islam should be appreciated within the framework of the principle of causality. That is to say that the prophets, by guiding and leading the people to the truth, cause their salvation (*sa'ada*; literally 'happiness'). Salvation must be earned and deserved, and the prophets and the Messengers of Allah provide us with the opportunity to earn and deserve salvation, that is to say, it is not the crucifixion and the cross that causes salvation, but it is the realization of the truth that causes it. Man is thus originally sinless, good, and peaceful, and the role of the prophets is a positive one: that of guidance and of being a paradigm, and not a negative one. Martyrs are the super-models of the divine message, too, and in this way they share a special responsibility and honour with the prophets. Islam means submission to the will of Allah. This means being prepared to die [martyrdom] in the course of this submission.

This devotion of one's whole life and death to God corresponds with the words in the Qur'an where God tells the Prophet Muhammad to say:

> My prayers and sacrifice, my life and death are all for God, the Lord of all the worlds. (6:162)

Any Human Good

It is not just dying that makes one a *shahīd*, but also living for God, and directing all one's actions towards Him. In a way very similar to the words of Aquinas, the Prophet is reported to have said:

> O people! Behold, action(s) are but (judged) by intention(s) and every man shall have but that which he intended. (Hadith: Bukhari)

And

> Anyone who seeks *shahadah* with sincerity will be ranked by Allah among the martyrs even if he dies on his bed. (Hadith: Muslim)

In such an instance, the word *shahadah* may well imply witnessing to God's truth, as well as dying in 'in God's way'.

In the Bible and the Qur'an it was Abraham's intention to obey God by sacrificing his son that pleased God so much that Abraham did not need to go through with the act. Likewise, in the Qur'an, God tells the believers making sacrifice during the Hajj pilgrimage, in remembrance of Abraham's submission to God: 'It is neither their meat nor their blood that reaches God, but your piety' (22:37). Thus the intention is the main deciding factor as to whether a person's death can be described as martyrdom or not. The Prophet is reported to have said:

> The first (whose case) will be decided on the Day of Judgement will be a man who died as a martyr. He shall be brought and Allah will make him recount His blessings and say, 'What did you do in return?' He will say, 'I fought for You until I died as a martyr.' Allah will say, 'You have told a lie. You fought so that you might be called a "brave warrior" and you were called so.' (Then) orders will be passed against him and he will be dragged with his face downcast and thrown into Hell. (Hadith: Muslim)

Not Acting in Anger

This devotion to God applies even in the heat of battle, and Islam lays down a host of regulations on how battle should be conducted in order to be 'in God's way' and not 'to exceed His limits'. The Qur'an describes the righteous as 'those who restrain their anger and pardon people' (3:134). One particular example here shows how the means and the ends converge:

> It was reported that Ali, the cousin of the Prophet Muhammad, was about to kill a man in battle, but then the man spat at him. Ali stopped and let him go. He asked why Ali had not killed him, and Ali replied that he would not kill a man out of anger. The man was so impressed that he became a Muslim.[12]

The point here is that the Muslim holds back his sword until he can overcome the impulse for vengeance – an individual and human motive – and strikes only when he can strike for God.

There are many other such examples in Muslim history, including the one mentioned in the Qur'an where an enemy, at the point of being killed, said the *Shahadah*. The Muslims thought that it was a trick and killed him anyway, but the Qur'an and the Prophet condemned them for doing this:

> So, you who believe, be careful when you go to fight in God's way, and do not say to someone who offers you a greeting of peace, 'You are not a believer,' out of desire for the chance gains of this life – God has plenty of gains for you. You yourself were in the same position [once], but God was gracious to you, so be careful: God is fully aware of what you do. (4:94)

According to Professor Clark McCauley, citing evidence found in the luggage of Muhammad al-Atta that was left behind when the 9/11 flights departed:

> If group identification can lead to anger for frustration and insults suffered by the group, it yet remains to be determined if there is any evidence of such emotions in the 9/11 terrorists. Our best guide to the motives of those who carried out the attacks of 9/11 is the document found in the luggage of several of the attackers. Four of the five pages of this document have been released by the FBI.[13] They are surprising for what they do not contain. There is no list of group frustrations and insults, no litany of injustice to justify violence. 'The sense throughout is that the would-be martyr is engaged in his actions solely to please God. There is no mention of any communal purpose behind his behaviour. In all of the four pages available to us there is not a word of an implication about any wrongs that are to be redressed through martyrdom, whether in Palestine or Iraq or in "the land of Muhammad", the phrase bin Laden used in the al-Jazeera video that was shown after September 11'.[14] Indeed the text cites approvingly the story from the Hadith about Ali ibn Abi Talib, cousin and son-in-law of the Prophet, . . .[15]
>
> Rather than anger or hatred, the dominant message of the text is a focus on the eternal. There are many references to the Qur'an, and the vocabulary departs from seventh century Arabic only for a few references to modern concepts such as 'airport' and 'plane' (and these modern words are reduced to one-letter abbreviations). To feel connection with God and the work of God, to feel the peace of submission to God's will – these are the imperatives and the promises of the text. Invocations and prayers are to be offered at every stage of the journey: the last night, the journey to the airport, boarding the plane, take-off, taking the plane, welcoming death. The reader is reminded that fear is an act of worship due only to God. If killing is necessary the language of the text makes the killing a ritual slaughter, with vocabulary that refers to animal sacrifice, including the sacrifice of Isaac that Abraham was prepared to offer.
>
> Judging from this text, the psychology of the 9/11 terrorists is not a psychology of anger, or hatred, or vengeance. The terrorists are not righting human wrongs but acting with God and for God against evil. In most general terms it is a psychology of attachment to the good rather than a psychology of hatred for evil. Research with US soldiers in WWII found something similar: hatred of the enemy

was a minor motive in combat performance, whereas attachment to buddies and not wanting to let them down was a major motive.[16] This resonance with the psychology of combat, a psychology usually treated as normal psychology, again suggests the possibility that terrorism and terrorists may be more normal than usually recognised.[17]

Victory over Worldly Things

As in Christian teaching, it is devotion to God above all the temptations of this world that makes death 'in God's Way' something to be aspired to. God urges, in the Qur'an:

> You who believe, be mindful of God, as is His due, and make sure you die in a state of devotion to Him. (3:102)[18]

This has also been translated as:

> ... make sure you devote yourselves to Him, to your dying moment.[19]

> The life of this world is nothing but a game and a distraction; the Home in the Hereafter is best for those who are aware of God – why will you [people] not understand? (6:32)

> Do not say that those who are killed in God's cause are dead; they are alive, though you do not realize it. (2:154)

It is also stated that:

> Those who believe, who migrated and strove hard in God's way with their possessions and their persons, are in God's eyes much higher in rank; it is they who will triumph ... (9:20)

Love of Enemy

Fighting is permitted by God in the Qur'an only in self-defence, and believers are advised to make peace as soon as it becomes feasible. Muslims should not retain hostility against anyone who has not harmed them, and indeed should even show exemplary patience and goodness towards their enemies.[20] The Qur'an contains several verses very similar to the one in Romans 12:21 mentioned above:

> Good and evil cannot be equal. [Prophet], repel evil with what is better and your enemy will become as close as an old and valued friend. (41:34)

The Prophet Muhammad, too, said:

> Hate your enemy mildly, for he may one day be your friend. (Hadith)

Do Not Seek Martyrdom

The Prophet Muhammad also said:

> O people! Do not wish to meet the enemy, and ask Allah for safety, but when you meet (face) the enemy, be patient, and remember that Paradise is under the shades of swords. (Hadith: Bukhari)

However, there are several other hadiths quoted by *jihadis* today (or by those who purport to represent their views) to support the merits of eagerness for death in fighting to uphold Islam against an enemy. It is a matter of *fiqh* ('interpretation') to explain the apparent contradictions between hadiths by means of ranking them for reliability. This is a highly developed science in classical Arabic scholarship, but has not yet been sufficiently translated into English to enable an intelligent discussion to take place on a textual basis between non-Arabic speakers. Accordingly, protagonists for one or other viewpoint have to rely on the *fatwas* ('legal opinions') of Arabic-speaking scholars who have varying degrees of training and understanding in the subject, some of which are consequently contradictory as they are based on different bodies of Hadith: for example, the Hanbali school of *fiqh* relies heavily on the large number of hadiths collected by Ahmad Ibn Hanbal and a tradition of later interpreters of these, which figure less strongly in other schools of Islamic law (*madhahib*). I try to explain some of the ongoing debate below (in the section 'Recent *Fatwas*').

Persecution

Most acts that involve martyrdom occur as a result of persecution of religious people by powers wishing to extinguish such religious beliefs by extinguishing the people who hold them. In the early history of Christians this power was the Romans, who first gave permission for Jesus' execution and afterwards persecuted Christians for refusing to worship the many Roman gods. In the early history of Islam it was the ruling classes of Mecca who tortured Bilal and Ammar ibn Yasir and killed Ammar's mother Summayah and his father. The persecution became so bad that the Prophet sent several hundred of his followers, including his cousin Ja'afar, to seek shelter with the Christian king of Abyssinia. Sanctions against the Prophet's clan led to the death of his wife and his uncle Abu Talib, and a plot was hatched to murder the Prophet himself. It was only when he was invited to Yathrib (Medina) that he found a haven from persecution for his followers and later himself.

In our times there has been persecution of Jews in Germany and Russia in particular, with some connivance from the Churches, and now of Muslims on a worldwide scale, from 'ethnic cleansing' in Bosnia and Kosovo to the Israeli oppression of Muslim (as well as secular and Christian) Palestinians, with the threat of 'transfers' of Palestinians. Muslims are still being bombed in Iraq (by fellow Muslims as well as by the occupying forces), as well as in Afghanistan and Chechnya, in the 'war on terror'. 'Terrorists' are being arrested in huge numbers in the USA and Uzbekistan, in North African 'Muslim' countries, and even some here in the UK, on the basis of sparse (and secret) evidence and with few, if any, convictions. Some are being held without charge or trial indefinitely, as in Guantanamo Bay. The ghost of McCarthyism is being resurrected in the USA to pursue Muslims 'under the bed'. Muslims have been burned alive in Gujarat by Hindus, and reportedly eaten (or so I read in my broadsheet newspaper)[21] in Indonesia by headhunters converted to Christianity, under the impression that Muslims are dangerous because 'they have to fight'. No doubt there are some Muslims who have given cause for anger to be vented against them, but it seems unlikely that all this persecution is a coincidence.

Is it inevitable that believers in God should face persecution? Of course, in so far as believers refuse to conform to the values of 'this world' they are always likely to be regarded as troublemakers. Nevertheless, if persecution were inescapable there would never have been periods in history when believers could live safely and develop great civilizations. Persecution seems to arise when some people, often imagining themselves to be threatened in some way, get up 'the fury of ignorance' (48:26) in their hearts and disseminate it, instead of listening to what others have to say. The word *kafir*, usually translated as 'unbeliever', actually describes this phenomenon of closing one's mind and refusing to listen.

The question that arises under persecution is 'How should one react to it?'. This can be compared with Hamlet's question 'To be or not to be? . . . whether it is nobler in the mind to suffer the slings and arrows of outrageous fortune, or by opposing end them.' The Islamic example goes through several stages, as outlined below.

Endurance with Patience

The Qur'an often (at least 21 times) exhorts Muslims to be patient and constant and endure hardship gladly in the way of God. During the first period of the Prophethood of Muhammad (*pbuh*) in Mecca, the Muslims were peaceful and did not use any form of violence. The message of Islam was preached, at first privately among those who were the most intimate friends and relations of the Prophet and then to the elders of his clan, who immediately rejected it and became very hostile, since they felt that it threatened the whole basis of their wealth and influence in Mecca. At first, the Meccan elders tried mockery, then bribery, then persecution and torture, then a boycott and, finally, an attempt at assassinating the Prophet. During all this time, the Prophet refused to allow any of the Muslims to fight back, saying that he had not been ordered by God to fight.

Warned in a dream of the assassination plot, Muhammad then migrated to Medina where he had already sent most of his followers who needed protection. Migration is recommended in the Qur'an for those who are so oppressed that they cannot maintain their own religious integrity. Muslims today migrate all over the world in search of better lives, and as asylum seekers and refugees, to escape persecution and oppression in their own countries.

Besides migration, there are various other forms of *jihad* (campaign/ struggle/effort) that can be used before resorting to violence. These include:

- righting wrongs
- *jihad* of the tongue
- jaw-jaw, not war-war
- propaganda
- keeping out of pointless quarrels
- peacemaking and arbitration
- repelling evil with what is better
- peaceful 'demonstrations'
- conscientious objection.

All these are further explained in my paper on 'Islam, Pacifism and Non-violence'.[22]

Fighting

Fighting is a last resort after all these options have been tried and is allowed only in self-defence when attacked, as happens in the final scene of *Hamlet* where he is forced to fight for his life, knows he is dying, and finally attacks the king, his uncle, who has set him up to be killed in a final, desperate act of retribution. In the Qur'an, God says:

> Those who have been attacked are permitted to take up arms because they have been wronged – God has the power to help them – those who have been driven unjustly from their homes only for saying, 'Our Lord is God.' If God did not repel some people by means of others, many monasteries, churches, synagogues, and mosques, where God's name is much invoked, would have been destroyed. God is sure to help those who help His cause – God is strong and mighty – those who, when We establish them in the land, keep up the prayer, pay the prescribed alms, command what is right, and forbid what is wrong: God controls the outcome of all events. (22:39–41)

Even in the event of fighting, rules and restrictions apply. Civilians are to be spared, non-combatants are to be spared, those who convert to Islam on the battlefield are to be spared. Fire is not a permitted weapon. During the Prophet's life there were no suicide missions of the kind we are now regrettably accustomed to.

However, in an e-mail circular purporting to be from the 'Chechen mujahidin', a hadith about one of the Prophet's Companions 'plunging into the enemy's ranks alone and without armour' is used as a precedent. On the basis of other such hadiths they say that to be 'killed by the enemy' is not a necessary qualification for martyrdom: 'the majority opinion is that the intention to resist is enough'. Even accidental self-killing in battle is allowed and deemed to be martyrdom. It counts as suicide (and is therefore prohibited) only if the intention is merely to end one's pain or despair. From all this they conclude that 'one who kills himself because of his strong faith and out of love for Allah and the Prophet, and in the interests of the religion, is praiseworthy'.[23]

The Chechen mujahidin's letter claims that 'at least 30 fatwas' have been issued to this effect. The following sections explore some of the arguments used by other, more widely recognized, Islamic scholars in the debate about the legitimacy in Islam of 'martyrdom operations'.

Recent *Fatwas*

Al-Qaradawi

Shaikh Yusuf al-Qaradawi is a well-respected and popular Egyptian scholar who broadcasts regularly from Qatar on al-Jazeera TV giving *fatwas* in answer to questions phoned in. In September 2001[24] he asserted that Muslim fighters are not allowed to kill except in face-to-face confrontation. They

> are not allowed to kill women, old persons, children, or even a monk in his religious seclusion. That is why killing hundreds of helpless civilians who have nothing to do with the decision-making process and are striving hard to earn their daily bread, such as the victims of the latest explosions in America, is a heinous crime in Islam.

However, during a recent visit to the UK he was quoted on BBC TV[25] as follows:

> I consider this type of martyrdom operation [sc. Palestinian operations against Israel] as an indication of the justice of Allah Almighty. Allah is just – through his infinite wisdom he has given the weak what the strong do not possess and that is the ability to turn their bodies into bombs like the Palestinians do . . . Islamic theologians and jurisprudents have debated the issue, referring to it as a form of *jihad* under the title of 'jeopardizing the life of the mujaheed' [fighter]. It is allowed to jeopardize your soul and cross the path of the enemy, even if it only generates fear in their hearts, shaking their morale, making them fear Muslims . . . If it does not affect the enemy it is not allowed.

He has also argued that:

... they are not suicide operations. These are heroic martyrdom operations, and the heroes who carry them out don't embark on this action out of hopelessness and despair but are driven by an overwhelming desire to cast terror and fear into the hearts of the oppressors.[26]

Asked whether these views extended to the situation in Iraq, al-Qaradawi said:

If the Iraqis can confront the enemy, there's no need for these acts of martyrdom. If they don't have the means, acts of martyrdom are allowed . . . I didn't say that the Iraqis cannot – it depends on their need.

Al-Tantawi

An *al-Ahram* report[27] says that the then Shaikh of Al-Azhar, Egypt, Mohamed Syed Tantawi, also gave a *fatwa* restricting the legitimacy of Palestinian attacks to those on fighters:

The actions of martyrdom undertaken by the Palestinians are in self-defence and are a sort of martyrdom as long as they are intended to kill fighters, not women and children.

Ash-Shaikh

Again, the same report shows the Saudi Grand Mufti Al-Sheikh as in doubt about the intention behind such attacks:

Jihad for God's sake is one of the best acts [in Islam], but killing oneself in the midst of the enemy or suicidal acts, I don't know whether this is endorsed by Shari'a [Islamic law] or whether it is considered *jihad* for God. I'm afraid it could be suicide. Fighting to hurt the enemy is required, but it should never violate Shari'a.

Shaikh Ali Gum'a

The new Egyptian Mufti, Shaikh Ali Gum'a, answering questions in October 2003, said:

The one who carries out martyrdom operations against the Israeli enemy and blows himself up is, without a doubt, a *shahīd* because he is defending his home from an occupying enemy who is supported by superpowers such as the US and Britain.

Asked whether he differentiated between operations against civilians and fighters, he replied:

The Zionists themselves do not differentiate between civilians and military personnel. They have set the entire people to military service. The civilian settler who is in a state of war is a *harbi* [that is, a non-Muslim living in an area regarded as Dar al-Harb, the domain of war].[28] Besides, everyone in Israel, civilians and military personnel, bear arms and are *Ahl al-Qital* [that is, those who deserve to be fought].

Some Hadiths Not Mentioned in the *Fatwas*

The following hadiths of the Prophet seem to go against the rising tide of justification for 'martyrdom operations'.

> The Prophet (pbuh) sent someone . . . and ordered the soldiers to obey him. One day the commander became angry and said, 'Didn't the Prophet (pbuh) order you to obey me?' They replied, 'Yes.' He said 'Collect firewood for me.' So they collected it. He said, 'Make a fire.' When they made it, he said, 'Enter it [i.e. the fire].'
>
> So they intended to do that, but then they started holding one another, and saying, 'We have run towards the Prophet [i.e. taken refuge with him (pbuh)] from the fire.' They kept on saying this until the fire was extinguished and the anger of the commander abated.
>
> When this news reached the Prophet (pbuh), he said, 'If they had entered it [i.e. the fire], they would not have come out of it till the Day of Resurrection. Obedience to somebody is required [only] when he enjoins what is good.' (Hadith: Bukhari)

This looks superficially like a clear parallel for a commander sending out an operative to blow himself up. The commander orders his men to burn themselves in a fire, as a suicide bomber burns himself using a bomb. According to this kind of analogy, such a command would clearly seem to be invalid as the commander is ordering his men to do something that is not 'good' – that is, to harm themselves.

However, it could be argued that the commander's intention here was merely to assert his authority and that he acted out of anger, whereas the commanders of 'martyrdom operations' are using their operatives as part of a calculated strategy against their enemies, as part of a lawful (and thus good) defensive *jihad*, retaliation or whatever, and that therefore the two examples are not similar. The importance of right intention (as noted by Aquinas) is brought out in the following hadith:

> . . . The Prophet asked, 'What has happened?' He replied, 'It is about the man whom you had described as one of the people of Hell Fire. The people were greatly surprised at what you said, and I said, "I will find out the truth about him for you." So I came out seeking him. He got severely wounded, and hastened to die by fixing the blade of his sword in the ground slanting towards the middle of his chest. Then he leaned on the sword and killed himself.' Then Allah's messenger

said, 'A man may seem to the people as if he were practising the deeds of the
people of Paradise, while in fact he is with the people of Hell Fire; another may
seem to the people as if he were practising the deeds of the People of Hell Fire,
while in fact he is from the people of Paradise.' (Hadith: Bukhari)

Jihadi websites have argued that this example, too, is different from
'martyrdom operations' because the man committed suicide out of despair
and impatience in his suffering, whereas the intention of the martyr is to
strike a blow for Islam against its enemies.

The following quotations from the Hadith and Qur'an emphasize that
suicide is forbidden, especially out of despair:

> The one who strangles himself will be strangling himself in the Fire, and whoever
> stabs himself will be stabbing himself in the Fire. (Hadith: Bukhari and Muslim)

> . . . do not despair of God's mercy – only disbelievers despair of God's mercy.
> (Qur'an 12:87)

> Let not any of you wish for death on account of any harm that has befallen him.
> (Hadith: Bukhari and Muslim)

Motivation: Real Suicide Bombers[29]

Kamikaze Boys: Nationalism

Possibly the first suicide bombers in living memory were the Japanese
kamikaze pilots. Some of their motivations have been explained as:

- *Social pressure*
  'Mama-san', who ran a restaurant where they ate their last meals, said
  of kamikazes: 'They flew their missions because the social pressures on
  them were so great, they could not back down.'
- *Culture/religion*
  The Japanese Shinto culture/religion advocates suicide as preferable to
  death with dishonour at the hands of another. This is similar to Roman
  ethic exemplified by Brutus in Shakespeare's *Julius Caesar*.[30]
- *Desperation against a winning enemy*
  At the time when the kamikaze operations began, it was clear that Japan
  was fast losing the war against the Americans and the British.

Palestinians: Nationalism/Religion

Palestinians, too, are motivated by nationalism, with religion playing a part.[31]
However, there are more direct, personal motivations involved as well. Here
are some quotes from newspaper reports of Palestinian suicide bombers.

Revenge, Fury, Desperation? – Or Just Retaliation?

[Palestinian suicide bomber] Ayat: Her neighbour was mortally wounded by Israeli soldiers while playing Lego with his children: 'Her shock and horror drove her to the act.'

Hiba Daraghmeh: Her brother was arrested by Israeli soldiers who stormed their home, her Qur'an and textbooks were torn up, and soldiers forced her to take the veil off. Her grandmother explained, 'She was very angry. She was full of hatred against Jews . . .'. Seeing people killed or injured, having your home demolished, having your landscape destroyed, these are the kinds of traumas Palestinian children have been subjected to, and from this pool of traumatised children, you have suicide bombers . . . The suicide bomber acts out of a sense of rage and a desire for revenge.[32]

A blow for justice?   Anger is not allowed as a motive for killing in Islam[33] but the right to *qisas* (lit. 'tracking down/prosecution' but widely understood as 'equal retaliation'[34]) or compensation is enshrined in the Qur'an with a recommendation to mercy on the part of the victim – after the offender has been caught (2:178). There is no law enforcement agency at present capable of guaranteeing this right of the Palestinians against Israeli aggression: talks and peaceful protests have failed to produce any just solution to their plight. Dr Ahmed Yousef, executive director of the United Association for Studies and Research in Annandale, Virginia, said, 'Muslims are obliged to seek peaceful solutions to injustice but are equally obliged to use physical force in self-defense when non-violent means fail to secure the basic human rights of both political and economic self determination and freedom of religion.'[35] Johann Hari, of *The Independent* newspaper,[36] is not the most obvious person to support suicide bombings, but having visited Palestine himself, he shows some sympathy and understanding,[37] saying, 'Far from nihilism, suicide bombing is a desperate attempt to effect political change. It is an act of hope, however perverted.'

Social pressure?   The Palestinians express great pride in their martyrs:[38] their pictures are posted on walls, young people aspire to be martyrs, and largesse is provided in support of families who lose their offspring as martyrs (although this is largely to compensate for the Israeli retaliation of destroying their family homes). Nevertheless, not all families support the martyrdom of their children, and they all seem to report that the loss of their child was a completely unanticipated shock to them.

Identity?   Professor Mark Harrison of Warwick University asks: 'Why may the shame and humiliation imposed by Israel . . . become a motive for suicide terrorism? Because shaming is another word for devaluing of the identity without which an individual has no status in society, that is why death is preferred to dishonour in many countries.'[39] He suggests that 'young men are generally more vulnerable to offers that will give them not only an identity but a place in community history for themselves and their families'.[40]

More Suicide Bombers

Hizbullah – Islamic National Liberation (Lebanon)   The suicide truck bombing of the US Marines' Beirut barracks on 23 October 1983 is thought to have 'persuaded' the USA to pull their troops out of northern Lebanon.

Tamil Tigers – National Liberation (Sri Lanka)   The Tamil Tigers are a Marxist–Leninist/Hindu group trying to liberate Tamils from Singhalese rule. They have carried out more suicide bombings than all Muslim groups put together (so far), with practically no publicity in the West. In 2002 Tamil Tiger rebels said that 240 of their members had carried out suicide attacks over the years.[41] (Many of their victims have been Sri-Lankan Muslims.)

Turkish–Political Liberation   Kurdish/Turkish left-wing nationalist groups carried out suicide bombings before the more recent attacks attributed to al-Qa'ida affiliates.[42]

Government Covert Action?

Turkey

According to a Kurdish website, the (secular) Turkish government actually encouraged an Islamic terrorist group, called Hezbollah:

> Until four years ago, Turkey, a Western-leaning, avowedly secular country, had tacitly encouraged Islamic extremism in this region, judging it a useful tool in a sometimes dirty war against Kurdish separatists. A brutal religious underground group known as Hezbollah received guns from government arsenals, according to official investigations, and several thousand killings widely attributed to the group were officially ignored.
> Now, after four truck bombs in six days have made Turkey what President Bush called 'a new front' in the war on terrorism, residents are raising fresh questions about the consequences of allowing extremism to flourish in the name of expediency. The three men from Bingol accused in the bombings had all been detained in their home town on suspicions of membership in Hezbollah, Turkish officials said. The Turkish underground organization has no relation to similarly named groups in Lebanon and elsewhere.[43]

Algeria

Although the Armed Islamic Group is generally portrayed as fighting the government in Algeria, its victims are more often helpless civilians. There is and was a widely held view that the Algerian government recruited at least some members of the AIG, via its secret service, to terrorize the members and supporters of the Islamic opposition party FIS.[44] The AIG is now widely linked to al-Qa'ida, a fighting unit set up originally by the CIA to fight the USSR's occupation of Afghanistan.

The USA

It is also on record[45] that the Saudi and Pakistani secret services supported the Taliban government. These countries were, and still are, considered military allies of the West. It is clear that the USA and Britain have maintained and still encourage, if not maintain, covert 'private' military forces that carry out actions for or against foreign governments. The notorious School of the Americas, also known as the Western Hemisphere Institute for Security Cooperation, based at Fort Benning, Georgia, was set up by the US government to train such forces to destabilize unfriendly countries – for example, the Contras in Nicaragua.

The UK

Widely reported in July 2004 was the arrest in Zimbabwe of ex-SAS man Simon Mann and a 'planeload' of mercenaries allegedly bound to aid a coup against the government of Equatorial Guinea. In 2002 a similar band of mercenaries, also led by Simon Mann of Sandline, was found to be assisting the government of Sierra Leone against rebels. Despite denials by Robin Cook MP, it became clear that some elements of the British government or civil service were complicit in this action, and Sandline claimed that it had government approval. In 2004 Sandline's former CEO, Tim Spicer, now acting under the company name Aegis, was controversially awarded a contract in Iraq.[46]

Israel

It was reported that the Israeli secret service Mossad was caught trying to recruit Palestinians to 'al-Qa'ida'.[47] Seymour Hersh attributes the creation of the whole 'Myth of al-Qa'ida' to Mossad.[48]

Russia

Boris Berezovsky and several other people,[49] including ex-*Financial Times* correspondent Andrew Jack,[50] have suggested that the Russian secret services under Vladimir Putin may have organized the tower block bombings in 1999 as an excuse to restart the war in Chechnya and smooth his path to power.

Al-Qa'ida

The stated aims of al-Qa'ida are to 'persuade' the USA to withdraw its troops from Saudi Arabia, and later also to stop both Israel's aggression against the Palestinians and the UN sanctions against Iraq, and to defend all Muslims from the war against Islam.

> What the United States tastes today is a very small thing compared to what we have tasted for tens of years. Our nation has been tasting this humiliation and contempt for more than 80 years. Its sons are being killed, its blood is being shed, its holy places are being attacked, and it is not being ruled according to what God has decreed . . . When these defended their oppressed sons, brothers, and sisters in Palestine and in many Islamic countries, the world at large shouted. The infidels shouted, followed by the hypocrites. One million Iraqi children have thus far died in Iraq although they did not do anything wrong. Israeli tanks and tracked vehicles also enter to wreak havoc in **Palestine**, in Jenin, Ramallah, Rafah, Beit Jala, and other Islamic areas and we hear no voices raised or moves made. But if the sword falls on the United States after 80 years, hypocrisy raises its head lamenting the deaths of these killers who tampered with the blood, honour, and holy places of the Muslims.[51]

As seen above, there is plenty of evidence of US training of covert and repressive, even terrorist, troops. The following is an extract from *U.S. Foreign Military Training: Global Reach, Global Power, and Oversight Issues*:

> The long-term legacies of foreign military training must not be excluded from current decision making about the costs and benefits of this exercise of foreign policy. Throughout the cold war, the U.S. government facilitated and condoned many human rights abuses by providing training and assistance justified in the name of fighting 'global communism.' Some of the unintended consequences of doing so are only now coming to light. Most notably, by arming and training local anticommunist forces in Afghanistan and Pakistan, the U.S. government helped establish the global network of militant anti-Western Muslim fundamentalists that it is now combating. If in this current effort U.S. forces intervene and provide training in support of regimes repressing legitimate political activism and/or using torture or coercion to maintain power, they are likely to foster, rather than diminish, political violence (terrorism) around the globe.[52]

If the USA can justify such activities in the name of fighting global communism, how much more appropriately can it justify them (and a vast weapons – including nuclear – development programme) in the name of the 'war on terror'?[53]

Hero-Worship or Veneration?[54]

Veneration of martyrs is difficult to avoid amongst their sympathizers. Jesus Christ himself (peace be upon him) was arguably a martyr, and most of the current Christian beliefs and religious practices centre around his martyrdom. Veneration is a way of rationalizing death and transforming it into something noble and lasting. National war heroes, too, are honoured for heroism in battle, often resulting in death. The rubric for awarding the Victoria Cross, a quasi-religious national medal, runs as follows: 'It is ordained that the Cross shall only be awarded for most conspicuous bravery, or some daring or pre-eminent act of valour or self-sacrifice or extreme devotion to duty in the presence of the enemy.'[55] Is this so very far from the kind of actions taken by 'martyrs' in their operations?

The Tamil Tigers, too, have an ambivalent attitude towards veneration of their suicide bombers:

> It is evident that the LTTE wishes to revive archaic Tamil hero worship by reviving the concept of the **natukal** [a stone memorial to a martyr]. This example clearly illustrates the traditionalism of the LTTE. But there is the rationalistic approach of the LTTE leadership counteracting an identification of the dead hero with the stone and a subsequent apotheosis and auspiciousness. It limits the worship to veneration and commemoration.[56]

Suicide Operations as a Military Tactic

As a tactic, suicide bombing is usually used by rebels against established forces of governments (including so-called liberal democracies). Such movements are unable to obtain weapons comparable to those of their 'oppressors' but have found suicide bombing to be a useful kind of 'smart bomb' for those without advanced technology, or access to large-scale funding. Suicide bombing as a tactic is not limited to religious or Islamic groups. The Tamil Tigers have used it more than all Muslim groups put together.[57]

Suicide operations are effective in narrowly military terms: more deaths are caused with fewer losses to combatants, as explained in the CDLR e-mail allegedly from the 'Chechen mujahidin':

> As for the enemy, their losses are high; after the last operation they had over 1,600 dead and wounded, and the most crucial concentration of Russian forces in Chechnya was completely destroyed. All this was achieved by the efforts of only four heroes. We feel sure that the Russians will not remain long in our land with such operations continuing . . . If they wish to keep matters under control, they would need more than 300,000 troops, and this is no exaggeration . . . As for the effects of these operations on the enemy, we have found, through the course of our experience, that there is no other technique which strikes as much terror into their hearts, and which shatters their spirit as much. On account of this they refrain from mixing with the population and from oppressing, harassing and looting them. They have also become occupied with trying to expose such operations before they occur, which has distracted them from other things. Praise is to Allah. Many of their imminent plans were foiled, and furthermore, Putin issued a severe condemnation of the Home Affairs and Defence Ministers, placing

the responsibility on them, and threatening high level reshufflings in the two ministries. Those troops who are not busy trying to foil martyrdom operations are occupied with removal of Russian corpses, healing the wounded, and drawing out plans and policies from beneath the debris.

This is all on the military level. But does it produce any progress in achieving peace and justice for one's people?

> Summing up after much rhetoric celebrating Palestinian suicide bombers as martyrs, [Ex-White House chief of staff John] Sununu addressed his audience at a recent conference of Arab journalists and academics in steely tones. 'Ask yourself what Sharon wants,' he said. 'Does he want more suicide bombers? Or does he want no suicide bombers?' Again and again he repeated the questions, as speakers from the hall tried in one way or another to evade his logic.[58]

This calls into question whose interests are best served by suicide bombings. In such attacks it is difficult to prove who did the bombings, and it is easy to attribute them to whoever you wish to discredit.[59] Israel uses each bomb to justify massive military operations by way of 'retaliation', as did George W. Bush with 9/11, and there are frequently political talks, decisions and elections that coincide with 'Palestinian' attacks.

As explained above, it is not unknown for powerful governments to use rebel movements to destabilize governments that they deem to be unfriendly, examples being the Iran-Contra scandal under Ronald Reagan and George Bush Senior, and many South African-sponsored rebel forces in neighbouring countries under apartheid. Israeli claims of help for suicide bombers coming from Iran and Syria and Saddam Hussein have arguably provided much support for the US invasion of Iraq. However, Israeli infiltration of resistance groups, and even support for them,[60] is on record as a 'counter-terrorist' tactic.[61] The rate of such infiltration had reached such a point that *Gulf News* reported that Hamas was forming new leadership to counter Israeli spies.[62]

Choice of Agent

The choice of agent to undertake suicide bombing missions ranges through the following:

- *Religious men, young and without family responsibilities*
  The following statement was allegedly made by a Hamas prisoner of Israelis, Salah Shehade, two months before he was killed by them (on 23 June 2002):

  > The choice is made according to four criteria: First, devout religious observance. Second we verify that the young man complies with his parents' wishes and is loved by his family, and that his martyrdom will not

[adversely] affect family life – that is, he is not the head of the family and he has siblings, as we will not take an only child. Third his ability to carry out the task assigned [to] him, and to understand its gravity; and fourth, his martyrdom should encourage others to carry out martyrdom operations and encourage Jihad in the hearts of people. We always prefer unmarried [men] . . .

If some of the youths do not follow the military apparatus's instructions, and [set out on military operations on their own] without being linked officially to this apparatus, this proves that the [entire] nation has become a nation of jihad on the threshold of liberation, and that it rejects humiliation and submission.[63]

- *Women (unusual for Muslim groups)*
  According to *Jane's Intelligence Review*, Islam has constrained the use of women suicide bombers, whereas 30 per cent of Tamil Tigers bombers were women, and so was a radical left-wing Turkish nationalist bomber in Ankara.[64]
- *Educated*
  The typical Hamas suicide bomber is
  - intelligent and doing well at school
  - sane and level-headed
  - trained and chosen by support groups.

Recent examples of a mother who carried out such an operation and a young boy of unsound mind are exceptions to these rules.[65]

Only God Knows

Hamlet's dying wish after killing his uncle, the king, was to ask his friend Horatio to tell the truth about what happened: 'Horatio, I am dead, thou livest: report me and my cause aright to the unsatisfied.' The truth is what he cared about, and this is what Muslims care about. In the Qur'an the Prophet is taught to pray:

'My Lord, make me go in truthfully, and come out truthfully, and grant me supporting authority from You.' And say, 'The truth has come, and falsehood has passed away: falsehood is bound to pass away.' (17:80–81)

Trying to find out and tell the truth about what is really going on is the first step towards achieving justice.

But can the truth ever be known completely? Pontius Pilate[66] put this question. God, in the Qur'an, claims throughout to be reminding people of the truth, distinguishing good from evil. The Prophet Muhammad himself said he, as a human being (unless he received a revelation about the case), could not know the whole truth when people came to him to judge between them, but had to go on the evidence available, as he could not know when people were lying. In such cases, all human beings can do is to speculate on the evidence available, and to look at *all* the available evidence, not just the bits that powerful people want to be seen. In this chapter I have tried to find out and explain as much as possible about the truth and the arguments behind 'suicide/martyrdom operations', but much remains hidden. Whoever and whatever is behind any one suicide/martyrdom operation, the question of whether or not it constitutes an individual act of martyrdom, self-sacrifice in the face of the enemy, rough justice, witness to the truth of God's Word striking a blow against evil, or cynical manufactured provocation by brainwashed victims is ultimately a *matter for God to decide*. Only He can know the true intention of the agent, or, for that matter, of the group that sends the agent to do the operation, and whether or not they were misguided. He is the One who sees all, knows all and rewards each person according to their deeds:

> Control of the heavens and earth belongs to God and He forgives whoever He will and punishes whoever He will: God is most forgiving and merciful. (48:14)

Grand Mufti Ekrima Sabri, Imam of al-Aqsa mosque, said:

> The person who sacrifices his life as a Muslim will know if God accepts it and whether it is for the right reason. God in the end will judge him and whether he did that for a good reason or not. We cannot judge him. The measure is whether the person is doing that for his own purposes or for Islam.[67]

Can a Christian or an Atheist be Described as a Martyr in Islam?

Islam means submission, or total devotion to God in life and death. The word 'Islam' is not restricted in the Qur'an to 'the followers of Muhammad' but is applied to all the previous prophets and their believing followers. In several places the Qur'an states that all who believe in God and the hereafter and do good deeds will receive their rewards. Believers are urged to stand up for justice as a witness to God. The Prophet (*pbuh*) is told to say, 'Call on God, or on the Lord of Mercy – whatever names you call Him, the best names belong to Him' (17:110). A believer is someone who *sadaq al-husna* ('testifies to the best') rather than *kadhab al-husna* ('calls the best a lie [or illusion]'). In all these senses, I would argue, anyone who devotes his or her life to the cause of justice, of defending the innocent, of testifying to goodness, might have a claim in Islam to be called a martyr, whether or not they had declared their faith to be Islam. Some brave Westerners, who have been killed defending Palestinians or reporting on their sufferings, have been treated like martyrs in Palestine. For example, on 16 March 2003, Rachel Corrie, 23, died under an Israeli bulldozer and became a heroine for Palestine. There are graffiti in Gaza in her honour – one slogan reads 'Rachel was a US citizen with

Palestinian blood' – and there is a picture of her on a website that usually reserves the honour for suicide bombers. Yasser Arafat has pledged to name a street after her.[68]

Although some traditional exegetes interpret some verses of the Qur'an to mean that the good deeds of the *kuffar* ('unbelievers') will be lost, the word 'good' does not appear in any of these verses, only 'deeds' and, as *kuffar* – those who shut out the truth and oppose it – their deeds can only be expected to be bad ones. The case of Abu Talib, the Prophet's uncle and protector, is an interesting one to examine. He was unfailingly kind, affectionate and supportive towards Muhammad (*pbuh*) but never accepted his religion. I have seen no evidence that anyone denied that his reward would be forthcoming. The Qur'an urges believers to treat people with kindness and justice, even when they are hostile to their religion:

> [God] does not forbid you to deal kindly and justly with anyone who has not fought you for your faith or driven you out of your homes: God loves the just. (60:8)

> You have your religion and I have mine. (109:6)

> Each community has its own direction to which it turns: race to do good deeds and, wherever you are, God will bring you together. God has power to do everything. (2:148)

Better known still is the case of Margaret Hassan, who was director of Care International's operations in Iraq. She was abducted on 19 October 2004, and a final video showed her being killed a few weeks later. Although reports were widely circulated in the international press[69] that she had converted to Islam, Margaret remained a practising Catholic married to an Iraqi Muslim. She lived in Iraq from 1973 until her death. She became an Iraqi citizen and worked tirelessly for the poorest and most vulnerable, raising money for medical supplies and warning of a humanitarian catastrophe resulting from sanctions. She told the United Nations that the Iraqi people 'do not have the resources to withstand an additional crisis brought about by military action'. After her death, billboards were posted throughout the city of Baghdad with a picture of her holding a sickly child. 'Margaret Hassan is truly a daughter of Iraq,' they said. Hospital patients took to the streets to protest against her abduction.[70] Despite media controversy about her religious allegiance there does not seem to be much disagreement that she is/was a martyr. According to this verse of the Qur'an she will get her reward from God, whichever religion she followed:

> The [Muslim] believers, the Jews, the Christians, and the Sabians – all those who believe in God and the Last Day and do good – will have their rewards with their Lord. No fear for them, nor will they grieve. (2:62)

As Dr Haider al-Najjar of Bristol has said, 'the people who did this have only unified all civilised people in their hatred for their barbarity. Many claim to be martyrs, Margaret has died a true Iraqi martyr.' On the same website Abbas Mohammed of Iraq said:

> I am very sad to hear about the killing of a peaceful person who helped and provided aid to our poor Iraqi people who are suffering from the criminals, the enemies of humanity. These disgusting acts show their savagery and the barbarity of those who are supporting them. Let Mrs. Hassan the martyr live forever in paradise and shame on her killers.[71]

In a similar vein, in a broadcast on 16 November 2004 Cardinal Cormac Murphy-O'Connor, Archbishop of Westminster, called her 'a martyr for truth and goodness', and repeated this affirmation at the requiem mass held for her in Westminster Cathedral, in the presence of her family and 2000 members of the public, on 11 December. In saying this, he in effect endorsed a broadening of the concept of martyrdom, well beyond the relatively narrow limits observed until recently by the Catholic saint-making authorities:[72] a move welcomed by several contributors to this book.

Conclusion

To sum up what it means to be a martyr, in the sense of 'witnessing unto death', there can be no better words than these from Qur'an 3:156–8:

> It is God who gives life and death; God sees everything you do. Whether you are killed for God's cause or die, God's forgiveness and mercy are better than anything people amass. Whether you die or are killed, it is to God that you will be gathered.

Notes

1   For the full text see Appendix 1.
2   *Summa Theologiae*, IIa IIae Q. 124, Art. 1.
3   Ibid., Art 3.
4   Ibid., Art. 5 ad 3 (my emphasis). The comparable Arabic phrase *fi sabil illah*, 'in God's way', is regularly attached to descriptions of *jihad* in the Qur'an. See Harfiyah Haleem *et al.*, *The Crescent and the Cross* (Basingstoke, Macmillan, 1998), p. 67, and Chapter One above.
5   http://www.newadvent.org/cathen/09736b.htm.
6   http://www.passia.org/meetings/rsunit/2002/files/1-5-02-text.htm.
7   *Summa Theologia*, IIa IIae Q. 188, Art. 6 ad 2 (my emphasis). No martyr is known to have been recognized from such orders, although some former soldiers have become martyrs – for example, St Alban.
8   This part of the above sura (chapter) refers to the Battle of Uhud, where the Muslims, having disobeyed the Prophet's orders, were defeated by an army coming from Mecca to attack them in Medina.

9   http://www.newadvent.org/cathen/09736b.htm.
10   See Qur'an, Haleem translation, p. 44 note b. All quotations from the Qur'an refer to this
     edition.
11   Tehran University, *Al-Serat*, Vol. XII (1986). See Chapter Seven.
12   http://www.islamanswers.net/jihad/religion.htm.
13   They have been translated and interpreted by Kanan Makiya and Hassan Mneimneh,
     'Manual for a "Raid"', in Michael Scott Doran, *Somebody Else's Civil War* in *Foreign
     Affairs* (January–February 2002), pp. 303–18. I am indebted to Hassan Mneimneh for his
     assistance in understanding this document.
14   Ibid., p. 21.
15   See above, page 27.
16   See S.A. Stouffer *et al.*, *The American Soldier: Combat and its Aftermath* (Princeton,
     Princeton University Press, 1949) cited by Clark McCauley (see note 17 below).
17   Clark McCauley, Professor of Psychology, Bryn Mawr College, University of
     Pennsylvania, *Psychological Issues in Understanding Terrorism and the Response to
     Terrorism* at http://www.paow.org/id110.htm.
18   3:102 (Haleem penultimate version).
19   Ibid. In Arabic *la tamatunna illa wa antum muslimun* – literally '[with emphasis] Do not
     die except [and/when?] you are surrendered/devoted [to God]'.
20   See Haleem *et al.*, *The Crescent and the Cross*, pp. 66–74, and Chapter One above.
21   Probably *The Independent*. See also http://news.bbc.co.uk/1/hi/world/asia-pacific/
     1186194.stm (February 2001).
22   See Appendix 3 below, and also Chapter One, above.
23   Committee for the Defence of Legitimate Rights (CDLR – a Saudi opposition group)
     e-mail forwarding 'letter from Chechen mujahidin', 17 May 2003. This letter does not
     tackle the question of civilian targets, but other scholarly sympathizers, such as the late
     Saudi Sh Humood bin Uqla al-Shu'aibi, have produced arguments to justify killing
     civilians mixed up with fighters. See also some of the *fatwas* below.
24   Islam Online, 13 September 2001.
25   BBC2 *Newsnight*, 7 July 2004.
26   Quoted as from *Al-Raya* newspaper, April 2003 on the Israelinsider website.
27   *Al-Ahram*, 3–9 May 2001.
28   See Haleem *et al.*, *The Crescent and the Cross*, p. 71.
29   For more detailed accounts of suicide bombing-groups see below, Part Three, Chapter
     Eight.
30   'The Masada mythical narrative [in which a group of Jews is held to have committed
     suicide rather than succumb to the Romans] has become a major and important ingredient
     in shaping the national and personal identity of the new secular and Zionist Jew –
     proud, rooted in his/her land and willing, indeed able, to fight for this land to the end
     if necessary', Nachman ben Yehuda, *The Masada Myth* at http://www.bibleinterp.com/
     articles/masadamyth9.htm.
31   See Chapter Eight, pp. 131–5 on the Palestinians.
32   Cited by Dr Eyed R. Serraj, a Palestinian psychiatrist, Director of the Gaza Community
     Mental Health Program in 'Suicide Bombers: Dignity, Despair and the Need for Hope',
     interview in *Journal of Palestine Studies*, Vol. XXXI, No. 4, Issue 124 (2 May 2002).
33   See above, pp. 53–5.
34   See also the 'eye for eye' passage referring to the law given to the Jews (Qur'an 5:45).
35   Dr Ahmed Yousef, *The True Clash of Civilizations: Zionism as Seen Through Islamic
     Eyes* (Annandale, Virginia, United Association for Studies and Research, 2002), p. iii.
36   *The Independent*, 21 May 2003.
37   So did the Liberal MP Jenny Tonge: see http://news.bbc.co.uk/1/hi/uk_politics/3421669.
     stm.
38   Donald Macintyre, 'Fathers of Suicide Bombers Declare Pride in Sacrifice of their
     "Martyr" Sons', in *The Independent* after the Ashdod bombing in 2004. Ibrahim Massoud

was proud of his son for avenging an Israeli attack on two Gaza refugee camps the previous week.

39 'The Logic of Terrorism', quoted in *The Guardian Unlimited* website 'What Makes a Martyr?', 29 April 2003.

40 For a full account with many interviews of the motivations and ideology of Palestinian 'martyrs' see Joyce M. Davis, *Martyrs: Innocence, Vengeance and Despair in the Middle East* (Basingstoke, Palgrave Macmillan, 2003).

41 http://news.bbc.co.uk/1/low/world/south_asia/2098657.stm and see below, Chapter Eight, pp. 127–30.

42 'Suicide Bomber Dies in Ankara Explosion' by Pelin Turgut, *The Independent*, 21 May 2003.

43 http://www.dozame.org/article.php?story=20031123230330690.

44 John Sweeney, *The Observer*, 16 November 1997 at http://www.algeria-watch.de/mrv/mrvmass/weaccused.htm; and *An Enquiry into the Algerian Massacres*, Bedjaoui, Aroua, Ait-Larbi (Geneva, Hoggar, 1999).

45 http://www.washingtonpost.com/ac2/wp-dyn?pagename=article&contentId=A38162-2001Sep15&notFound=true.

46 Mary Pat Flaherty, 'Iraq Work Awarded to Veteran of Civil Wars: Briton Who Provided Units in Asia and Africa Will Oversee Security', *Washington Post*, 16 June 2004 at http://www.washingtonpost.com/ac2/wp-dyn/A44945-2004Jun15?language=printer.

47 Michele Steinberg, 'Mossad Exposed In Phony "Palestinian Al Qaeda" Caper', 11 February 2003 at 8:45 a.m. at http://www.indybay.org/news/2003/02/1572495.php.

48 http://www.uslaboragainstwar.org/article.php?id=5730.

49 http://www.theage.com.au/articles/2004/02/13/1076548219210.html?from=storyrhs& oneclick=true.

50 'Bleak House', *The Economist*, 13 January 2005.

51 Usama bin Laden, Afghanistan, 7 October 2001.

52 Lora Lumpe, FPIF Special 5/02, *U.S. Foreign Military Training: Global Reach, Global Power, and Overnight Issues* at http://www.navyseals.com/community/dropzone/dropzone15.cfm. The full report of the think tank 'Foreign Policy in Focus' can be found at http://www.fpif.org/pdf/papers/SRmiltrain.pdf.

53 'US missiles to have global reach' at http://www.guardian.co.uk/usa/story/0,12271, 988612,00. html.

54 See also Chapter Five below, on the veneration of martyrs.

55 The most recent example is that of Private Johnson Beharry who won the VC in Iraq in 2004. His award was 'a classic in the VC mould – he was rescuing colleagues' according to Gary Sheffield, a historian of the modern British army. See *The Guardian*, 18 March 2005.

56 http://www.tamilcanadian.com/eelam/maaveerar/ps4.html#The%20veneration%20of %20martyrs%20by%20the%20LTTE.

57 1980–2000: Tigers 168; All Muslims 102 (Nationalists Pbk 15); Sikhs 1.

58 Martin Wollacott, *The Guardian*, 26 July 2002.

59 Israel has been accused of fabricating terrorist attacks to discredit the Palestinians, most recently the one by a young boy, Hussam Abdu. See http://english.aljazeera.net/NR/exeres/8C7BCBC3-CA2C-4F33-B27D-80AF0AF830E2.htm. The BBC reporter Orla Guerin was criticized by Israeli Minister Without Portfolio Natan Sharansky for biased reporting: 'Sharansky quoted Guerin as describing to viewers how the IDF "paraded the child in front of the international media," then "produced" the child for reporters, "posed" him a second time for the cameras, and then "rushed him back into a jeep." He continued that she reported that the entire event was under "Israeli army control," which meant that "we were not allowed to get his [the child's] version of events." Such language, Sharansky said, casts doubt on what has happened. The report ends with her saying, "This is a picture that Israel wants the world to see."' See http://www.freerepublic.com/focus/f-news/1108304/posts.

60 "'The thinking on the part of some of the right-wing Israeli establishment was that Hamas and the others, if they gained control, would refuse to have any part of the peace process and would torpedo any agreements put in place," said a US government official who asked not to be named. "Israel would still be the only democracy in the region for the United States to deal with," he said. According to former State Department counter-terrorism official Larry Johnson, "the Israelis are their own worst enemies when it comes to fighting terrorism. The Israelis are like a guy who sets fire to his hair and then tries to put it out by hitting it with a hammer . . . They do more to incite and sustain terrorism than curb it," he said.' See http://www.upi.com/print.cfm?StoryID=18062002-051845-8272r; cf. also 'Turkey' above.

61 See also *The Stevens Enquiry*, 17 April 2003 (3) into British army complicity in Northern Ireland attacks: Conclusion 4.9: 'Informants and agents were allowed to operate without effective control and to participate in terrorist crimes' (http://humanrightsonline.net/stevensreport.pdf).

62 *Gulf News*, 10 October 2003.

63 Jewish Virtual Library at www.us-israel.org.

64 *The Independent*, 21 May 2003.

65 Arabs have accused Israel of fabricating the whole incident. See note 32 above.

66 John 18:33–38.

67 http://search.csmonitor.com/durable/1997/08/11/intl/intl.1.html.

68 http://www.smh.com.au/articles/2003/03/28/1048653861570.html?oneclick=true.

69 Justin Huggler, *The Independent*, London, 17 November 2004; *Agence France Presse*, English, 17 November 2004; *Daily Mirror*, London, 28 October 2004.

70 These details were given in the brief account of Margaret Hassan in the pamphlet distributed to those attending her requiem mass at Westminster, 11 December 2004.

71 http://news.bbc.co.uk/2/hi/talkingpoint/4017529.stm.

72 See below, Appendix 2; and also Chapter Four, pp. 91–? and Appendix 1 (*Summa Theologiae* IIa IIae Q. 124, Art. 5 ad 3).

PART TWO

Chapter Four

Still a 'Noble Army' after 11 September 2001?[1]

Brian Wicker

Martyrdom and Suicide

One of the most troubling innovations that has hit the world since the end of the Cold War, and especially since 11 September 2001, has been the adoption of suicidal bombing as a strategy. The victims take it simply as murderous terrorism; the perpetrators as martyrdom. Which is true? What is meant by martyrdom in such a context? How can an increasing multitude of suicidal terrorists be thought of (to use Cranmer's phrase) as a 'noble army'?[2]

Of course, there have been suicidal martyrs before. St Augustine discussed some of them in the early chapters of the *City of God*. And there have been suicidal killers, like the Japanese kamikaze pilots of the Second World War, who flew their guided bombs into American warships in the Pacific, blowing themselves up in order to destroy their targets.[3] But kamikaze tactics were soon overtaken by the arrival of more efficient weapons, such as cruise missiles. By the 1980s or thereabouts, smart technology had made military suicide as a tactic in major international conflict obsolete. Even nuclear deterrence was never *designed* to be suicidal. It simply proposed the suicide of civilization as a practical possibility, perhaps a virtual certainty in the long run.

Of course, in the Second World War there was plenty of heroic self-sacrifice for one's friends. But intentionally committing suicide for a cause is quite a different matter, for the suicide's death is not an unwanted side-effect of some larger operation. It is a consciously *chosen* end, as well as a means to an end. Death itself, in this context, appears as a solemn vocation, or calling: part of the very purpose of the suicidal action, which is designed not just to kill people, but to reveal to the world what the whole conflict is about. The suicidal crimes of al-Qa'ida and the other terrorist organizations have brought back into sharp focus a question implicitly posed to us when we saw the airliners flying into the World Trade Center on 11 September 2001: what is the individual life worth? What is it for?[4]

My answer is: the purpose of life is to *die well*. And that means dying with love, not hate, even if life is a battle. Shakespeare understood this. I am constantly reminded of the little-known or noticed sentence he gives to Williams, a common soldier in King Henry V's army, the night before the battle of Agincourt: 'I am afeard there are few die well that die in a battle; for how could they charitably dispose of anything when blood is in their argument?'

Now, dying well is a theological matter, as Shakespeare saw in his reference to charity. Gandhi, too, understood the point of dying well: 'Just as one must learn the art of killing in training for violence, so one must learn the art of dying in the training for non-violence.'[5] But Christianity goes much further: for the death of Jesus is the quintessential case of dying well. Yet his terrors in the garden of Gethsemane show that he was revolted, even panicked, by the death he was going to be sentenced to. He did not *choose*, let alone want, to be executed as the dangerous troublemaker he clearly was. The point is, rather, that it was obvious from the start that the sort of life he was leading would inevitably end in execution. He knew this early on, as Mark points out: 'He began to teach them that the Son of Man was destined to suffer grievously, to be rejected by the elders and the chief priests and the scribes, and to be put to death . . .' (Mark 8:31). But what was this sort of life? Herbert McCabe got the point exactly right when he wrote:

> When we encounter Jesus, in whatever way we encounter him, he strikes a chord in us; we resonate to him because he shows the humanity that lies hidden in us – the humanity of which we are afraid. He is the human being that we dare not be. He takes the risks of love which we recognise as risks and so for the most part do not take . . . Mostly we settle for being what we are, what we have made of ourselves. We settle for the person that we have achieved or constructed; we settle for our own self-image because we are afraid of being made in the image of God.[6]

In other words, to put it bluntly, if you become fully human, if you love people enough, you will be killed. This is clear from the lives of people who are like ourselves except that they *do* take the necessary risks. What is more, they are killed by people like us, who fail to take the risks. The deaths of Gandhi, Martin Luther King, Edith Stein, Maximilian Kolbe, Oscar Romero, Dietrich Bonhoeffer, Franz Jagerstatter exemplify this truth.

In short, the life of Christ shows us what being fully human demands. And his execution shows what happens to people who live up to these demands. As Herbert McCabe went on to say:

> The cross shows that whatever else may be wrong with this or that society, whatever may be remedied by this or that political or economic change, there is a basic wrong, persistent through history and through all progress: the rejection of the love that casts out fear, the fear of the love that casts out fear, the fear that without the backing of terror, at least in the last resort, human society and thus human life cannot exist.[7]

This love that casts out fear is the opposite of violence, as St Paul's understanding of the Passion makes clear. John Robinson got this right when he wrote:

... the only way evil ever wins victories is by making a man retort by evil, reflect it, pay it back, and thus afford it a new lease of life. Over one who persistently absorbs it and refuses to give it out, it is powerless. It is in this kind of way that Paul sees Christ dealing with the forces of evil – going on and on and on, triumphantly absorbing their attack by untiring obedience, till eventually there is nothing more they can do. Or, rather, there is one thing more – and that is to kill Him. This they do. But in the very act they confess their own defeat.[8]

Here surely lies the definitive answer to the temptation of seeking revenge. But it is also the answer to the temptation of suicide.

But, we may ask, what does becoming fully human mean? Are we not human already? How can we become more so? The answer to this question is given by the picture from Genesis which governs our Judaeo-Christian culture, but also the culture of Islam. By eating of the fruit which gives knowledge of good and evil, people fall either for becoming subhuman, like the snake which seduces them in the myth, or for becoming superhuman, like the gods whose extraordinary power we foolishly think we can be relied on to wield responsibly.[9] In short, Genesis teaches that we are condemned to oscillate endlessly between two nightmares, for fear of being truly human, for fear of reality. Some people think that this is a hopelessly obsolete way of seeing things: part of a fundamentalist myth we have grown out of. But the history of our time demonstrates its validity all too dramatically. For, as we all know, the myth in Genesis goes on to tell us that the first crime fallen humanity is lured into is the deliberate killing of the innocent. And we are still at it: constantly tempted, in this twenty-first century, either to enter into the brutishness of actual war or to grasp at being gods by brandishing virtually omnipotent weapons in the hope of preventing it. In either case, the killing of the innocent, those who have done us no harm, is accepted as inevitable. That much is clear from 11 September and its aftermath, even if it has not been clear to everybody since 1945.

If this is a true picture of how things are in the world, then I think we can make sense of the suicidal terrorist. He or she is a person who has partly understood the picture, but thinks it is possible to take a short cut to becoming the person he is called to become. Suicidal terrorism is a travesty because it seeks to avoid the need to overcome 'the fear of the love that casts out fear' by going through the garden of Gethsemane. The genuine martyr is one who does confront that fear, and fulfils his vocation by loving people to the end despite it. His or her death is unavoidable only because the world cannot understand the sign that his death provides, the sign of its own sin, its refusal of love, and therefore decides to destroy him. This sin is what caused both traditions, of Christianity and Islam, to turn the act of being a legal witness into the inevitability of being killed, as writers in this book have shown. In being killed, the genuine martyr shows up the mess we have made of the world, a mess we can cope with only by hiding it from ourselves, by making the martyr into a scapegoat. The point of martyrdom, then, is that it publicizes the bad job human beings have made of becoming human. It shows up the 'sin of the world' for what it really is. This is also part of the purpose of the suicidal terrorist's action, as I have already suggested. But he or she cannot completely fulfil it, because a decision has been taken to pay back the evil forces in their own coin, and thus to abort the process of becoming fully the person the terrorist is called to be. He kills himself because he cannot wait to let the world kill him instead.

The Christian Theology of Martyrdom

At this point the question arises, how to tell the genuine martyr from the fake? This is of course a theological question. Aquinas tackles it in his classic exposition of Christian martyrdom in the *Summa Theologiae*, IIa IIae, Q. 124.[10] First of all, martyrdom, he says, is a gift from God; a vocation. This comes out in his first article, which asks the seemingly dry question: is martyrdom the act of a virtue? To this he answers yes, for he intends to go on to discuss which virtue(s) are necessary for genuine martyrdom. But there are difficulties. The first is that the 'Holy Innocents' – that is, the children killed by Herod to try to ensure that Jesus would not survive beyond infancy – have been universally regarded by the Church as genuine martyrs. Yet they were too young to have developed any virtues. How come, then, that they are martyrs? The answer has to be that they won the glory of martyrdom as a divine gift. Following Augustine, Aquinas argues that 'the shedding of blood for Christ's sake is a substitute for Baptism'; and, of course, baptism is a gift. In other words, 'just as when infants are baptized, Christ's merit works through baptismal grace to win for them eternal glory, so when they are killed for Christ his merit effectively achieves for them the glory of martyrdom'. Because martyrdom is a gift, not something you can earn by your own efforts, it follows that you cannot become a martyr simply by courageously committing suicide in however just a cause. Indeed, to rush into martyrdom is presumptuous and dangerous.[11] Aquinas points this out as a possible objection to the view that martyrdom is an act of virtue. And although he gets round the difficulty in his reply, the point about presumption seems valid, as I shall argue in a moment. Meanwhile, further objections need to be considered: for example, that of Samson.[12] For, of course, Samson is a suicidal terrorist: almost a model for the modern variety. Yet he is also a kind of martyr. Christians who defend Samson as a martyr sometimes use arguments that are parallel to those adopted by modern terrorist theorists. Aquinas's solution is that God told Samson to do what he did, as recorded in Judges 16:28. Furthermore, the Letter to the Hebrews praises Samson as one who 'through faith conquered kingdoms, did what is right and earned the promises', albeit that he could not come fully into the glory of martyrdom until Christ had risen from the dead.[13]

One implication of this argument is clear: whether someone is or is not a martyr is a matter of fact, not of mere private opinion. Describing somebody as a martyr is no mere 'periphrastic study in a worn-out poetical fashion'.[14] It is a matter of sober truth. But in the absence of either scriptural warrant or the tradition of the Church, how are we to discover whether someone has or has not been given the vocation of martyrdom? This is a very modern question, as I shall argue shortly. Here is the point at which Aquinas's discussion of the virtues comes in. For Christians receive the gift of martyrdom only if they live up to the virtues which Christ taught, and which scripture and/or the Church teach on Christ's authority, to be necessary. In other words, Aquinas's argument gives us a basis for establishing the truth of martyrdom from a consideration of the candidate's virtues. The question is whether these same virtues might warrant similar consideration being given to people of other faiths.

Aquinas's central concern is how to relate the virtues of charity and courage, and the fact of dying for the faith, to each other. First of all, the chief incentive to martyrdom is the virtue of charity, without which martyrdom is valueless: as St Paul says, 'if I even let them take my body to burn it, but am without love, it will do me no good whatever' (1 Cor. 13:3). So, in brief, Aquinas argues that while faith is the final good of martyrdom, and courage, especially in the form of endurance, is the disposition which brings about the act, charity is the 'directing virtue' without which the act of martyrdom has no value.[15] But he adds one or two further thoughts about martyrdom which are relevant to our present purpose. Endurance of death is praiseworthy only as it is directed towards some good found in an act of virtue – for example, faith and love of God. And of all acts, martyrdom is the most perfect, being the mark of the greatest love, for there is no love greater than that of laying down one's life for one's friends.[16] So martyrdom entails death; for as long as life lasts the person has not yet shown *complete* indifference to temporal things. Hence sufferings short of death are martyrdoms only in a figurative sense.[17] (Aquinas takes as a given the development of *martyr* from 'witnessing' to 'dying': a development which Christianity had long since undergone, as Harvey and Finn document in this book.[18]) Again, the martyr is certainly a witness, but not just to any good, only to the truth involved in our duty to God. Yet martyrdom can extend beyond confessing to the faith: the suffering involved in striving to perform any good act, or to avoid any evil one, *for Christ's sake*, can count as martyrdom. Indeed, Aquinas goes further than this: any human good can become a reason for martyrdom, inasmuch as it is directed to God.[19]

Early writings about martyrdom suggest that there was a dispute between those whose thinking was essentially Greek in origin and influence (for example, Clement of Alexandria, d. *c.* 215 CE) and contemporaries of Roman persuasion like Tertullian (*c.* 160–225 CE). Tertullian, a profound Latinist in his intellectual orientation, thought and felt in many ways like an 'old pagan Roman' in the line of Cato the Younger. If it was all right for the

Stoic Roman nobleman who found himself in a jam to commit suicide for a pagan principle, like Cato after defeat by Caesar's legions in 46 BC, or like Seneca after the plot to kill Nero was uncovered in 65 CE, surely it was better still for a Christian to be prepared to do the same for the true faith? This was the argument for suicidal martyrdom. But Greek-influenced Platonists like Clement or Origen thought of suicide as a form of cowardice. In his *Stromateis ('Miscellanies')* Clement insisted that the essential thing about martyrdom was that it was a 'witnessing' to Christ, a way of confessing that Christ was Lord.[20] Any death following upon such confession was (to use a modern piece of jargon) just collateral damage (as some modern political Islamists also seem to argue).[21] Although there were some Christian sects who praised, or even advocated, suicide as a form of martyrdom, Clement regarded them as heretical cowards. By provoking their own deaths, people following this route failed to attain to the status of genuine martyrs. Clement brought St Luke in to clinch the argument: 'if anyone openly declares himself for me in the presence of men, the Son of Man will declare himself for him in the presence of God's angels' (Luke 12:8). Clement interprets this text as defining true 'martyrdom'. Death is not absolutely necessary for martyrdom, for 'anyone who has lived purely in the knowledge of God, and has obeyed the commandments thereby witnesses both by life and word, in whatever way he or she may be released from the body'.[22] In short, the death consequential on such an open declaration must be forced upon the victim, if he or she is to be a genuine martyr. You cannot win the martyr's crown by volunteering for it. You can only win it by witnessing and then taking the consequences. Worse still, Clement thinks, the suicidal martyr commits an extra sin, by forcing the magistrate who condemns him to sin in turn, by unjustly condemning him.

The very strength of Clement's language here indicates the contemporary attractions of suicidal martyrdom in his own time. He perhaps sympathized with the Jewish tradition (and many Christians were of course Hellenized Jews) which viewed violent death with a special horror, and associated it with diabolical things like necromancy. If so, perhaps Clement's opposition to suicidal martyrdom stems partly from this horror. Later, Cyprian of Alexandria (*c.* 210–258 CE – another Latinist of Roman sympathies, writing in the wake of Tertullian's enthusiasm) had to work hard to disentangle genuine martyrdom from suicide.[23]

In the end, it was St Augustine who put an end to the acceptability, if not quite the attractions, of suicidal martyrdom for Christians. Of course, there are many passages of the New Testament which indicate that volunteering for death is unacceptable,[24] but these presumably did not weigh with those who were fascinated by the idea of volunteering to die in the Christian cause. Anyhow, the psychological fascination with suicide, to a certain kind of mind, however morbid it may be, is probably ineradicable, as too is the tendency to venerate popular heroes as martyrs. Augustine cites the case of Cleombrotus, who, having convinced himself, from the teaching of Plato, of the immortality of the soul (but presumably not of Plato's objections to suicide), immediately threw himself to death from a wall. Augustine coolly comments, 'leaving this life, [he] went unto another which he believed was better'.[25] There have been many such enthusiasts: people who have thought that, once 'saved' by Christian faith, they had better get out of this world as soon as possible, before doubts or other temptations set in to disturb their new-found certainties.[26] Of people like these Augustine tersely says: 'If any man think that this is fit to be persuaded, I say not that he dotes, but I say that he is plain mad.' Be that as it may, it is certainly clear that the fascination with suicidal martyrdom had not completely died out by the time Augustine came to write Book I of the *City of God*: the Donatists, in particular, were attracted to it and, clearly, it still had some influence in the West.[27] But Augustine's praise of acknowledged Christian martyrs such as Pelagia, who committed suicide in order to escape rape, and his discussion of Samson, who committed suicide at the suggestion, perhaps the command, of God, was definitive. He excused Pelagia by allowing the possibility that the Church has 'sufficient testimonies that the divine will advised it to honour these persons' memories'.[28] As for Samson, his action was excusable because 'the Holy Spirit within him, which wrought miracles by him, did prompt him unto this act'.[29] Samson's suicide was no sin because it had been sanctioned by God. Without this sanction the suicidal hero would be committing homicide against himself, contrary to the injunction 'Thou shalt not kill' (Deut. 5:17). Here Augustine and Aquinas are at one. They offer a justification which has its echoes in the protestations of modern suicidal-terrorist ideologues like al-Zawahari.[30]

Nevertheless, the example of Samson presents us today with a problem than it did not present to Augustine and Aquinas, because of our own ethical and scholarly concerns. These throw doubt on the Augustinian and Thomist conceptions of the historical authority of scripture. Today, the story of Samson, in so far as it presents the hero as an instrument of divine purposes, cannot help suggesting that God is contradicting Himself. For if suicide and the intentional killing of the innocent are both, without exception, sins, it is difficult to see how God could, without logical self-contradiction, command somebody to do it. And, of course, a logical contradiction says nothing at all. Why should we bother with stories like Samson's? How can he possibly be an instrument of divine purposes?[31]

The Samson story is a test case for two reasons. First, Samson commits suicide and, second, he indiscriminately kills both the guilty (that is, the Philistine rulers and military) and the 3000 innocent spectators sitting on the roof of the building to watch the sport.[32] Now, in his discussion of Samson's suicide Augustine fails to mention the innocents; he merely talks about Samson having killed himself along with his 'enemies'.[33] (Is Augustine here regarding all of the Philistine population as 'guilty', rather as Hamas regards all Israelis as 'combatants'?) Aquinas follows Augustine's example. Neither of them considers Samson's action in the context of the killing of innocents,[34] For both would have regarded Samson's killing of the innocent, as well as his suicide, as forbidden by divine and natural law. Is it not clear that, leaving aside the excuse of divine sanction, Samson is just a suicidal killer who (we ourselves might be tempted in AD 2005 to point out) commits his crime in the Gaza strip! How, then, can he be presented as an instrument of God's purposes, a kind of Hebrew, or even proto-Christian, martyr? Augustine and Aquinas both get round the problem by saying that Samson acts under the influence of the Holy Spirit, who of course is not bound by any moral rules laid down for us. But today this answer looks dangerously weak: why should something be forbidden to everybody else (including, say Hamas and al-Qa'ida) when it is apparently quite acceptable if done by 'our side'? Furthermore, Samson's action is done out of personal vengeance, not out of the love of others which casts out fear, and which alone gives value to martyrdom, as Aquinas points out.[35]

Modern terrorism has made the traditional 'solution' of the Samson problem look increasingly threadbare. This is doubtless why many modern commentators approach it by a different route, saying that it is a rattling good folk-tale which we do not have to take seriously as revelation.[36] But this solution has its own difficulties. If we can get round corners in 'sacred history' thus easily, perhaps the whole concept of God's revealing himself in the scriptures begins to unravel. Was Milton the last person whose beliefs forced him to take Samson seriously as a problem in moral theology?[37] A sign that Milton takes the Samson story seriously is that he deliberately alters the text of scripture. In *Samson Agonistes* Milton's messenger reports that the innocent spectators escaped the fate of the guilty Philistine leaders.[38] He presumably does so because otherwise, in his opinion, the story renders impossible the idea of Samson as an instrument of God's justice. But playing about with the text in this way can be just another way of opening the moral floodgates. More troubling still, Milton solves the suicide problem by presenting the case *for* suicidal martyrdom all too persuasively. First, he does so by confining the apparent logical contradiction that, in order to further His plan of deliverance, God persuades Samson to do things which God Himself has forbidden,[39] to the relatively minor cultic context – that is, he explains Samson's taking his first wife from an ethnically forbidden source at Timnah. His Chorus does not similarly wrestle with the weightier actions of suicide and murder; they simply appeal to God's infinite exemption from His own laws. But more significantly than this, Milton's Samson blames himself for his present predicament. As I have indicated, the Book of Judges does not make heavy weather of Samson's many breaches of his Nazirite vows, which anyway may not have been included in the original tale.[40] But Milton's Samson sees his own death as a vengeful penance for his past sins, as well as a way of singlehandedly getting his own back for humiliations received. In other words, Milton's Samson becomes something like a 'martyr' in the sense nowadays given to that word by the apologists for Islamic and other atrocities.[41] He presumptuously volunteers for death, and thus for revenge, while claiming that what he is going to do has divine sanction. And the Chorus seems to accept this 'solution'. In short, Samson sees himself, and the Chorus sees him too, as a singlehanded fighter for his own tribe in a liberation struggle.[42] Given Milton's own political sympathies, this is understandable. This Samson does not lay down his life out of love for his friends any more than the original Samson did. He cannot *charitably* dispose of things, because blood is in his argument. In this respect, Milton stays close to the original Judges story. But he fails, as a result, to make Samson a saint and martyr motivated by charity, as, following 1 Corinthians and the Letter to the Hebrews, Augustine and Aquinas try to do.[43] Perhaps this does not bother Milton too much since, for him, ritual veneration of saints and martyrs reeked of popish and prelatical superstition, and he had his own notion of how to celebrate the 'victorious agonies' of martyrs and saints.[44] But this was not all. I suspect there is a great deal of Milton himself in his Samson, both in his sense of humiliation in having been made blind by excessive work in defence of liberty, and in his desire singlehandedly to 'pay back' the tyrants and traitors who had betrayed the Protestant revolution.

To put it bluntly in our own context, if it was all right for Samson to kill himself and large numbers of innocent Philistines, as a way of showing up the sin of the world, why is it wrong for Hamas or al-Qa'ida to do the same? It seems to me this is a deep question which needs a better answer than Augustine and his followers can give.[45]

Extending the Range of Martyrdom

The answer, I think, has to be that suicidal terrorism involves a distortion of the theological virtue of hope. It amounts, for example, to counting on God's pardon without repenting, or on heavenly glory without merit.[46] In other words, it is hope for the impossible. Such distorted hope is a sin against the Holy Spirit, because it dismisses or disdains the Holy Spirit's assistance in calling us back from sin.[47] I have already noted[48] that Aquinas points out that volunteering for suicidal martyrdom is a form of presumption, since it envisages obtaining the martyr's crown without having gone through the necessary sufferings for Christ's sake. And it is surely this that gives the lie to the suicidal martyr's hope for glory. But on this account, presumption is an offence against a theological, not a moral, virtue. Is it possible to give an account of it which can appeal to those who do not share the theological perspective which makes presumption a sin against the Holy Spirit? For without such an argument presumption may be understood as a mistake but hardly as a sin. Aquinas raises this possibility himself,[49] and counters it with a good moral, as distinct from theological, argument. Presumption, he argues, comes from vainglory ('*inani gloria*'). It is vainglorious to count on the worldly glory of achieving things which are beyond one's own powers or on an unmerited expectation of heavenly glory. Such expectation stems from the pride ('*superbia*') of thinking so well of oneself that divine punishment is not expected. I think it is here that the suicidal terrorist goes morally, as well as theologically, wrong. For presumption is not just a distortion of the theological virtue of hope; it is also a kind of pride – that is, a vainglorious sense of satisfaction with oneself.

As we have seen, from Augustine's time onwards, martyrdom was clearly distinguished from suicide. But the concept was further complicated when the concept of martyrdom was taken over into Arabic, in the Muslim tradition. It seems clear, as we have seen, that martyrdom in Islam emerges from contact with Christian roots, probably during the conquest of Palestine by Muslims, when Greek-speaking Christian churches were still in existence there. But for Islam the 'witness' of martyrdom can often be the martyr's death in battle before the infidel. This is something that does not appear in the Christian context. The Church does not celebrate martyrdom for soldiers who die in a just war, as Aquinas points out,[50] whereas in Islam the martyr in battle can count on great rewards in the afterlife. And often anyone who thus dies in battle for Islam is regarded as a martyr, as we have seen in recent years. A recent Muslim writer has noted that 'the belief that anyone killed "in the way of Allah" (that is, in self-defence, or defence of the Muslims, or of Islam) will go straight to Paradise, with all its rewards as mentioned in the Qur'an and Hadith, gives Muslim fighters a courage which Western writers and journalists marvel at, in a bemused way, as a kind of admirable insanity'.[51]

It might be concluded that, for Islam, a person can attain martyrdom by his own efforts. But perhaps this is too crude and simple. For Islamic martyrdom is affected by a peculiarity of the Arabic language. G.W. Bowerstock maintains that the verb *shahīd* means both 'to witness' and 'to be witnessed'.[52] It follows, he says, that in the passive sense, the martyr's death can only properly be witnessed – that is, the significance of his death can only be understood and rewarded – by God, or perhaps by an angelic power. Thus Allah is the primary witness of what the martyr suffers and does for the faith, just as Apollo was the witness of Socrates' sufferings. However, I am told by competent Arabists that *shahīd* does not have the passive sense attributed to it by Bowerstock. Rather it has an 'intensive' mode, unknown in English. In this use, *shahīd* means being *al-Sahid*, the ultimate witness, who can only be Allah, who witnesses everything. But either way, Muslim teaching comes close to the Christian teaching that martyrdom is a gift from God.[53] Hence, too, the preoccupation of the Qur'an with people dying in the struggle of life (*jihad*), and being rewarded for their fortitude by the promise of joy in the afterlife, as a due recompense for their work, given by the one who has 'ultimately' witnessed it. On the other hand, unlike Christianity, Islam does not seem to give the central emphasis to *charity* (rather than courage) in the martyr's soul. Instead, steadfastness (*sabr*) in doing good, even in a battle, is understood as a defining virtue of the true believer. Steadfastness (*firmitas*) is a virtue mentioned by Aquinas too, as a grace from God. As the essence of courage it is an essential component of martyrdom, though of course not in battle.[54]

Asma Afsaruddin has shown that it has never been necessary for a person to die in battle in order to become an Islamic martyr.[55] Pious Muslims who died en route for Mecca have been popularly called 'witnesses' – that is, martyrs for the faith. Although the faithful soldier of Allah might be less than 'afeard there are few die well that die in a battle', the importance of right intention was stressed by the Prophet Muhammad. What matters in the next world is being recognized by God, who knows everyone's innermost thoughts, since this is what matters for happiness in the next world. This acceptance of martyrdom in battle has arguably led, in the twentieth and twenty-first centuries, to suicidal attacks as acts of resistance by the weak, for the sake of faith in Allah, against overwhelming oppression, becoming seen by some as praiseworthy and deserving of the highest reward. This acceptance comes closer to the doctrines of Montanism or Donatism than to those of orthodox Christianity. Anyhow it has had profound repercussions in our own day, especially in the light of the *Intifada* in Palestine and of 11 September 2001 in New York.

As we have seen, Aquinas rejects suicidal martyrdom as contrary to the inclination to love and cherish the self, as injuring the community of which we are a part and as wronging God who gives us our life.[56] Yet the 'rabbit out of the hat' case he puts for Samson marks the thin end of a very large wedge. Popular acclaim for martyrs cannot be avoided, however powerfully, and perhaps rightly, religious authorities want to control such manifestations. As Enda McDonagh has said, 'it would be foolish to resist extending the range of Christian martyrdom . . . to those who give their lives for their neighbour in political contexts'.[57] How far should we go in this direction? Should Christians today be widening the scope of martyrdom to include other faiths? This is clearly a difficult, but potentially explosive, political as well as theological issue, and Aquinas cannot give us much help in dealing with it. He does not ask whether any other kind of 'faith', such as Islam, could be an adequate basis for martyrdom. This is not surprising, given his historical context, despite his obvious debts to Muslim philosophers in other parts of his work. On the other hand, he admits the Holy Innocents as martyrs although they were evidently not Christians, but Jews. Furthermore, if *praying* with people of many faiths, on behalf of the world, as happened in Assisi in 1986, and more recently at the instigation of Pope John Paul II after 11 September 2001, is to be encouraged,[58] may it not be possible for *martyrs* of many faiths to emerge and be recognized by the Church for what they are?

Perhaps the Nazi-era cases of Edith Stein and Maximilian Kolbe could lead the way here. In the case of Edith Stein, a Carmelite convert of Jewish origin, her fellow Jews were profoundly upset by the insistence of the Catholic saint-making authorities that she died not because she was a Jewess, but because she was a *Christian* witness. The immediate cause of her death was said by the Church authorities not to be the fact that, as a Jewess, she was sent to Auschwitz but that she was arrested, along with all Catholics in Holland with Jewish blood, after the archbishop of Utrecht, contrary to the express demands of the Nazis, had made public the Nazi order deporting Jews from Holland in July 1942. In short, according to the Church officials, Edith Stein suffered because the Church had defied the Nazis, not because of the Nazi persecution of Jews as such. They said that she had suffered for her Christian faith, despite her own awareness that her passion was bound up with her Jewish identity.[59] Their argument followed the line taken by Aquinas. But they failed to note his concession to the significance of the human good as potentially divine. Hence the understandable fury of Jewish protesters, who saw no reason why her death should be singled out from the deaths of millions of other Jews killed by the Nazis. Their protestations were eventually understood, if not wholly accepted, by the Vatican. Certainly, the case broke new ground, as the pope's homily on her beatification in January 1987 showed. 'In the extermination camp she died as a daughter of Israel "for the glory of the Most Holy Name" [but] . . . because of her great desire to unite with the sufferings of Christ on the cross she gave her life for "genuine peace" and "for the people".'[60] A martyr for peace was a new idea, whose time was coming even if, for the saint-making officials of the Church, it has not yet quite come.

The beatification of Maximilian Kolbe moved the process of widening the concept of martyrdom yet further on. Kolbe was almost fanatically devoted to the Virgin Mary. In July 1941 he volunteered to take the place of another prisoner in a group sentenced to be starved to death in the prison camp because somebody had escaped. By 1972 he was already being venerated as a confessor and had two healing miracles credited to him. Nobody doubted his sanctity. But he had not been treated as a martyr, because he was not arrested *for his faith*, but only in a general Nazi sweep of potential troublemakers before the invasion of Russia. Nevertheless, despite reservations from various dignitaries who formed a special commission to review the evidence, John Paul II drew on his personal authority to decree, on 10 October 1982, 'that Maximilian Maria Kolbe . . . shall henceforth be venerated also as a Martyr'.[61] His death, the pope said, exemplified the truth of St John's Gospel: 'There is no greater love than this, that a man should lay down his life for his friends' (John 15:13). As Kenneth Woodward has written, in quoting St John, 'John Paul II sanctioned the concept of the martyr for charity as a new category of saint – and with it the possibility of bestowing the title of martyr on a wider range of candidates'.[63]

The case of Franz Jagerstatter may eventually take the process of expanding the category of martyrs still further. Jagerstatter was a pious Austrian village sacristan beheaded for refusing to join the Nazi army, despite advice to the contrary from all sorts of people, including his own bishop. Up until the early 1990s, the Austrian bishops were refusing to take up his cause, probably because they did not wish to give support to pacifism among Catholics. Jagerstatter's beatification 'could go beyond a declaration of sanctity of one individual to imply a preference for pacifism, which would have serious implications for the [Church's] just war theory', according to an official of the congregation for saint-making. Kenneth Woodward was told in Rome that the Austrian bishops did not want to endorse pacifism by promoting the canonization of Jagerstatter.[63] But time has moved on, and now the Austrian bishops have decided to support his cause, doubtless because of popular demand, and the relevant evidence is now with Rome awaiting its final outcome.

If the process for Jagerstatter is successful, the grounds for recognizing martyrdom will include political considerations since fear of endorsing pacifism, as a reason for denying someone the martyr's crown, is clearly political, as well as theological. But, of course, martyrdom has always been a political matter.[64] It cannot be otherwise, for defying the powers-that-be in defence of the faith is always and necessarily a political act.[66] The question is: what does 'defence of the faith' mean today? Should it not include cases such as those of Mahatma Gandhi, as well as of overtly Christian martyrs? Confining martyrdom to the familiar circle of private matters, such as defence of chastity, has never worked and cannot work today. Woodward rightly thinks that the process of 'politicization' of martyrdom is bound to go much further. He cites the examples of numerous South American Christians murdered for the sake of social justice and popularly venerated for that reason: 'Their stories, told and retold, already constitute a modern *Acta Martyrum*; in some countries their names are inserted alongside those of the early Christian martyrs for remembrance at Mass.'[66] Yet most of these people were not killed by powers hostile to the faith, but by fellow Catholics. Nor are they 'martyrs of charity' like Maximilian Kolbe, who gave his life for a single individual. They have become martyrs for whole communities of the oppressed and the poor, and have been killed for political reasons, as troublemakers. Some have even been agents of guerrilla forces. And most of them cannot be said to have died 'for the Church': most died, like Archbishop Romero, because they identified the cause of Christ with the cause of political liberation. The same can be said for Fr Jerzy Popieluszko, a priest killed in 1984 by the Polish secret police because of his identification with the cause of Solidarity, the Polish workers' liberation movement. His beatification as a martyr is apparently certain to be achieved in due course.[67] More intriguing still may be the proposal to declare John Paul II a martyr because 'he shed his own blood in St. Peter's Square on 13 May 1981'. As *The Tablet* has pointed out, 'the allusion was not insignificant. Recently a Polish priest who died of cancer after being released from a 36-month prison sentence was beatified as a martyr [because] his Communist prison guards caused him spiritual and physical suffering which eventually led to his death'.[68]

Much more recently Margaret Hassan, of Care International, was murdered in Iraq around 14 November 2004 despite having devoted her life to the improvement of the lives of ordinary Iraqis. She was extremely critical of the 2003 war, and indeed of the UN sanctions policy that had preceded it.[69] The motives for her murder are not wholly clear, but the fact that she was a 'Westerner' (despite being married to an Iraqi Muslim), and was of

British–Irish nationality (as well as having Iraqi nationality), who continued to work for the poor and dispossessed in Iraq during the period of the invasion and subsequent mayhem around Fallujah, must have had something to do with it. Shortly after her death Cardinal Cormac Murphy-O'Connor went on BBC television to say publicly that she should be regarded as 'a martyr for truth and goodness'.[70] This statement is perhaps a landmark in the 'development' of the concept of martyrdom, as it were straddling the two religions. More recently still, a 74-year-old American nun, Sr Dorothy Stang, who was shot by gunmen employed by commercial interests determined to exploit the American forests' tropical hardwoods, could soon be recognized as another 'martyr for goodness', on account of her defence of the forest and its subsistence farmers. She had already faced death-threats in a region where slave labour and illegal logging are rife.[71]

This development presents a challenge, for if, as the argument runs, witnessing to human justice and peace is a category of martyrdom, may it not also be a calling by God from within some other faith, or even from within a mixture of faiths? The example of Gandhi springs to mind, profoundly influenced as he was by both Christianity and by Indian religion. Indeed, Jan Sobrino asks for a new kind of holiness, a 'political holiness', which would require the Church to think in a 'new key', even though the virtues required, and the temptations to be avoided, would not be very different from those traditionally required of the Christian martyr.[72] But may it not be possible to conceive of going further still? What about the passengers in the airliner which crashed into a field near the Pentagon, who overpowered the hi-jackers and forced it off its course for the White House, thus saving many innocent lives on 11 September 2001? Were they not martyrs, whether Christians or not? Is it possible to conceive of (say) Muslims or Israelis who die for their friends being acknowledged as martyrs by the Church?[73] After all, if, as was wrongly reported by some newspapers, Margaret Hassan had been a convert to Islam, it would still have been logically right for Cardinal Murphy-O'Connor to dub her a 'martyr for goodness' because of what she did for her fellow citizens of Iraq.

I suggest that the implications of opening up the concept of martyrdom, in response to current political events, are quite enormous as well as being unavoidable. I think we ought to be thinking about them now. Here is a potential growing point in our understanding both of human sanctity and of the meaning of 'church' – and indeed of Islam too.

Notes

1   A shorter version of this chapter was published in *Theology*, Vol. CVI, No. 831 (May/ June 2003), pp. 159–67.
2   A phrase from Cranmer's translation of the *Te Deum* in the *Book of Common Prayer*.
3   See below, Chapter Eight, pp. 123–7.

4 'The martyr bets his life on a future of freedom and justice; the suicide bomber bets your life on it.' Terry Eagleton, 'A Different Way of Death', *The Guardian*, 26 January 2005.

5 Quoted in Lacey Baldwin Smith, *Fools, Martyrs, Traitors* (New York, A. Knopf, 1997), p. 274.

6 Herbert McCabe OP, *God Matters* (London, Geoffrey Chapman, 1987), pp. 93–94.

7 Ibid., p. 97.

8 John A.T. Robinson, *The Body: A Study in Pauline Theology* (London, SCM Press, 1952), p. 40.

9 Genesis 3:5. Today the most obvious way in which we fall for the temptation to become superhuman is by imagining that we can make and responsibly control the 'virtually infinite destructive power' of nuclear weapons. The giveaway quoted phrase comes from Sir Michael Quinlan, former permanent secretary at the Ministry of Defence, in his *Thinking About Nuclear Weapons*, Royal United Services Institute 'Whitehall Paper' series (London, 1997).

10 See below, Appendix 1.

11 *Summa Theologiae*, IIa IIae Q. 124, 1:3.

12 Ibid., Q. 64, Art. 5 ad 4.

13 Hebrews 11, 32–40.

14 T.S. Eliot, *East Coker* II.

15 *Summa Theologiae*, IIa IIae Q. 124, Art. 2.

16 Ibid., Art. 3.

17 Ibid., Art. 4.

18 See Chapter Two.

19 *Summa Theologiae*, IIa IIae Q. 124, Art. 5.

20 Clement of Alexandria, *Stromateis (Miscellanies)*, Book IV, Chapter 4, in *The Ante-Nicene Fathers Vol. 1* (Edinburgh, T&T Clark, 1994), p. 412.

21 See Introduction, p. 8.

22 Clement of Alexandria, *Stromateis, loc. cit.*

23 Tertullian was, of course, working under Montanist influence. Montanist 'enthusiasm' was exemplified by the readiness of Quintus the 'Phrygian' (that is, Montanist) to volunteer for execution. He had put himself forward with Polycarp in AD 155, but took fright when he saw the wild beasts and was dissuaded by the Roman proconsul. See *The Martyrdom of Polycarp, 4* in *The Library of Christian Classics* (London, SCM Press, 1953), Vol. 1, p. 150.

24 Obvious examples include: Matt. 10:23; John 7:1; 8:59; 10:39; Acts 13:51; 17:14; 19:30, 31.

25 St Augustine, *City of God*, Book I, Chapter 21, Healey translation in Everyman Books (London, Dent, 1945), Vol. 1, p. 27.

26 Ibid., Book I, Chapter 26, p. 32.

27 See Peter Brown, *Augustine of Hippo: A Biography* (London, Faber and Faber, 1967), ch. 19.

28 St Augustine, *City of God*, Book I, Chapter 25, p. 30. See also Appendix 1, p. 140; this translation differs somewhat from that given in the Introduction, p. 8 and in note 37.

29 Ibid., Book I, Chapter 20, p. 26.

30 See Introduction, p. 9.

31 I have discussed the Samson example in more detail in 'Samson Terroristes: A Theological Reflection on Suicidal Terrorism' in *New Blackfriars*, Vol. 84, No. 983 (January 2003), pp. 42–60.

32 Judg. 16:27.

33 St Augustine, *City of God*, Book I, Chapter 21.

34 Doubtless this is because their discussion of war is confined to *ad bellum* questions. Milton's *Samson Agonistes* evades Samson's killing of the innocents by simply altering the text of scripture (see l. 1659). By Milton's time Vitoria had elaborated just war principles to include the prohibition on killing the innocent, and Grotius (whom Milton

had met during his grand tour in Paris in 1638) had laid the foundations of international law and published his *De Jure Belli et Pacis* (1625). Perhaps Milton was influenced by their arguments. To defend the indiscriminate killing by Samson on 'double effect' lines must have seemed to Milton implausible since the text itself points out, with apparent satisfaction, that the hero has at last excelled himself, by killing more people in his final act than in all his previous exploits combined (Judg. 16:30). Presumably this is why Milton took the extraordinary step of changing the text of sacred scripture.

35   The text of Judges makes it perfectly clear that Samson's motive is revenge, as in 15:7. For Milton too, Samson's primary motive is vengeance, as *Samson Agonistes* ll. 1201–5 shows, referring to the 30 spies who had been sent to watch over Samson, threatening his wife:

>   When I perceiv'd all set on enmity
>   As on my enemies, wherever chanc'd,
>   I us'd hostility, and took thir spoil
>   To pay my underminers in thir coin.

The Chorus commends Samson's revenge thus (ll. 1660-68):

>   O dearly-bought revenge, yet glorious!
>   Living or dying thou hast fulfill'd
>   The work for which thou wast foretold
>   To Israel, and now ly'st victorious
>   Among thy slain self-kill'd
>   Not willingly, but tangl'd in the fold,
>   Of dire necessity, whose law in death conjoin'd
>   Thee with thy slaughtered foes in number more
>   Than all thy life had slain before.

Of course, Milton's Samson also wishes to revenge himself against women, perhaps reflecting the poet's own private feelings. See my 'Samson Terroristes', pp. 42–60.

36   Saint-Saens saw it as material for a popular opera. Mary Joan Winn Leith points out that 'the Samson story reflects an early stage of actual Philistine–Israelite confrontations, but it is rooted in Danite folk-tales and perhaps Philistine story traditions'. She suggests that Samson's obliviousness to his Nazirite status suggests that it is not original to the Samson legend. See *Oxford Companion to the Bible*, ed. Bruce M. Metzger and Michael D. Coogan (New York and Oxford, Oxford University Press, 1993), p. 673. Bernhard Anderson says: 'It is unnecessary to go into the details of these lusty stories, which have as their theme the discomfiture of the Philistines by an Israelite Tarzan whose fatal weakness was women. The Samson stories are more legendary than any other material preserved in the book of Judges.' Bernhard Anderson, *The Living World of the Old Testament*, 4th edn (London, Longmans, 1975), pp. 200–201.

37   For most people in the seventeenth century, scripture had to be taken as fact even if other kinds of sagas, such as the Arthurian legends, were mere fiction. Part of the reason why Milton finally chose to write an epic based on Genesis rather than one on the Arthurian legends, as he had been tempted to, lies in his preference for the strenuous arts of biblical fact over the more relaxed fancies of fiction *à la* Spenser. But the earliest stirrings of the 'higher criticism' had begun during Milton's lifetime, with the work of Grotius, Spinoza and Richard Simon.

38   Milton, *Samson Agonistes*, l. 1659.

39   Ibid., ll. 293–325.

40   See note 36 above.

41   For example, consider the following, from a conversation between the late Hamas leader Abdul-Aziz Rantissi and Robert Fisk, of *The Independent on Sunday*, 28 April 2002:

'We believe that our lifetime is always predicted and that our death has been determined by God, and this cannot change. There are many different reasons that could lead to the end of a person's life – a car accident, cancer, a heart attack – so I'm not saying I am making a choice to shorten my life. But the preferred way of ending my life would be martyrdom.' Compare this with Milton's conception of Samson's martyrdom in notes 34 and 35 above.

42   For Milton, contrary to what many commentators on Judges had observed, Samson was not just a 'private person' who 'presum'd Single Rebellion and did Hostile Acts' but was:

> no private but a person rais'd
> With strength sufficient and command from Heav'n
> To free my Countrey; if their servile minds
> Me their Deliverer sent, would not receive,
> But to thir Masters gave me up for nought,
> Th'unworthier they; whence to this day they serve. (*Samson Agonistes*, ll. 1211–16)

43   Hebrews 11:32–34.
44   Cf. John Milton, *The Reason of Church-Governement* in *Milton: Complete Poetry & Selected Prose* (Glasgow, The Nonesuch Library, 1952), p. 559.
45   The recently published Vatican *Compendium of the Social Doctrine of the Church* seems to solve the problem when it says that martyrdom 'cannot be the act of a person who kills in the name of God'. This thesis seems to rule out Samson as any kind of martyr. In doing so, the *Compendium* is presumably abandoning altogether the ancient tradition of Hebrews, Augustine and Aquinas on this matter.
46   *Summa Theologiae*, IIa IIae Q. 21, Art 1.
47   Ibid., Art. 2.
48   See p.   above.
49   *Summa Theologiae*, IIa IIae Q. 21, Art 4:3.
50   Ibid., Q. 124, Art 5:3.
51   See Introduction p. 9 and also 'War and Peace in Islamic Law' in Harfiyah Haleem *et al.*, *The Crescent and the Cross* (Basingstoke, Macmillan, 1998).
52   G.W. Bowerstock, *Martyrdom and Rome* (Cambridge, Cambridge University Press, 1995), pp. 19–20.
53   Qur'an, 3:140 (and note b, p. 44 in Haleem translation).
54   *Summa Theologiae*, IIa IIae Q. 124, Art. 2 ad 1.
55   See above, Chapter One, p.   .
56   *Summa Theologiae*, IIa IIae Q. 64, Art. 5.
57   Quoted in Kenneth Woodward, *Making Saints: Inside the Vatican* (London, Chatto and Windus, 1991), pp. 154–55.
58   See William Johnston in *The Tablet*, 16 March 2002, pp. 4–6.
59   See Oliver Davies, 'Edith Stein' in *The Oxford Companion to Christian Thought*, ed. A. Hastings (Oxford, Oxford University Press, 2000), p. 687.
60   Woodward, *Making Saints*, p. 144.
61   Ibid., p. 147.
62   Another martyr canonized purely for an act of charity towards another individual is Gianna Molla, who sacrificed her life for her unborn daughter, who would otherwise have been sacrificed in an operation to save her mother's life through a hysterectomy. See Jean Olwen Maynard, *Gianna Lolla, Mother, Doctor and Martyr* (London, Catholic Truth Society, 2000). Clearly, she was not killed for refusing to deny that faith. Gianna Molla was beatified as a martyr in 1994.
63   Woodward, *Making Saints*, pp. 150–51.
64   The formal processes whereby the Church had to pronounce on the venerability of any individual, instituted by Gregory IX in 1234, and of canonization, as regulated by

Benedict XIV, in *De servorum dei beatificatione et beatorum canonizatione* (1734–38), were partly designed to curb the enthusiasms of those who wanted to venerate their favourite heroes.

65   'One of the aspects of the ecumenical encounter not often noted is the real growth in our celebrating together someone else's martyrs, not only our own, and being grateful for what someone else has given.' Dr Rowan Williams on BBC Radio 4, 8 April 2005, interviewed with Cardinal Cormac Murphy-O'Connor on the day of John Paul II's funeral.

66   Woodward, *Making Saints*, p. 153.

67   See Kevin Ruane, 'The Holiness of Defiance' in *The Tablet*, 3 July 2004, p. 15.

68   *The Tablet*, 2 July 2005, p. 32.

69   See the tribute printed in the booklet for the requiem mass held for her in Westminster Cathedral, 11 December 2004.

70   BBC TV *Newsnight*, 16 November 2004. He repeated the statement at a requiem mass celebrated for her in Westminster Cathedral on 11 December 2004.

71   *The Tablet*, 19 February 2005, p. 35 and obituary in *The Guardian*, 21 February 2005.

72   Woodward, *Making Saints*, p. 155.

73   For Karl Rahner's thoughts on this issue see below, Appendix 2. See also *Concilium* 2003/1 on *Rethinking Martyrdom* (London, SCM Press, 2003).

Chapter Five

The Veneration of Martyrs: A Muslim–Christian Dialogue

Harfiyah Haleem and Brian Wicker

The Muslim Perspective

How do Muslims and Christians regard their martyrs? Chapter Two of this book explores the changing and ambivalent attitudes of Christians to the veneration of saints and martyrs, and how the Church came to impose limits on this by seeking to legitimize some candidates as saints and martyrs, while rejecting others. Criteria for canonization by Roman Catholics eventually came to include the working of miracles.[1] In the Qur'an, on the other hand, the power to work miracles is reserved for God, who uses a little of it from time to time on behalf of prophets, like Moses and Jesus, in order to evoke belief in the truth of the messages they bring from Him. The Qur'an is fairly scathing, though, about those who need miracles to help them believe:

> When the disciples said, 'Jesus, son of Mary, can your Lord send down a feast to us from heaven?' he said, 'Be mindful of God if you are true believers.' They said, 'We wish to eat from it; to have our hearts reassured; to know that you have told us the truth; and to be witnesses of it.' Jesus, son of Mary, said, 'Lord, send down to us a feast from heaven so that we can have a festival – the first and last of us – and a sign from You. Provide for us: You are the best provider.' God said, 'I will send it down to you, but anyone who disbelieves after this will be punished with a punishment that I will not inflict on anyone else in the world.' (5:112–15)

The truth of God's message is self-evident, to 'those who use their reason', 'those who have minds' and so on, and is backed up by the witness of prophets, believers, angels, and oaths based on the phenomena of God's creation. The Qur'an hails Christians as the 'closest in affection' to Muslim believers because:

> ... there are among them people devoted to learning and ascetics. These people are not given to arrogance, and when they listen to what has been sent down to the Messenger, you will see their eyes overflowing with tears because they recognize the truth [in it]. They say, 'Our Lord, we believe, so count us amongst the witnesses ...' (5:82–83)

97

Yet there were others who remained unmoved and defiant, even though:

> . . . all they were ordered to do was worship God alone, sincerely devoting their religion to Him as people of true faith, keep up the prayer, and pay the prescribed alms, for that is the true religion. (98:4–5)

The Qur'anic concept of miracles (even natural wonders) as proof of God's power is a subtly but radically different concept from that of the Christian Church, where miracles are recognized as proof of God's power working in individual human beings.

Although the Qur'an says that those who die 'in God's way . . . are alive, though you do not realize it' (2:154), they have no power to intercede to help anyone in this world, and even on the Day of Judgement it is only those to whom God gives permission who can intercede on anyone's behalf:

> On that Day, intercession will be useless except from those to whom the Lord of Mercy has granted permission and whose words He approves. (20:109)

The strongest message of the Qur'an, therefore, confirming the First Commandment in the Law of Moses, is that all prayer and worship should be directed to God, who is 'closer to man than his jugular vein' (50:16), and not to others lesser than Him, who 'can neither benefit nor harm even themselves' (13:16). Even 'the Messiah would never disdain to be a servant of God, nor would the angels who are close to Him' (4:172). In practice, though, the attitudes of Muslims to the veneration of saints have always varied. Muslims live in nearly all parts of the world and no one Islamic government, even the caliphate, has ever had the power to control or even influence the remoter rural areas to any great extent. Reform movements have arisen in different parts of the Muslim world at different times, based on a return to strict monotheism. The twelfth-century Almohads (*muwahhidun*) in North Africa (*wahid* means 'one'), and the eighteenth- to twenty-first-century Wahhabis in Saudi Arabia are examples. However, amongst the general Muslim population, veneration of saints and martyrs has persisted. For instance, in Egypt the veneration of the Prophet's descendants (not all of them martyrs) dates from the Shi'i Fatimid dynasties in the early centuries following the Prophet's death and has some echoes of Pharaonic worship of Isis,[2] as well as the influence of the Christian Coptic Church.[3] Strictly monotheistic reform movements do not appear to have had a great deal of influence there. Shaikh Shaltut,[4] a respected shaikh of al-Azhar,[5] in a book of *fatwas* (1965), disapproved of some of the practices associated with the veneration of saints:

> . . . visits to the tombs of deceased good Muslims are lawful, if they are conducted simply to invoke divine mercy on the souls of the dead . . . remind people that death is [not?] the ultimate end and . . . induce them to submit to the will of God.[6]

But

... it is forbidden to build on top of tombs (domes for instance), clothe the tombs, surround them with (silver) railings, adorn their domes, place turbans on them, or light candles, keep lamps or chandeliers around them. People should not stand at a distance from these tombs and knock on the wall in a gesture requesting permission from those buried there to enter the shrine area. They should not extend their hands in supplication to the interred saints, submit written complaints to them or tell them of their problems. It is forbidden to pray inside these shrines ... or in their direction, to circumambulate them, touch the railings surrounding the tombs, to kiss these railings or embrace them.[7]

Nonetheless Shaikh Shaltut did not adopt the very strict and even violent attitude of the Saudi Wahhabis, who have sometimes destroyed shrines and tombs of saints to make their point. He argued that:

Those who follow these customs must not be treated severely, judged harshly, denounced as not being Muslim, accused of *shirk* [believing that God has associates] or of worshipping idols, for it is known, as their behaviour in other respects indicates, that they do believe in the creed of Islam and Islamic duties ... People should be taught and guided rather than denounced ...

Furthermore, he maintains that:

... such practices [as slaughtering an animal when the body of the deceased was taken out of the house] were encouraged by some who pretended to understand Islam, and have also been tolerated by some who are learned in Islam ... these traditions are expressed in an Islamic idiom and are coloured by Islam to the point that non-Muslims will think they are part of Islam. Those responsible for carrying out the rules of Islam should put an end to the practice of these traditional customs.

Despite such *fatwas* (scholarly legal opinions), the practices of veneration and respect for the deceased members of the Prophet's family continue to be observed in Egypt, even by some educated, wealthy professional women, who come to pray in the mosques attached to the tombs of female relatives of the Prophet in Cairo. (The tombs are not inside the main prayer area of the mosque but in separate rooms.) The cult of saints in Egypt also involves many women and poor people in prayer and charitable giving, mainly of food, making pledges in return for answers to their prayers,[8] and in many places seems to act as a temporary stand-in for the more expensive religious obligation of pilgrimage to Mecca.

Even the strict Saudi Wahhabis of modern times are not immune from being turned into martyrs and venerated. In an article in *The Independent* on 28 October 2004, Niko Meo describes the veneration paid in Afghanistan at the graves of al-Qa'ida and Taliban martyrs, who are even said to cure illnesses. He concludes:

Ironically the strict Wahhabi Arabs buried at Khost and the other shrines were opposed to Afghan burial customs they considered idolatrous. One of the reasons they were so hated in Afghanistan was their habit of tearing down flags and decorations on Afghan graves. They would surely have hated to think that, in death, with an obsession for *jihadis*, they would be invested with magical powers and be prayed to by the superstitious tribesmen they looked down on in life.

The Christian Perspective

It has often been suggested that the cult of saints and martyrs became popular in Western Christianity because of mass conversions of polytheistic pagans in the late Roman period, especially after Constantine. Many of these converts were supposed to have retained their old polytheistic attachments, by simply transferring them to the new Christian context through devotion to the multitude of the saints and martyrs instead. The cult is thus alleged to have arisen because it was an easy way of keeping up belief in a multiplicity of beings to adore and celebrate, while at the same time adhering to the new faith. It was admitted that Church authorities tried at times to control the growth of the new superstition, but could not afford altogether to discourage the 'vulgar' from their new enthusiasms.

Very influential post-Enlightenment thinkers – for example, David Hume and Edward Gibbon – endorsed this version of what happened. While, according to Hume, 'no rational enquirer can, after serious reflection, suspend his belief a moment with regard to the primary principles of genuine Theism and Religion', he clearly thinks that the cult of saints and martyrs is a superstitious absurdity, from which he himself is, of course, exempt. 'The heroes in polytheistic paganism correspond exactly to the saints in popery, and holy dervises [*sic*] in Mahometanism', he says. 'The place of HERCULES, THESEUS, HECTOR, ROMULUS is now supplied by DOMINIC, FRANCIS, ANTHONY, AND BENEDICT.'[9] Although Gibbon, too, professed what he called 'the pure and perfect simplicity if the Christian model', he also held that 'the worship of saints and relics corrupted' it.[10]

This 'two-tiered' model, of popular superstition over against elite enlightenment, has been challenged by modern scholars such as Peter Brown, according to whom it was for the most part the solidarity between the living and the dead members of Christian families that established the cult of the martyrs.[11] This had nothing to do with popular superstition, but rather with belief in the possibility of bridging the gulf between this world and the next (something abhorrent to pagan polytheism):

> The philosophers and the orators have fallen into oblivion; the masses do not even know the names of the emperors and the generals; but everyone knows the names of the martyrs better than those of their most intimate friends.[12]

This belief, that those who died as saints and martyrs are our intimate friends, albeit on the far side of the grave, lay at the root of the cult. Indeed, influential Christian families often appropriated the body of a dead member of their own group, by burying it in a place to which they alone had access, in order to gain spiritual benefits for themselves. Bishops commonly deplored such 'privatization' of a spiritual asset which ought to be available to the whole community. They saw the Church as an extended *family* based on spiritual kinship, all of whose members were entitled to the benefits of praying to and with their close friends, the saints and martyrs. Privatization of the cult of martyrs by influential families was often the target of authoritative wrath, as in the case of St Augustine's *De cure gerenda pro mortuis*.[13] Brown chronicles numerous examples of the tension between prominent Christian families who sought privately to care for, and indeed seek intercession from, their own dead in their own burial places, and the Church authorities who sought to make the tombs of saints and martyrs accessible to the whole community.[14]

As the Church's wealth grew, buildings and ceremonies associated with those who had died for the faith became more elaborate, and feasts were held near their tombs with the saint 'presiding'. The martyr would be 'the good *patronus*, whose intercessions were successful' and whose *potentia* was exercised without violence, so that 'loyalty could be shown without constraint'.[15] Typically, martyrs' graves in Late Antiquity were outside town centres, so pilgrimages to shrines naturally developed, especially with the practice of the transfer of relics to other places. More importantly, the cult brought the poor and women into prominence. It 'offered a way of bringing [women and the poor] . . . under the patronage of the bishop, in such a way as to offer a new basis for the solidarity of the late-antique town'.[16] The cult gave women a public role they had lacked, both as recipients of blessings and as givers of alms to the poor.

This picture of the martyrs as our intimate family friends, who are happy to give us their help as servants of God who have demonstrated ultimate perseverance, even to death, in love of the faith, bears little resemblance to the 'two-tiered' concept of popular superstition which later became a Protestant and Enlightenment cliché. In medieval England devotion to, and intercession for and by, the martyrs included all social levels, from knight to miller, as the *dramatis personae* of Chaucer's *Canterbury Tales* shows. Even King Henry II himself had to make amends for the murder, and accept the subsequent canonization, of his erstwhile friend, Thomas Becket.

It is easy to see that there is plenty of room for superstition and abuse in the Christian cult of martyrs and saints, and no doubt over the centuries many people have fallen into superstitious habits because of it. It was at least partly in reaction to such abuse that the churches of the Reformation made a clean sweep of all shrines and cults associated with any saints or martyrs other than those of the apostolic age, and both the Protestant and the Reformed traditions have tended to exclude them altogether from liturgical commemorations, stressing always that the believer has direct access to God through faith. But in the Catholic and Orthodox traditions, at any rate, praying with, and to, the martyrs is not seen as implying the need of any kind of mediation for being able to pray to God; instead, it is seen as praying with and in God, because it is praying with and in Christ who is God. This is why all such prayer is 'through Jesus Christ Our Lord'. But for Muslims, every time Christians pray 'through Jesus Christ Our Lord' they cut themselves off from Muslims, Jews and others, including some Christians, who pray directly to God. God, in the Qur'an, asks Christians to agree with Muslims that:

> . . . we worship God alone, we ascribe no partner to Him, and none of us takes others beside God as lords. If they turn away, say, 'Witness our devotion to Him.' (3:64)

To Muslims, only God is 'our Lord'.

At the deepest level, then, this difference between the faiths over the veneration of martyrs and saints raises profound theological questions which lie beyond the scope of the present book.

Notes

1 In 1983 Pope John Paul II reduced the centuries-old miracle requirement for martyrs from four miracles to one, once beatification by proof of the 'heroic virtue' of martyrdom has been achieved. But Cardinal Bertone, secretary of the Congregation for the Doctrine of the Faith which deals with these matters, has recently gone much further, suggesting that miracles to prove 'heroic virtue' are 'anachronistic'. It thus appears that abolition of the miracle requirement is under serious consideration. See *The Tablet*, 1 January 2005, p. 24.
2 Nadia Abu Zahra, *The Pure and the Powerful* (London, Garnet, 1997), pp. 125–26.
3 http://www.coptichymns.net/mod-pagesetter-viewpub-tid-1-pid-20.html.
4 Abu Zahra, *The Pure and the Powerful*, pp. 104–106.
5 In Cairo, al-Azhar is the oldest and most venerable institution of Islamic learning in the world. It opened in 972 CE.
6 *Fatwa* 222; Abu Zahra, *The Pure and the Powerful*, p. 105.
7 *Fatwa* 195; ibid.
8 Ibid., p. 233. See also Peter Brown, *The Cult of the Saints* (London, SCM Press, 1981), p. 50. A Christian member of the group responsible for this book remembers a visit made to the Delhi tomb of the Sufi saint Shaikh Nizamuddin Awlia. He writes: 'Many pilgrims were making their devotions. Men were filing through the tomb and kneeling to kiss the place where the saint's feet were under a cloth. Women were not allowed (within the tomb) . . . but all were able to tie ribbons around the tomb representing wishes which they would follow up, if their prayers were granted, by returning with a thank-offering to untie them.' See also William Dalrymple, 'The Gateway to the Heart', *The Guardian*, 30 November 2004, who describes this shrine as 'Islam's most tolerant and syncretic incarnation just when that face of Islam is most needed'.
9 David Hume, *The Natural History of Religion*, quoted from David Hume, *Hume on Religion*, ed. Richard Wollheim (London, Fontana Library, 1963), pp. 68–69. For a refutation of this idea see St Augustine, *City of God*, Chapter 28:10.
10 Edward Gibbon, *The Decline and Fall of the Roman Empire*, ed. Revd H.H. Milman (London, Ward Lock and Co., n.d.), Vol. 1, Chapter xxviii, pp. 762ff.

11 Brown, *The Cult of the Saints*.
12 Theodoret, *Curatio affectionum graecarum* 8.67, quoted in ibid., p. 50.
13 Ibid., p. 27.
14 Brown notes a parallel here with some early Muslim examples. He contrasts 'the bleak self-effacement . . . where all believers are equal under God' characteristic of most early Sunni burial rites with the social distinctions preserved by families in the Mausoleum of Cairo's 'City of the Dead' (also mentioned above, p. 99).
15 Brown, *The Cult of the Saints*, p. 41.
16 Ibid., pp. 41ff.

Chapter Six

The Drama of Martyrdom:
Christian and Muslim Approaches

Brian Wicker

This chapter compares and contrasts the concepts of martyrdom in two twentieth-century plays: T.S. Eliot's *Murder in the Cathedral* (1935) and *Murder in Baghdad: the Tragedy of Al Hallaj* by 'Abd al-Sabur (1965). The comparison is illuminating because 'Abd al-Sabur, a well-established Egyptian poet and teacher of literature, was deeply influenced by Eliot's modernism, and seems to have conceived his Arabic drama as a companion piece to Eliot's. Each writer is concerned to bring out what he conceives to be the essence of genuine martyrdom. Eliot does so as a Christian in the Catholic tradition, while 'Abd al-Sabur is a Sunni Muslim confronted by a Sufi-influenced Shia 'saint'.[1] How much do they have in common?

In discussing a Christian martyrdom it is necessary to distinguish two separate, but connected, aspects. The first is what the martyr him- or herself was and did. This is a matter of history and biography – that is, of what can be discovered or recovered from the accounts of what happened leading to the martyrdom, together with any available information about the state of the martyr's mind at the time of his or her confrontation with death. The second aspect is the process by which, at least in the case of Catholic martyrs, public recognition emerges, leading to the formal canonization of the martyr as a saint. Obviously this second aspect depends heavily on the first, for it requires answers to the question whether the virtues or characteristics of the person concerned qualify her or him for inclusion in the calendar of martyrs. But it also involves theological questions: namely, how far do these qualities measure up to the requirements for martyrdom? What exactly do we mean by 'martyr'? What tests are to be applied to any particular claim for martyr status? Of course, formal public recognition of martyr status in no way prevents others, who do not become recognized, from being genuine martyrs as well. Anyone whose acts and dispositions leading to death are of the required kind, in the appropriate situation, will be a martyr whether or not the Church knows this. In any case, cults centred on people regarded by a local church as martyrs cannot be prevented from arising. Indeed, it is usually because of such local cults that a formal process of canonization takes place (as in the case of Thomas Becket). Part of the function of the formal process of canonization is to prevent spurious and undesirable claims gaining public favour. But canonization in no way limits martyrdom status to those who gain favour with the Church 'authorities' and get their names on the calendar. A question that arises here is whether persons who find themselves in what we may call 'martyr situations' may be formally or informally recognized as martyrs even when they are not members of the community of the Christian baptized. This is the question that underlies any consideration of the case of al-Hallaj, who is the protagonist in 'Abd al-Sabur's play.

Murder in the Cathedral

T.S. Eliot's *Murder in the Cathedral*[2] is about the killing, on the orders of King Henry II, of the archbishop of Canterbury, Thomas Becket, in late AD 1170. Thomas, himself of Norman descent, had been appointed the senior judicial authority in England in 1155. As such, he enjoyed the worldly pleasures of being the king's closest confidant and adviser on matters of state. The only higher position to which he could aspire was the archbishopric of Canterbury, to which the pope appointed him in 1162. Almost as soon as he was made archbishop, Thomas forsook his former worldly life and pleasures, including his friendship with the king, and singlemindedly took upon himself the pastoral and spiritual responsibilities of leading the Church in England. It was this change of direction in Thomas's life that infuriated Henry. When it led Thomas to oppose the king's interference in Church affairs, the latter decided to get rid of Thomas, and ordered his murder. Knights loyal to Henry carried out the order, in the cathedral, on 29 December 1170. Almost immediately, a popular cult grew up around Thomas's martyrdom, and he was canonized in 1173.

The action of Eliot's play consists primarily of Becket's confrontation with four different spiritual temptations. The first three are temptations he has already anticipated. The first is to return to 'the good times past' and to be easygoing with those who were once his friends. This is hardly a temptation at all; it has come 20 years too late, as Thomas points out. Next comes the temptation to regain the political power that was once Thomas's as chancellor, in order to dispense justice to the poor and needy, the very people whom Thomas is called to serve. Thomas dismisses this temptation by challenging the tempter:

> [shall I] Who bind and loose with power from the Pope,
> Descend to desire a punier power?[3]

Third comes the temptation to create 'a happy coalition of intelligent interests' against 'the tyrannous jurisdiction of king's court over bishop's court' – in short, to side with the Norman barons, who think of themselves as the 'backbone of England', against the misgovernment of the king. Thomas dismisses this temptation too, with a contemptuous shrug:

Pursue your treacheries as you have done before:
No one shall say that I betrayed a king.[4]

At this point Thomas thinks that he has finished with temptations, but there is an unexpected fourth challenge to be confronted. This tempter offers Thomas just what he most desires, namely to be a saint; that is to:

Seek the way of martyrdom, make yourself the lowest
On earth, to be high in heaven.[5]

This is the hardest, most subtle temptation of all, because the tempter is simply a version of what Thomas himself still is, in the here and now. This temptation does not come from a past which Thomas has already overcome; it expresses what Thomas wants now, which is to be a martyr and to be recognized as such. He has to overcome it by struggling with himself in our presence, in front of the chorus, and in the presence of three priests and the tempters collectively, who meanwhile reflect on the depths of Thomas's dilemma, his Gethsemane experience. In the end he does so. As he says:

Temptation shall not come in this kind again.
The last temptation is the greatest treason:
To do the right deed for the wrong reason.[6]

The core of Eliot's conception of martyrdom lies here, in the struggle of Thomas with the fourth temptation. So it is in scrutinizing it in more detail that we can begin to understand the key point of the play – namely, that you cannot become a martyr by your own choice. Martyrdom is not a matter of allowing yourself to be killed, for whatever cause, however just or meritorious. It is a matter of allowing God to choose (or not to choose) whether you should be martyred. Martyrdom is the ultimate abnegation, because it is not only giving up your life, but also giving up all your *desire* – even, and perhaps especially, including the desire to be a martyr. For that desire is the last gasp of the overwhelming, perpetual temptation to do what *you* want to do, rather than doing what God wills for you. So the essence of martyrdom is the conquest of desire itself. The mere will to live has already been overcome, but this is not enough. The will to die has to be conquered also. The martyr's death has to come as a gift, not as the fulfilment of any wish, any ambition or any aspiration on his part.

This becomes clear in the sermon that Thomas preaches on Christmas morning, between the two main Acts of the drama. For he has now confronted the last temptation, and already knows what is going to happen:

A Christian martyrdom is never an accident, for Saints are not made by accident.
Still less is a Christian martyrdom the effect of a man's will to become a Saint, as

a man by willing and contriving may become a ruler of men. A martyrdom is always the design of God, for His love of men, to warn them and to lead them, to bring them back to His ways . . . the true martyr is he who has become the instrument of God, and who no longer desires anything for himself, not even the glory of being a martyr.[7]

Eliot emphasizes the temptation to become a saint as the effect of a man's own will, by later putting some of Thomas's opening words, as he enters upon the stage, into the mouth of his last tempter. On his entrance, Thomas had said this to his priests, referring to the women of Canterbury who form the chorus to the drama:

> They speak better than they know, and beyond your understanding.
> They know and do not know, that action is suffering
> And suffering is action. Neither does the agent suffer
> Nor the patient act. But both are fixed
> In an eternal action, an eternal patience
> To which all must consent that it may be willed
> And which all must suffer that they may will it,
> That the pattern may subsist, for the pattern is the action
> And the suffering, that the wheel may turn and still
> Be forever still.[8]

The worldly priests do not understand any of this mysterious speech. The fourth tempter is the only person who does understand it, because he is reflecting back to Thomas what Thomas already knows from theology books, but which he cannot fully make his own until his alter ago, the tempter himself, has uttered them. But what do we, as audience, make of it? We, too, have to learn what it really means by looking at, and indeed participating in, the making of the martyr. For we, too, are those for whom the martyrdom of Thomas has to be endured: we are as much the 'chorus' as the women of Canterbury are. Their words, as they begin to understand what it is all about after the murder is over, have to become ours too.

But what do these words signify? Thomas's final struggle is the struggle to come to terms, in his own life, with their meaning. His only action now is to suffer: he can do no more, having conquered the temptations of worldly activity. But to suffer is itself a form of action, since being acted upon by God in His execution of His Will is the only response now open, and responding is itself an action. To submit to being God's patient is the ultimate *deed*. But even this act of suffering must not be the product of a desire to suffer, for that would be to reinstate desire at the very point where desire itself has been extinguished. As a Christian thinker and scholar, Thomas has already learnt this from books of theology and from the Christian tradition. But now he has to do more: he has to embody this understanding in his own action, in his own body. And this is what the fourth temptation is about. The tempter says directly to Thomas the very thing that Thomas has said to his priests, 'You know and do not know, what it is to act or suffer',[9] but now this truth is to be absorbed into Thomas's own body and soul. He has to face the fact that what he already knew, as a matter of theology, is about to be enacted in himself. He not only *knows* now what a martyr is, he has to *show* what it is, by going through with it in his own death.

Eliot's thesis is that the conquest of all desire, including even desire for holiness, lies at the root of all true sanctity, of all martyrdom. For without this, he argues, the martyr cannot wholly submit his own will to the will of God. But the thesis about the abnegation of desire cannot be safely generalized for all martyrs: for many martyrdoms are not sufficiently well recorded for such knowledge of the victim's state of mind to be available. And people have died as martyrs because of a thirst for justice rather than through a complete and conscious renunciation of all desire, including the desire for justice. In this respect, Eliot underestimates, or perhaps misrepresents, the second temptation posed to Thomas. Of course, simply resuming the life of a public administrator would be an ignoble choice. The second tempter's suggestion that 'Power obtained grows to glory, / Life lasting, a permanent possession'[10] is a genuine and dangerous possibility that Thomas rightly spurns. But the tempter has a better case to make than this:

> To set down the great, protect the poor,
> Beneath the throne of God can man do more?
> Disarm the ruffian, strengthen the laws,
> Rule for the good of the better cause,
> Dispensing justice make all even,
> Is thrive on earth, and perhaps in heaven.[11]

In rejecting even this plea I think that Thomas spurns the administrator's life too easily. After all, setting down the great and protecting the poor is what many have been martyred for, as the example of Oscar Romero shows. Yet to do so may well involve collaboration with the powers of this world. The administrators of (say) Amnesty International or Oxfam know this well enough. They have to cajole worldly businessmen, and even make deals with governments, in order to achieve the justice they seek. Thomas More showed that the political life is not absolutely incompatible with sanctity. Plainly such a life requires the individual to harbour the desire to do good, rather than to deny all desire for the sake of the higher claim to submit to the divine will. Thus, in spurning the second tempter's argument, Thomas is allowed to avoid the necessary dilemmas which many saints have had to grapple with and solve, each in his or her own way. That success in such an enterprise is impossible without God's grace is obvious enough. But that such grace can come from the purification of desire, as much as from its elimination, is also clear.

Murder in Baghdad

The immediate reason for the murder of al-Hallaj, according to 'Abd al-Sabur in *Murder in Baghdad*, is not that he has incited rebellion against the sultan (as Thomas had opposed the will of Henry II), for, although he is accused of this in the trial scene of the play, it is announced that the sultan has personally cleared him of this charge. The accusation on which he is condemned is heresy: namely that 'God reveals Himself to him' or 'God manifests Himself in him'.[12] The judges have been asked by the sultan's vizier whether al-Hallaj 'claims that God manifests Himself in him, and such other things inspired by the devil'. In other words, they think they have to decide whether al-Hallaj is claiming to be a specially favoured soul who has a mystical relationship to God which is denied to orthodox Muslims. As a Sufi, al-Hallaj is here being tried for unorthodoxy.[13] The play's translator says, in his Introduction, that among other unorthodox beliefs within Sufism, one is that God 'is immanent, whereas orthodoxy holds that God is transcendent'.[14] Belief in God's immanence seems to be al-Hallaj's crime, for which he is condemned:

> The Sultan may grant amnesty for a crime committed against the State,
> But God does not forgive one who sins against Him.[6]

Underlying al-Hallaj's claim that God is manifested in him (but, of course, not uniquely in him) is a profound theological idea: God is Love. It was God's love which first led al-Hallaj into the Sufi order, with the purpose of developing a fuller spiritual understanding of divine love, and then out of it again into the world, in order to preach God's love to the poor and dispossessed. Within orthodox Islam the Sufi doctrine of divine love (expressed in the play by Shibli, the shaikh of the Sufis) could be permitted to flourish only as long as it remained enclosed within a closed circle of mystical persons who made no attempt to preach it to the masses. This was doubtless because of a fear that such a doctrine of divine love, through which God becomes manifest in human loving, would prejudice the concept of God's utter transcendence which is central to Muslim theology. This is the underlying reason why al-Hallaj's decision to preach God's love to the world leads to his condemnation: because his belief in God's love, especially of the poor and oppressed, is both a political threat to the absolute authority of the sultan's regime and a theological threat to the religious claims of orthodox Islam.

In defending himself at the trial, al-Hallaj has to explain what led him to the way of martyrdom. He tells his judges that he has been through the process of becoming learned, and that he has sought God in prayer. But neither of these, on its own, has overcome his 'fear of death, fear of life, fear of the unknown'.[16] In going through these stages of spiritual progress he has come to understand that 'what I was worshipping was my fear, not God – I was worshipping more than one God: my God was also my fear . . . [and] I felt that I was selling my prayers to God . . . greed was also my God'.[17] In making fear and greed into objects of worship al-Hallaj asks himself:

> Is associating other Beings with God preordained?
> Otherwise, how would I worship Him alone?
> And concentrate my thought upon Him alone?[18]

Here al-Hallaj is acknowledging his own Muslim orthodoxy. The fierce monotheism, or anti-Trinitarianism, of Islam is at its strongest in al-Hallaj's soul at this point. But he is also aware of something else about God, as he recalls the words spoken to him at his Sufi robing:

> True love is the death of the lover,
> So that he may live in the Beloved.
> You are not a lover until you have discarded your own identity,
> And have assumed His.[19]

This surely is the crux of al-Hallaj's predicament: his love of fellow human beings leads him to preach the 'secret' of God's love, namely that it (which, of course, is the pattern of ordinary human loving) leads us to 'assume the identity' of the Beloved. Hence the claim that God is manifest in him simply by loving him – the claim for which he is condemned. It is this mystery which the orthodox characters in the play cannot understand, and certainly cannot accept, because they think it undermines God's aseity and utter oneness. Hence, too, their anxiety that the 'secret' of this love might be exposed.

Al-Hallaj goes on to explain to the orthodox law officer who comes to arrest him that 'my being is a part of Him which shall return to Him', and when the law officer perspicaciously protests 'Do you mean that this worn out frame is part of God?', al-Hallaj continues: 'Yes, a broken frame is a part of Him when it is pure.'[20] Of course, the law officer is right. Other than metaphorically, nothing can be a part of God, and certainly nothing so inadequate as a fallen human being. God is not divisible into parts. Al-Hallaj is certainly taking a risk of being misunderstood in putting his point in this way, thus misrepresenting what he truly means.[21] But, more importantly, in saying these words he gives away something that Sufism insists is a secret that must never be betrayed:

> Do you now know that love is a secret between two lovers?
> It is a relationship which, if made public, defiles our honor.
> We had made a covenant that I should keep the secret
> Until I lie in my tomb, silenced by death.[22]

This betrayal of the secret of divine love, which seems to be modelled on the secret of the sacred sexual union of man and woman, is what haunts al-Hallaj. He expects and even thirsts for the punishment which comes from betraying

the secret. From his point of view it is the giving away of the secret which is
the real cause of his death.

A Theological Comment

I find it hard to see why the reality of God's love has to be kept a secret,
rather than being at the core of preaching about God. Is it because all love
between God and man is conceived as a kind of marriage contract, the
innermost reality of which has to remain secret between the partners? Or is it
because it is part of a closed Sufi tradition, not to be revealed outside the
order? Anyhow, theologically it is hard to see the rationale for such secrecy.
Furthermore, there are good *philosophical* reasons for al-Hallaj's claims
about God's being manifest in himself – that is, that God 'is in every man
without distinction'.[23] Although al-Hallaj in the play does not suggest these
reasons, they would have been plain once Aristotle's philosophical inheritance
had been absorbed into Islam. For, of course, it is central to Aristotle's account
of causality, which was later absorbed into both Christian and Muslim
philosophy, that causes are present in, and manifested in, their effects. Just as
the sunshine is *in* the cornflakes (to quote the very Aristotelean Kellogg's
advertisement), so too God, as cause of everything's existence, is *in* His
creatures, and especially in His supreme earthly creation, humankind. Is it
the absence of this Aristotelean insight that leads the orthodox characters in
'Abd al-Sabur's play – rather surprisingly, given the enormous debt to
Aristotle in other areas of Muslim thought – to deny al-Hallaj's most telling
claim about his relationship to God? For I see no good reason why it should
be thought that God's being manifested in his creatures, as the cause of their
existence, is any kind of threat to His oneness or transcendence. Why then the
'secret'? Aquinas had no difficulty with it: why should any Muslim theologian?
If God is Love (as Sufism and Christianity both proclaim), why should there
be any difficulty in believing that God is manifested in human beings? Why
should any Muslim wish to deny this?

Part of the answer may lie in a further theological point. If God is Love,
and the source of all love in this world, then it seems to follow that there must
be some distinction of lover and beloved within the undoubted oneness and
aseity of the Godhead. Al-Hallaj admits as much when he says that love is
necessarily a secret between two lovers and implies that this is true of divine
love as well as of human love.[24] Anyhow, a thoroughgoing Thomist must
say[25] that the very concept of loving demands that there be a beloved 'other'.
It seems quite inappropriate to think of God's love as merely self-love. Since
love is an outpouring of the lover as a gift to the beloved, love even within
the Godhead must indeed be a gift of lover to beloved. This is the fundamental
reason for the doctrine of the Trinity, which (as Aquinas, not to mention the
Nicene Creed, never fails to insist) in no way whatever prejudices the absolute
oneness of God. Whether the Sufi doctrine of the divine love, as manifested

in al-Hallaj's life and martyrdom, shows any sign of recognizing this truth I leave to others to decide.

Murder in Baghdad contains an unresolved mystery about al-Hallaj's fate. How is the preaching of divine love, which is the fundamental cause of his martyrdom, to be reconciled with Muslim orthodoxy? And why is it something to be kept a secret so sacred that its betrayal, even in the act of preaching God's love for all of us, is a capital offence and is welcomed as such by those who profess it? The lack of an answer to this question in the play tends to emphasize the possibility that political reasons account for al-Hallaj's murder, despite his own protestations to the contrary. How far, then, does Eliot's claim, that martyrdom necessitates the overcoming of all desire by the victim, in order that she or he becomes wholly submissive to the divine will, also apply to 'Abd al-Sabur's play? It is not a prominent theme there; and indeed the political effects of al-Hallaj's decision to go out and preach his doctrine of divine love comes across clearly as something that results from what al-Hallaj *wants* to do. His is an active, not a passive, martyrdom. He can mount a good challenge to Eliot's second temptation. Indeed, sometimes he positively seeks martyrdom, even perhaps to the extent of doing the right deed for the wrong reason:

> Punish me, O my Beloved, for I have divulged the secret
> And betrayed our covenant.
> Do not forgive me; my heart can bear no more . . .
> Make my frail body, my wrinkled skin,
> The instruments of your punishment.[26]

Yet the emphasis in the play on al-Hallaj's insight about God's love is implicitly in tune with Eliot's conception. For God to be truly manifest in him is for him to be identified with God's will, and, to that extent, the overcoming of all desire other than to do what God wants seems implicit in the subtext if not so much in the words put into his mouth.

However, there is a tension, if not a downright contradiction, at the heart of al-Hallaj's predicament. He is right to insist that God's love is manifested, as first cause, in the very existence of his creatures. But if, as the orthodox characters in the play also imply in their condemnation of al-Hallaj, God's love does not involve a beloved 'other' within the Godhead, then this love necessarily requires a beloved 'other' within creation, and perhaps especially in God's supreme creation, humankind. If there is no beloved within the Godhead, then the part of the beloved has to be taken by human beings. To this extent we are *necessary* to God. And this surely compromises God's transcendence. This is the dilemma which al-Hallaj poses, not only to himself but to the orthodox Muslims who confront him. 'Abd al-Sabur's play does not attempt to resolve the tension, but it manifests it in a particularly striking way. Perhaps this is its primary value as a study of an Islamic martyrdom.

Notes

1   It should be pointed out that, having no Arabic, I am relying wholly on the English translation of 'Abd al-Sabur's work, by Khalil I. Semaan (Leiden, E.J. Brill, 1972).

2   First performed in Canterbury Cathedral in June 1935. The text was published by Faber and Faber, of London, at the same time. In concentrating on the theological aspects of Eliot's drama I am unable adequately to discuss the play's great literary importance, especially the fact that it virtually inaugurated the modern revival in English of the classical Greek form of tragic drama in verse – a revival later taken up not only by Eliot himself, but also by a number of other authors.

3   T.S. Eliot, *Murder in the Cathedral*, 4th edn (London, Faber and Faber, 1938), Part 1, p. 30.

4   Ibid., Part 1, p. 34.

5   Ibid., Part 1, p. 39.

6   Ibid., Part 1, p. 34.

7   Ibid., Interlude, p. 49.

8   Ibid., Part 1, p. 21.

9   Ibid., Part 1, p. 40.

10 Ibid., Part 1, p. 27.

11 Ibid., Part 1, pp. 27–28.

12 Al-Sabur, *Murder in Baghdad*, p. 74.

13 On this see the major study of al-Hallaj by Louis Massignon. See Louis Massignon, *Hallaj, Mystic and Martyr* (originally published in French in 1922), trans. Herbert Mason (Princeton, Princeton University Press), Vol. 2, pp. 337–436.

14 Ibid., p. xix.

15 Ibid., p. 71.

16 Ibid., p. 64.

17 Ibid., p. 65.

18 Ibid., p. 65.

19 Ibid., p. 21.

20 Ibid., p. 30.

21 Whether 'Abd al-Sabur himself understands how misleading these words are is not altogether clear. I am assuming that there is no evidence that the historical al-Hallaj actually said them.

22 Massignon, *Hallaj*, pp. 30–31.

23 Ibid., p. 30.

24 Ibid.

25 As Peter Geach does say, in his very Thomistic discussion of the virtue of charity, in *The Virtues: The Stanton Lectures 1973–74* (Cambridge, Cambridge University Press, 1977). See also Herbert McCabe OP, *God Matters* (London, Geoffrey Chapman, 1987), p. 98.

26 *Murder in Baghdad*, p. 33.

PART THREE

Chapter Seven

The Concept of Martyrdom: A Shia Perspective[*]

Abolfazl Ezzati

Islam as an all inclusive systematic religion is an interrelated set of ideals and realities covering the entire area of human notion and action, beliefs and practices, thought, word, and deed. Islamic principles and concepts cannot be fully and properly appreciated unless they are analysed and realized within the framework of Islam as a whole.

The concept of martyrdom (*shahada*) in Islam can only be understood in the light of the Islamic concept of Holy Struggle (*jihad*) and the concept of *jihad* may only be appreciated if the concept of the doctrine of enjoining right and discovering wrong (*al-amr bi'l-maruf*) is properly appreciated, and good and bad, right and wrong, can only be understood if the independent divine source of righteousness, truth, and goodness (*tawhid*), and how the Message of the divine source of righteousness and truth has been honestly and properly conveyed to humanity through prophethood, are understood. Finally the divine message may not be fully appreciated unless the embodiment of this divine message, or the Model of Guidance, and the Supreme Paradigm (*imama* or *uswa*) is properly recognized.

We can thus see how the concept of martyrdom in Islam is linked with the entire religion of Islam. This whole process can be somehow understood if the term 'Islam' is appreciated. This is because being a derivate of the Arabic root *salama*, which means 'surrender' and 'peace', Islam is a wholesome and peaceful submission to the will of Allah. This means being prepared to die (martyrdom) in the course of this submission. Thus the concept of martyrdom, like all other Islamic concepts, can be fully and wholly appreciated only in the light of the Islamic doctrine of tawhid, or the absolute unity of Allah and full submission to His will and command. It cannot be fully appreciated in isolation.

In this sense, the concept of *shahada* is no exception. All Islamic concepts are interrelated, and should be appreciated within the framework of the doctrine of tawhid.

* This article is by Abolfazl Ezzati of Tehran University and is reprinted without revision (except for the omitting of endnotes), from *Al-Serat*, Vol. XII (1986) from a website at: http//www.al-islam.org/al-serat/Concept-Ezzati.htm, with kind permission of the Muhammad Trust of Great Britain and Northern Ireland.

The concept of *shahada* in Islam has been misunderstood by both Muslims and non-Muslims. As stated above, *shahada* is closely associated with the concept of *jihad*. Most non-Muslim scholars, intentionally or unintentionally, have defined *jihad* as only the Holy War, and thus have understood neither *jihad* nor *shahada*. The Muslims, mostly taking into consideration the martyrs of the early days of Islamic history, define martyrdom in terms of the fatalistic death of those dear to Allah, and do not see the close link between continuous struggle in the cause of Allah (jihad) and martyrdom.

Martyrdom is not the monopoly of Islam (though it is the monopoly of spiritual, religious, and divine systems, and cannot be claimed by followers of materialistic schools). Islam introduces its own concept of martyrdom. An Islamic concept should be explained within the framework of Islam, and not, by Muslims or by non-Muslims, in the light of non-Islamic concepts such as guilt and suffering. Muslims are not allowed to explain Islamic principles without taking due consideration of the entire conceptual system of Islam. *Shahada* thus cannot be explained purely in terms of intercession and mediation. That is to say, those early martyrs of Islam volunteered for death to be able to intercede and mediate for sinners on the Day of Judgement.

The Islamic concept of intercession and mediation (*shafa'a*) should be appreciated within the framework of the principle of causality, and not solely as spiritual mediation. Islam rejects the Christian concept of mediation without the personal responsibility for the salvation of oneself.

The concepts of martyrdom and Holy Struggle in the cause of Allah are interrelated. Both words have been frequently used in the Holy Qur'an. In fact, there is no martyrdom without struggle in the cause of Allah and for the cause of the truth. Both words have literal meanings different from their terminological meanings, although these terminological meanings were originally based on the literal meanings. They developed their terminological meanings later on, though the term *shahada* was used in the Qur'an for those who were martyred too. The Islamic concepts of both *shahada* and *jihad* have been misunderstood, particularly by non-Muslims, mainly by Orientalists.

The word *shahada* is derived from the Arabic verbal root *shahada*, which means to 'see', to 'witness', to 'testify', to 'become a model and paradigm'. *Shahada* therefore literally means to 'see', to 'witness', and to 'become a model'. A *shahid* is the person who sees and witnesses, and he is therefore the witness, as if the martyr witnesses and sees the truth physically and thus stands by it firmly, so much so that not only does he testify it verbally, but he is prepared to struggle and fight and give up his life for the truth, and thus to become a martyr. In this way, and by his struggle and sacrifice for the sake of the truth, he becomes a model, a paradigm, and an example for others, worthy of being copied, and worthy of being followed.

In this process, the keyword is 'truth' (*haqq*), its recognition and declaration, the struggle and fight for it, and the preparedness to die for its sake and thus set the model for the seekers of truth. The goal, motive, and the whole aim is the establishment of the truth. *Jihad* is the means for establishing the truth, and may lead to martyrdom, but does not necessarily lead to being killed for it in the battlefield, although it necessarily involves the continuous Holy Struggle, and death in the cause of the struggle.

We may therefore conclude that there is neither *jihad* nor martyrdom outside the realm of truth, that martyrdom applies only when it is preceded by *jihad*, that *jihad* is an inclusive struggle for the cause of the truth, that a *mujahid* dies the death of a martyr even though he does not fall on the battlefield. He dies as a martyr even though he is not killed, on the condition that he stays loyal to the divine truth and stands ready to fight for the truth and to defend it at all costs, even at the cost of his own life. He is a *mujahid* while he lives, and a martyr if he dies or is killed for it.

We have explained that a martyr establishes himself as a paradigm and a model. Both *shahid* (martyr) and *shahid* (model) are derived from the same Arabic root. In this sense, the concept of *shahada* is closely related to the concept of prophethood in Islam. Both the martyrs and the prophets are regarded as paradigms (2:143).

In Islam man needs guidance to the truth. The true guidance is from the whole truth, God, the Source of Truth and Guidance (50:6, 71, 88, 92:12). But since it is man who is to be guided, the guide should naturally be a man. Islam is the message from the source of truth, given to the Messenger as the guideline for leading mankind to the truth. Guiding humanity requires leading humanity. The true faith is united with righteous living in Islam, and there is unity of belief and practice in Islam. A comprehensive guidance therefore involves leading in thought, words, and behaviour. The guide should therefore practise what he preaches, and should himself be the supreme incarnation and the perfect embodiment of the message he spreads. He should be a paradigm, a model, and a model-maker.' Muhammad was thus the Messenger who brought the comprehensive universal Message of Allah, and he was the incarnation of the divine message, and the living example of his mission, the model (*shahid*), the paradigm (*uswa*). The key word in the concept of prophethood in Islam is thus human guidance. This involves the recognition of what humanity should be guided to, what guidance is, how it should be done, and the realization of the guidance by being the true model of the actual guidance. This is why Muhammad was himself the first Muslim and the best model of Islam. And thus his practice is recognized as the guideline and standard pattern (*sunna*) for the Muslim community, the members of which are supposed to become models (*shuhada*) for the entire human community. The prophets, including Muhammad, were thus models and model-makers, and their disciples and companions were models. Thus those who carry on the struggle in the cause of the truth are *mujahid*s and *shahid*s at the same time.

The position of the prophets as the paradigms and model-makers in Islam gives the Islamic concept of prophethood a unique characteristic. Their main responsibility is thus leading and guiding humanity to the truth by being the true incarnation of God. They do not intercede and mediate between the source of the truth and humanity spiritually, in the sense that they come to be crucified to pay for the sins committed by humanity through Adam. In Islam, everybody is responsible for his or her own actions. Nothing and nobody can intercede between the sinner and God. The concept of intercession in Islam should be appreciated within the framework of the principle of causality. That is to say that the prophets, by guiding and leading the people to the truth, cause their salvation (*sa'ada*). Salvation must be earned and deserved, and the prophets and the Messengers of Allah provide us with the opportunity to earn and deserve salvation, that is to say, it is not the crucifixion and the cross that causes salvation, but it is the realization of the truth that causes it. Man is thus, originally sinless, good, and peaceful, and the role of the prophets is a positive one that of guidance and of being a paradigm, and not a negative one. Martyrs are the super-models of the divine message, too, and in this way they share a special responsibility and honour with the prophets.

Because the responsibility of the prophets is partly to provide the living example of the divine message, their message should be practical so that the rest of humanity, like them, is able to copy and follow them and practise the Message too. What Jesus did, according to Christian doctrine, was a unique action by a unique being (the crucifixion of the Son of God), not possible and necessary for humanity to copy. But what Muhammad did was to convey the practical guidelines of righteousness, and he himself lived within those guidelines to prove their practicability for the rest of humanity. This is why the prophets are called *shahids* (paradigms and witnesses) in the Qur'an, a term used for martyrs later on in the early days of Islamic history. Muhammad, therefore, like other Messengers, is the incarnation of Islam, full surrender to God, the universal religion of all of creation, including man. He was the model of what he taught, and a paradigm for humanity. A model attracts and leads people to the truth. He does not force them. This is in full harmony with the concept of man in Islam. Islam rejects the incarnation in man of the essence of the actual divinity, but fully encourages the incarnation of God's guidance, will, and command, to become the living example of God's full code of thought and life (*din*, religion) for man. The prophets are the living examples of the divine message, and by being so make others the examples. Martyrs are also full examples of the divine message, and thus the embodiment of the divine will. There are a few Islamic traditions which introduce the blood of the martyrs as the blood of God (*thar Allah*).

Shi'ism being one of the fundamental and original sects of Islam, and staying loyal to all authentic Islamic doctrines, lays great emphasis on the doctrine of the leadership (Imamate) of the Muslim leadership. I believe it is not inappropriate to suggest that all of Shi'ism revolves around one major principle, that of the leadership of the Islamic community (*umma*).

The keyword in Shi'ism is thus Imamate, which means leading and guiding those in need of guidance. If the community is to be led and guided, the leaders themselves should be the leading examples of the faith in what they try to lead the community to believe in, and models of the code of thought and practice they try to lead others to practice. The concept of leadership involves three elements: (i) those who lead (*imam*), (ii) those who are to be led (*shia, mamum*), and (iii) the actual leadership, guidance, and code of leadership. The community cannot be lead unless those who lead believe in what they practice and in what they preach others to practice. In short, *imams* should themselves be the living examples and models for those they try to lead.

If prophethood and messengership involve two major responsibilities, namely, introducing and spreading the divine message, and setting the model and being the living example of the divine message, the Imamate involves only the latter responsibility. This is why every Messenger is also an Imam, but an Imam is not necessarily a Messenger. In fact, the office of the Imamate is the responsibility for providing the model for the office of messengership, and this is how he leads. We can therefore understand that Shi'ism (following the leader) based on the doctrine of the Imamate (leadership) is more directly involved with the idea of setting the model, providing the example, and producing the paradigm. The entire history of Shi'ism, and the lives of the Shi'i Imams should be appreciated in this context and within the concept of the Imamate, which is the leading of humanity to salvation by guiding them to the full implementation of Allah's code for the salvation of humanity, by being the supreme example in word and deed of that divine code. That is to say that they live a life of continuous struggle in the cause of Allah and of truth, and that is why they are all regarded as martyrs, whether they die on the battlefield or in bed.

The event of Karbala', the martyrdom of the Imam Husayn on 'Ashura', and the whole struggle he undertook, plays a very crucial role in the history of Shi'ism. Yet this unique historical event is seen by the Shi'a as a model event to inspire the Muslims. This is explained in the well known narration frequently quoted 'Every day is 'Ashura', and every place is Karbala'. This is partly why it has kept its dynamic, resilient, and revolutionary spirit, and features throughout history, and this is how Shi'ism truly reflects this spirit.

Chapter Eight

Martyrdom and Murder: Aspects of Suicidal Terrorism

Brian Wicker, Peter Bishop and Maha Azzam

The Kamikaze Suicides

Everybody has heard of the suicidal kamikaze fighters of Japan who played a key role in the final stages of the war in the Pacific in 1944–45. But not everyone has understood their reasons for doing what they did. A study of these raises the question: were they martyrs for their cause? If not, why not?

Kamikaze is a word widely used in the West, meaning 'divine wind' in Japanese. It originally referred to the typhoons of 1274 and 1281 CE which reputedly saved Japan from Mongol invasions. As such, it was adopted in 1944 to designate the project of a suicidal attack unit within the Japanese navy towards the end of the Second World War.[1] By means of this new unit it was hoped to prevent an otherwise inevitable American invasion.

The new, emergency tactic of suicidal attack from the air against the allied Pacific fleets ultimately failed to achieve its aim, even without the *coup de grâce* of the atomic bombs on Hiroshima and Nagasaki. By late 1944 Japan was already in desperate straits, and shortages of all kinds of military equipment, including fuel, as well as numerous mechanical failures resulting from the haste and the material inadequacies with which the tactic was put in place, helped to make the kamikaze tactic futile in the long run. But in the immediate circumstances of the approaching end of the war, especially in the Philippines from October 1944 and, above all, Okinawa in 1945, it had its local successes, sinking ships and killing a large number of allied sailors. By the end of 1944, 500 kamikaze sorties had been flown, even though it was already clear that Japan was losing the war. By the end of the war it is estimated that 5000 kamikaze pilots had died. Not all of these used the specially constructed light aircraft designed for the purpose; sometimes the Japanese used ordinary fighters to ram American B29 bombers in the air. They also had suicidal midget submarines designed to sink ships in port.[2]

From the beginning, the kamikaze pilots were genuine volunteers. And even when conscription into the suicide squadrons was introduced, late in the war, their enthusiasm was undiminished. There was no shortage of men willing, indeed eager, to commit suicide for the cause. No doubt there were those who tried to avoid being recruited – for example, by reporting sick. But the effect of peer pressure tended to have the opposite effect. And hatred of the Americans, especially after the carpet-bombing of Japanese cities and the viciousness of the Pacific Island campaigns, also had its effect. Some men would even sign up by writing their names in their own blood, to show how determined they were to take part. In one case, a married man with several daughters who wanted to volunteer found his family connections an obstacle. But the obstacle was removed when his wife and daughters collectively killed themselves in order to release him for his chosen mission.[3] Even more appalling was the mass suicide of Japanese soldiers and civilians in Saipan in July 1944. After 3000 fit men had voluntarily charged into concentrated American machine-gun fire, and been mown down, a crowd of wounded then followed suit. After that, whole units of men were decapitated by their officers, who then committed harakiri. Finally, hundreds of civilians, including women and children, flung themselves off cliff-tops to avoid being captured.[4] Events such as these raise the question of personal motivation. As one American witness of a kamikaze attack confessed, in a documentary broadcast on 14 July 2004 on UKTV History, it seems impossible for anyone to get personal satisfaction out of committing suicide; after all, once you are dead you can't gain anything for yourself. How, then, is it possible for large numbers of people to volunteer to do something from which they could gain absolutely nothing? This is the point at which the concept of martyrdom might begin to be relevant in accounting for what happened. Yet virtually nowhere, since the seventeenth-century massacres of Christians, do the Japanese themselves use the language of martyrdom to describe what their own fellow countrymen were doing. As for those in the West who are more used to talking about martyrs, virtually nobody has described the kamikaze in these terms either. Why not?

The history of Japanese culture can explain a good deal. Suicide is not forbidden, let alone a sin, in the traditional Japanese tradition. On the contrary, it has been an honour, even a privilege, to commit harakiri, particularly to avoid humiliation, defeat or capture in battle. Japanese history is littered with stories, some legendary from the distant past, others well documented or even physically witnessed by disinterested visiting observers in modern times,[5] of heroes who have stabbed themselves in the neck (to cut the carotid artery) or, more usually, disembowelled themselves, in order to avoid disgrace. Such suicides of failed heroes are widely felt to be the epitome of the true Japanese spirit. Among disgraces, defeat in battle, or imprisonment as its consequence, seem to be the most prominent reasons for self-killing. 'Don't survive shamefully as a prisoner', wrote General Hideki Tojo in his *Instructions for the Military* in the Second World War; 'die and thus escape ignominy.'[6] A similar resolution was expressed (though eventually not carried out) by Admiral Ugaki Mantome, commander-in-chief of the Fifth Air Force with special responsibility for the kamikaze pilots. He wrote in his diary of his resolution 'when and how to die as a samurai, an admiral or a supreme commander. I renewed a resolution today of entrusting my body to the throne and defending the empire until death takes me away.'[7] Where possible, ritual self-disembowelment has usually been followed by decapitation by a willing accomplice, partly to shorten the excruciating pain but also to make sure it 'works'. From the legendary Yorozu in 587 CE to groups of generals at the end of the Second World War, harakiri has been practised and praised as a virtuous act, especially for the defeated. Indeed, being defeated is part of the point. For the Japanese have cultivated the 'nobility of failure' for their tragic heroes, as Ivan Morris's splendid book of that title illustrates. Most of their greatest men have failed to achieve great things. Whereas in the West heroism and its rewards, in terms of honours and memories, has been associated with great achievements, even in death (for example, Nelson), in Japan the most revered men have been those who have achieved nothing in worldly terms, but who have been famous for their other-worldly virtues, including their renunciation of life itself by means of suicide.[8] How is this possible?

A man's self-disembowelment is first the public exhibition, and then the extinction, of everything that makes him to be the person he is. For in Shinto and then Zen tradition, the lower abdomen is the seat of the will, the emotions, the virtues, the very personality of a man. So harakiri, or 'belly-slitting', is not only a way of demonstrating courage and the manly conquest of pain (mere self-poisoning is a 'womanish' means of suicide), but of self-abnegation, the giving up of a man's whole existence and his *raison d'être*, for some greater cause.[9] By the twelfth century CE this greater cause had been accepted by the medieval hereditary warrior class, or samurai, as absolute loyalty to the emperor, seen as divine head of the nation and identified with Dai Nippon or 'Greater Japan'. The Shinto insistence of cleanliness of body and mind, together with the impossibility of defining good and evil in any other terms, reinforced the Zen faith in a transcendental wisdom to be attained only by rigorous discipline, asceticism and indifference to physical needs. This combination led to a warrior ethic of instant action. 'The Zen adept is "right thinking": without ratiocination, by intuition alone, he acts immediately, decisively and correctly in all circumstances.'[10] Fujio Hayashi, who helped with the selection of volunteers but never flew himself as a kamikaze, admits to studying Zen ideals: 'In Zen teaching there is no life or death. Even if one lives a bit longer or dies younger, when one thinks of one's life against all the living things in the world, it is quite insignificant. If one can think like this it is no big deal.'[11] This is the ethic which underlies the readiness of the kamikaze fighter to volunteer for suicide, in the name not only of the nation and its honour, but also (especially in the case of young unmarried men who formed the majority of the volunteers accepted for the role) of the family and its honour too. For most of the volunteers were well-educated, well-adjusted, well-respected sons of respectable families – far removed from the caricatures often prevailing in the West of a caste of subhuman, bloodthirsty, thoroughly brainwashed barbarians.

But the ethic just outlined also justified the emphasis on the tragic element in the kamikaze make-up. For it is essentially an other-worldly ethic, scornful of success in financial, political or even ideological terms. Like the suicides of the long Japanese tradition, in which nothing succeeds like failure,[12] the kamikaze pilots were not giving up already-successful careers or promises of a great future. They were giving up themselves and thus, too, the very idea of worldly 'achievement'. Ironically, of course, their veneration tended to encourage others to take up this same cause. As O'Neill points out, in the case of Field-Marshal Takamori Saigo, who disembowelled himself after defeat at the battle of Shiroyama (24 September 1877), he 'won a great victory for those virtues of which he had feared the loss and which he had sought to defend'.[13] The very success of Vice-Admiral Onishi Takijiro, in creating the kamikaze units in 1944, was built on a widespread cult of venerating great heroes of failure in the past. No wonder the Americans at the time could not understand what was going on. Only in retrospect have Western thinkers been able to appreciate the Japanese cult of suicide for what it is.

What were the virtues which the kamikaze pilots and their tradition epitomized? First, it was gratitude for everything that had made their lives possible. This gratitude was summed up in their love of the emperor, who was himself not a particularly notable 'personality' (perhaps this was part of the point). Nevertheless he represented, in his own person, the tradition and the moral riches of the nation. 'It is an honour to be able to give my life in defence of these beautiful and lofty things,' writes Yamaguchi Teruo on the eve of his death.[14] Above all, 'these beautiful and lofty things' included the pilot's own family. Sometimes a pilot even associated his parents with his own mission, as if they were physically with him in his final moments.[15] A second virtue which is frequently cited by the kamikaze fighters themselves is 'sincerity'. This comes out in the lack of any hope for a successful outcome of the kamikaze tactic. One surviving final kamikaze pilot's letter reads: 'Is it true that self-sacrifice is the only thing that gives meaning to death? To this question the warrior is obliged to reply "yes", while knowing full well that his suicide mission has no meaning.'[16] But this is perhaps overdoing it, for while the mission may have no military meaning, it can lead to a spiritual rebirth. Indeed, military defeat may be the condition of this 'victory'. But, of course, there is no question of a spiritual rebirth for the hero himself. He himself gains nothing, as the American sailor quoted earlier rightly points out. Indeed, 'if by some strange chance, Japan should suddenly win this war, it would be a fatal misfortune for the future of the nation . . . [so] it will be better for our nation and people if they are tempered through real ordeals which will serve to strengthen [them]'.[17]

Underlying this outlook is the insistence that the point of living well is not to achieve worldly success, but to die well. A good death is what the right-thinking person most wants from life: 'His final, blazing meeting with his fate is the most important event in his life.' 'Think constantly of your death,' advised one of Japan's earliest failed heroes, Masashige. A later samurai scholar wrote: 'One's way of dying can validate one's entire life.'[18] But, of course, there can be a paradox here: for the end of your life is not an event in your life, unless there is personal survival after death. And such survival is not part of the Japanese Shinto or Zen creed, which is more about avoiding any personal need for survival than it is about seeking to survive through cultivating the virtues and doing good works.

From the Christian or Muslim point of view, two things seem to prevent the kamikaze pilot from being a martyr. The first is the nature of the 'mission' which brings about his death. For it is in fighting for a sense of personal or national honour that the Japanese 'hero' typically dies. Is this an adequate or even a laudable objective? How is it to be distinguished from mere idolatry, the worship of an 'unworldly' worldliness? What is this 'honour' which it is death to lose and which the exercise of the virtues is designed to promote? Are not the unworldly virtues of the Japanese hero, and even the welcome he gives to failure, a kind of 'higher' worldliness – a seeking, for others if not for himself, of a certain status in the eyes of 'the world'?

Deeper, perhaps, is the rejection of the belief that life is a *gift*. For the Japanese hero, his life is his own, to be disposed of as he thinks fit. Death, after all, is not a prelude to something greater, for life is not a gift to be treasured and preserved for eternity. Indeed the whole Christian/Muslim understanding of the cosmos as freely created, metaphysically contingent through and through – given to itself, as it were, as an act of grace – is foreign to the Japanese mind. (Perhaps this explains the extreme measures taken in the seventeenth century to extirpate Christianity not only from Japanese territory but from the Japanese soul.) Hence there is nothing morally repugnant about suicide, for it is not a rejection of something that God has given to us, but is rather a conquest of self taken to the limit. In so far as martyrdom is giving back to God a gift that can only be kept for oneself at a morally intolerable cost, it is quite alien to the kamikaze pilot's outlook, despite the many features which both share: especially the need for endurance in face of appalling dangers and the value of other-worldly virtues, including the recognition that ultimately the point of living well is to die well.

The Tamil Tigers

During the past two decades the Tamil Tigers of Sri Lanka have been among the most vigorous and successful exponents of suicide attacks in the pursuit of political aims. However, their motivation and ideology need to be distinguished from those of other groups using similar tactics.

The early history of Sri Lanka (formerly Ceylon) is of a mixed community of Sinhalese Buddhists and Tamils who are predominantly Hindu but who include a substantial number of Muslims and a smaller number of Christians. Some of the Tamils are indigenous to the island, as are the majority Sinhalese community; others are the result of migration over a long period from the nearby Tamil-speaking area of south-eastern India, just 20 miles away across the water. The Hindu kingdom of Jaffna existed between the thirteenth and

the fifteenth centuries following a succession of invasions during the period
of the Chola kings of South India. In the nineteenth century the British policy
of despatching the poorest people from their Indian dominions to other parts
of the Empire as indentured labourers resulted in the addition of further
Tamils to work in the tea plantations.

The Portuguese ruled parts of the island from the early sixteenth century,
and the Dutch established control of most of the littoral of Ceylon between
1658 and 1795. The British began to establish bases in Ceylon in 1796, had
conquered the whole island by 1815, and in 1833 put in place a centralized
British government. Later, they introduced 'communal representation' in
legislative councils as they had done in India, with votes allocated according
to perceived religious or ethnic community membership.

In February 1948 Ceylon gained its independence. The population of the
island was then approximately 15 million, of whom about 30 per cent were
Tamils. Some Sinhalese Buddhists, although enjoying a substantial majority,
had misgivings not only about a Tamil minority, but also about the existence
of another 50 million Tamils in nearby India. Tamils of Indian origin – that is,
the descendants of indentured labourers – were denied citizenship, and there
were attempts over many years to repatriate the 'Indian' Tamils to India. The
last 100 000 of them were granted citizenship by the Sri Lankan government
in 1986. For their part, the Tamils, as represented by the Tamil Federal Party,
proposed a policy of a federal Sri Lanka with the northern and eastern
provinces under local Tamil control and using the Tamil language, whilst the
major part of the island would remain Sinhalese-speaking and culturally
Buddhist. In January 1956 (the year in which the 2500th anniversary of the
Mahaparinirvana of the Buddha was celebrated by Buddhists throughout the
world) Sinhala was formally adopted by a newly elected Sri Lanka Freedom
Party as the sole official language, replacing English which had been the link
language between Sinhala- and Tamil-speaking people. This prompted a
campaign, initially non-violent *satyagraha* on Gandhian lines, on the part of
the Tamils. The official name of the country was changed in 1972 from the
English 'Ceylon' to the Sinhalese 'Sri Lanka'. Over the next decade, Tamil
groups became increasingly militant. The ambush of an army truck and the
killing of 13 Sinhalese soldiers in 1983 was followed by a major outbreak of
Sinhalese violence against the Tamils. By that year more than 10 000 Tamils
had fled the country; most to India, some to Europe.

Although at the height of the troubles there were 37 militant Tamil groups,
the most ruthless was that of the Liberation Tigers of Tamil Eelam (*eelam*
translates as 'home'). Led by Velupillai Prabhakaran, the LTTE became a
formidable force of men and women, wearing around their necks the cyanide
pills with which they were prepared to end their lives to avoid capture and
what might follow. The strong impetus of Tamil nationalism which drove
the movement reflected to some degree the confidence and enthusiasm of
the Tamil cultural revival in India, which, from the 1920s onwards, had
established a political party espousing the values of Tamil language (over

against what was perceived to be the linguistic nationalism of the northern states with their Sanskrit-based languages) and of working people against the privileged high-caste people. The Tamil nationalist party (the DMK – party for the uplift of the Tamils) came to power in Madras State in 1967 and promptly changed the name of the state to Tamilnadu. In the 1970s and 1980s there was some enthusiasm in Tamilnadu for the LTTE, and training and staging bases for Tigers were located there. This support largely evaporated when Rajiv Gandhi was assassinated during a visit to Tamilnadu in May 1991. His assassin was a woman who concealed explosives under her sari, knelt at the feet of the great man in true Indian fashion, and in doing so touched not his feet but the detonator on the explosives, blowing them both apart.

Women play an important part in the LTTE struggle. On International Women's Day in 1992, the LTTE leader said: '. . . the courage, determination and heroism of our women fighters has served to awaken their sisters and brothers, break down centuries old social barriers and ways of thinking and behaving, and restructure society on a free and equal basis'.[19] By the end of 1992 the total death toll of women fighters had reached 381. Adele Balasingham claims that:

> The women who have joined the Tamil liberation army as well as the majority of the women who participate in the civilian mass protests, constitute the backbone of the Tamil national struggle.[20]

The LTTE claimed its first 'martyr' in 1982, although it continued to practise some non violent action, with members undertaking 'fasts to death' in 1987 and 1988. An LTTE text of the period described the offering of one's life for the cause as the way to achieve the liberation of the motherland.[21] Rituals adopted by the LTTE included:

1 initiation and the taking of an oath;
2 the symbolic planting of a seed, in recognition of the belief that a martyr plants his body as a seed to germinate in a new harvest – 'The LTTE does not bury its dead, it plants them';
3 commemoration rituals on the anniversary of martyrs' deaths;
4 renaming roads after martyrs;[22]
5 displaying texts on posters, such as 'the sepulchres of the martyrs shall glimmer as cornerstones for the new land which is to be born'.[23]

Although most of the Tamil Tigers are Hindu Shaivites by religion, the giving of life for a cause does not appear to be motivated by religious belief. Far more important are the concepts of the Tamil nation and Tamil language. Interestingly, this appears to mirror the deep concerns of Tamil nationalism in India, where it may be claimed that nationalism in the north revolves around religion, whilst in the south it focuses on language.

Peter Schalk, in identifying some of the main ideological sources for the LTTE concepts of martyrdom, does include some references to religion, but they do not appear to be the dominant factors. Among his sources are:

- the revival of sacrificial language, expressed in the word *arppani* ('dedication', as to a god)
- the Tamil bhakti tradition, a religious tradition of devotional worship which includes concepts of dedication and asceticism
- a Christian element, expressed in language similar to that used by Christians of martyrs
- Dravidian nationalism, related to the idea of a linguistic Tamil nation-state
- the martial feminism of the female Tigers.[24]

Despite this mixture of what appear to be the sacred and the secular, it is clear that the main driving forces have to do with language and ethnicity, not with religious sanctions or supernatural rewards. Schalk concludes that there were Marxist influences at work among the Tigers in the 1980s, but argues that they later disappeared. He also points out that the word 'martyrdom' is not reserved for those who deliberately set out to kill themselves in a suicide attack: 'Every freedom fighter who sacrifices his or her life is a martyr', whether they die by suicide or in battle.[25] The visible wearing of a cyanide capsule around the neck is said to be an attempt to shift responsibility for the fighter's death to the enemy, so that it may not be regarded as suicide in a strict sense.

However, there is a special group of fighters, the 'black tigers', who undertake tasks that they know will lead to their deaths. Here a distinction is drawn between the LTTE and Hamas, even though Tigers may have trained with Hamas in the past:[26] namely, that whilst Hamas may invoke religious concepts of martyrdom, the Tamil Tigers act in a secular setting, with no reference to religious authority or to compensations in an afterlife.[27] The Tigers do not encourage the idea of an afterlife for the dead hero, only the possibility of a life remembered in history.

It would appear that the Tamil freedom fighters must be categorized separately from those who are motivated by religious concepts of martyrdom. For the Tamils, there is no expectation of a future reward, of a supernatural deliverance that will compensate them for their struggle and their death. The individual Tamil Tiger is sacrificing his or her life for the sake of the Tamil 'nation' and so for a future in which the dead hero will not share. In this respect, it may appear to be a more noble and self-sacrificial act than that of the conventionally religious martyr.

Palestinian Terrorism

The Historical Dimension

The Palestinian struggle has used religious terminology almost from its inception. This was partly because of the historical link of the Palestinians to the Ottoman caliphate and the collective memory of the Ottoman wars which were seen as just Islamic wars, partly because in the post-Ottoman anti-colonial struggles in the Middle East, the religious lexicon was almost universally adopted and partly because the nature of the Jewish colonization itself had a religious dimension.

We find in folk-songs celebrating the 1936 uprising that fallen Palestinian guerrillas are referred to as *Shuhada* (*Shaheed* in the singular), commonly translated as martyr, but in fact literally meaning 'one who bears a strong witness (to God's omnipotence)'. The significance of this lies in the fact that what later developed into the secular liberation movement of the Palestinian people had its roots in this early uprising and continued to adopt its quasi-religious references.

By 1948, when the Jewish settlement movement had overwhelmed the local Arab population, the specifically Islamic reference to a just war was being used by the landed elite in their failed attempt to halt the establishment of the Jewish state. This elite, although they had distanced themselves from the Ottoman government, were in many ways the inheritors of the legacy of that government. After all, members of the Palestinian landed elite themselves formed part of the ruling Ottoman elite up until the fall of the Levant in 1917. Thus the militia hastily formed to meet the nascent Israeli army in the field was called *al-Jihad al-Muqaddas* or the Holy Struggle.[28] The total defeat of that amateur militia heralded the demise of the influence of the landed elite and the withering of any tenuous link with the past as the leadership passed to the middle classes. However, the new 'nationalist' leadership of the Palestinians, partly because of its roots in the 1936 uprising, continued to use the religious terminology of *Shaheed* when describing its fallen even as it moved to a more secular socialist agenda.

Finally, the Levantine Arab nationalist movements were greatly influenced by Christian Arab thinkers. In the context of the Arab–Israeli struggle, that Christian influence manifested itself in the use of Christian religious terminology to define the struggle. This is best illustrated in what became known as the Songs of Return (*Aghani al Awdah*) sung by Fairuz and others after the 1967 defeat following the pre-emptive strike by the Israeli army. In perhaps the most famous, *Zahrat al-Mada'in*, Fairuz sings of the Baby Jesus and Mary crying for the Palestinian people and predicting that the River Jordan shall 'wash away the barbaric footprint' in a clear reference to baptism. In another, she sings of a 'White Christmas night, like the first Christmas night, a child of twenty is given the gift of a machine gun' in a reference to the gifts of the Magi.

Therefore within the context of the Palestinian struggle, what might otherwise be seen as Islamic religious terminology has long been used by nationalist secular elements and has often had a Christian dimension when used by Christian Palestinians. This can be clearly seen in the First Intifada of 1976, which erupted when several unarmed demonstrators were shot dead by Israeli forces within the Green Line. They became the first martyrs (or *shuhada*) of the newest phase of confrontation. However, the demonstration was organized by Palestinian communists, and many of the 'martyrs' were Marxist–Leninists.

Suicide and Terror

By the end of the 1960s and the start of the 1970s, the Palestinian guerrilla movement had adopted terror as a legitimate weapon against the Israelis. The lead in this came from the socialist Popular Front for the Liberation of Palestine headed by the Christian George Habash. In many ways this represented the introduction of the Leninist maxim that 'the objective of terrorism is to terrorize' into the Arab–Israeli arena.

Possibly because of the lack of military resources, and possibly as an imitation of Viet Cong tactics, this terror campaign was combined with the idea of 'suicide' missions in which the terror missions were carried out by activists expecting and willing to die in the process. Perhaps the most infamous of these attacks was the one in 1974 on an apartment block in Kiryat Shmona in northern Israel that resulted in the massacre of children. Suicide, even in war, is prohibited under Islamic law, as is the targeting of innocent civilians. Yet the propaganda machine of the Palestinian movement, aided and abetted by the Arab media, extolled those attacks as heroic and habitually referred to Palestinians who were killed in perpetrating them as martyrs, an Islamic religious reference often bestowed on socialist secular fighters.

In fact, this terror campaign was counterproductive, in that it turned world opinion firmly against the Palestinian liberation movement, and ineffective, in that it never gathered enough momentum to seriously tilt the balance against Israeli military superiority.

Ideologically, matters became even more confused when the Palestinian movements fell out with various Arab regimes, first in Jordan in 1970 and later in the Lebanese civil war with the fascists and the Syrians. All Palestinian dead (and, for that matter, Jordanian and Syrian dead as well) were referred to as martyrs, thus robbing the term of any religious dimension and placing it firmly within the nationalist context.

The Islamist Dimension

As with Egypt in the early years of Sadat's rule in the 1970s, the Israelis encouraged the Islamist movement to develop in the occupied territories as a counterbalance to the various factions of the PLO. Not only did the Israelis make the same miscalculation as Sadat in allowing space for the development of an implacable opposition, but they also failed to take into consideration demographic dimensions peculiar to Palestinians living in the occupied territories. The long years of the occupation had resulted in the migration of two segments of Palestinian society: the more Westernized landed elite and, more significantly, the Christians, who made up most of the middle class. They were thus left with primarily the Muslim working-class and farmer segments of the Palestinian society who were traditionally more conservative and more open to religious influence.

The rise and popularity of Hamas underlines this shift. Hamas, freed from having to incorporate Christian Palestinians (since most had left), reintroduced an Islamic dimension into the discourse of the anti-Israeli struggle and, in so doing, tried to reclaim the Islamic interpretation of martyr and *jihad* from the secular Palestinian movement. In this they have only been partially successful, in that both factions continue to use this terminology.

The first suicide bombings proper were perpetrated by the military wing of Hamas, partly in response to the very high casualty rate suffered by the Palestinian civilian population in the Second (and better-known) Intifada. Whether this was initially simply an act of revenge for the Palestinian civilian death-count that was derived from the local tradition of suicide missions or a more considered imitation of the tactics of the Tamil Tigers who pioneered its use remains a matter for speculation. What is clear, however, is that Hamas's terminology continued to mix elements of Islam (martyrdom) with nationalist elements (the struggle for the homeland). Moreover, until the recent writings of al-Qa'ida's Ayyman al-Zawahiri, suicide bombings had no theological foundation in Islam and were thus viewed as un-Islamic even by the most ardent supporters of the Palestinian struggle in the Muslim camp, including the leading theologian of the al-Azhar university and the mufti of Saudi Arabia.

Unlike al-Zawahiri, Hamas has never sought to find a theological argument for the use of suicide bombings, relying instead on the popular acceptance among the Palestinians of the legitimacy of such attacks and the 'martyrdom' of its perpetrators.

The Secular Dimension

Israeli academics have long pointed to the Islamic religious dimension of suicide bombings as evidence of a fanatical religious motivation among the Palestinians who support its use. In evidence they have pointed to the contents of the usual pre-attack videos recorded by the bombers that often talk of rewards awaiting martyrs in heaven.

However, this misses the point in that secular Palestinian fighters who died for the cause were also seen as martyrs bound for heaven by the Palestinian population. It also fails to take into account the rapid adoption of suicide bombing by factions among the non-religious PLO, including the al-Aqsa brigade which used the same references as the Hamas bombers (martyrdom and the promise of heaven). Nor does it explain the occasional Westernized female bomber who fails to fit the profile used by the Israeli security services.

It might be tempting to see the problem as two separate issues with two separate ideologies, one applying to the Islamist movement and the other to the secular movement. However, there is too much of an overlap between the two to support such a supposition.

A Weapon of the Weak

Given the historical use of religious terminology by the Palestinian movement, it might be profitable to move away from a religious explanation for the ideology of suicide bombers, even for those who belong to Hamas, and instead to suggest that the ideology for suicide bombings in the Palestinian context lies within the parameters of a nationalist anti-colonial struggle that, for historical reasons, makes allusions to religious metaphors. In a society where all attacks against the occupier were seen as *jihad* and all the fallen were seen as martyrs, it is natural that any new military tactic would adopt the same terminology.

The Palestinian resistance to the encroachment by the Israeli state has been marked by constant military defeat and retreat from 1948 to the present. All military tactics adopted by the Palestinian side failed to have any meaningful impact on the enemy. The traditional military endeavours of the Palestinian militia at the outset of the fight failed, as did those of the Arab armies in 1967 and ultimately in 1973. The attempt to copy the guerrilla tactics of other struggles in Asia also failed. Likewise, the attempt at a civilian uprising pitting stone-throwing youths against armoured columns also failed. The history of Palestinian resistance has thus been a history of failure – politically, materially and psychologically.

In this context, suicide bombing gave the Palestinian movement two advantageous elements. First, it met the need to extract some kind of bloody revenge for both the defeat and the civilian casualties of the Intifada. Second, it gave the Palestinian movement a sense of power in that they could now employ a weapon which they knew had a profound impact on the psyche of the enemy and, as such, could be seen as levelling the playing field a fraction more in their favour.

The Cult of Suicide

Finally, it is worthwhile looking at an important element of suicide bombings that relates to the perceived status of the bomber and his family. Certainly from the inception of the PLO, there has been a peculiarly exalted place in the Palestinian perception for those who sacrifice their lives for the cause. This is no different from other societies at war. In the pressured atmosphere of the occupied territories with its inherent economic hardships, the 'cause' overwhelms all other pursuits as the main concern of all citizens.

Suicide bombers are seen as the ultimate symbol of self-sacrifice. For the young, aspiring to be part of this exalted group becomes an ambition. We are told that volunteers have to ask many times before they are selected, thus adding to the mystique of a select few. They know that their memory would become sacred in the folk memory of the Palestinian people and that their status, and ultimately that of their families, would be exalted not as some analysts have suggested because of financial reward (in fact, the financial consequences are dire in that they always result in the demolition of the family home), but as the ultimate symbols of national self-sacrifice and national pride. This applies equally to those with strong religious beliefs and to secularists.

Conclusion

Despite the use of religious terminology by Palestinian suicide bombers, the ideology of this movement can be firmly placed within the context of a national liberation struggle. The long-term use of terms such as martyr and *jihad* among the Palestinians to describe their fighters have long robbed these words of any true religious dimension, despite the efforts of Hamas to reclaim that religious heritage. Suicide bombing is another facet of the Palestinians' attempt to inflict damage on their enemies and to reclaim some of what has been lost in an almost continuous history of defeat. As such, it owes more to the ideology of Ho Chi Minh and George Habash than to fanatical Islam.

Notes

1   Ivan Morris, *The Nobility of Failure: Tragic Heroes in the History of Japan* (Harmondsworth, Penguin Books, 1980), pp. 288–89.
2   Richard O'Neill, *Suicide Squads* (London, Salamander Books, 1981), p. 38.
3   A programme on kamikaze pilots broadcast on UKTV *History* channel, 14 July 2004.
4   Morris, *The Nobility of Failure*, p. 299.
5   Ibid., p. 368.
6   O'Neill, *Suicide Squads*, p. 12.
7   *Fading Victory: The Diary of Admiral Matome Ugaki, 1941–45* (Pittsburgh, Pittsburgh University Press, 1991), p. 659 (11 August 1945), quoted by Ian Nish in *Preparing for Peace and Survival: The Japanese Experience 1943–46*, Annual Lecture of the Liddell Centre for Military Archives, King's College, London (4 November 1996).
8   Morris, *The Nobility of Failure*, pp. 14ff.
9   Ibid., p. 367.
10 O'Neill, *Suicide Squads*, p. 11.
11 Programme on kamikaze pilots, note 3 (translation by Takako Mendl).
12 Morris, *The Nobility of Failure*, p. 15.
13 O'Neill, *Suicide Squads*, p. 14.
14 Morris, *The Nobility of Failure*, p. 309.
15 Ibid., p. 310.

16   Ibid., p. 312.
17   Ibid., p. 313.
18   Ibid., p. 14.
19   Peter Schalk, 'Resistance and Martyrdom in the Process of State Formation of Tamililam',
     in Joyce Pettigrew (ed.), *Martyrdom and Political Resistance: Essays from Asia and
     Europe*, Comparative Asian Studies 18 (Amsterdam, VU University, 1997), p. 71.
20   Adele Balasingham, *The Will to Freedom. An Inside View of Tamil Resistance* (Mitcham,
     Fairmax Publications, 2001), p. 286.
21   Schalk, 'Resistance and Martyrdom', p. 65.
22   Ibid., p. 68.
23   Ibid., p. 83.
24   Ibid., p. 66.
25   Ibid., p. 67.
26   See S.J. Tambiah, *Sri Lanka. Ethnic Fratricide and the Dismantling of Democracy*
     (Chicago, University of Chicago Press, 1986), p. 115: In response to 'the rumour' that
     Tamil rebels have established links with the PLO, he adds that it is 'an established fact
     that the UNP government has imported Israeli government agents from the Mossad and
     British ex-SAS commandos considered experts on fighting "terrorism" to help eradicate
     the rebels.'
27   Schalk, 'Resistance and Martyrdom', p. 78.
28   *Jihad* is often translated as 'holy war'. In fact, its literal meaning is to struggle or to exert
     effort. See Chapter One of this book, p. 15 ff.

APPENDICES

Appendix 1

Thomas Aquinas on Martyrdom*

We must now consider martyrdom; about which there are five points of inquiry:

1. is martyrdom the act of a virtue?
2. to which virtue does this act belong?
3. the act's perfection.
4. the suffering involved in martyrdom.
5. the cause of martyrdom.

article 1. *is martyrdom the act of a virtue?*

THE FIRST POINT: 1. It appears that martyrdom is not the act of a virtue. For every virtuous act is voluntary. But sometimes martyrdom is not voluntary, as is clear in the case of the Holy Innocents who died for Christ, about whom Hilary says that *by the glory of martyrdom they were raised to the attainment of eternal life.* Therefore martyrdom is not the act of a virtue.

2. Moreover, no unlawful deed is an act of virtue. But suicide is unlawful, as was stated earlier. Yet it is by suicide that martyrdom is achieved. For Augustine says that *certain holy women in time of persecution hurled themselves into a river to avoid those who attacked their chastity, and thus they died. Their martyrdom is the subject of a very popular cult in the Catholic Church.* Therefore martyrdom is not an act of virtue.

3. Moreover, it is praiseworthy for someone to volunteer to perform a virtuous act, but not to rush into martyrdom, indeed this appears presumptuous and dangerous. Therefore martyrdom is not an act of virtue.

ON THE OTHER HAND, only virtuous action receives as its due the reward of blessedness. But according to *Matthew* martyrdom receives this reward, *Blessed are they who suffer persecution for justice's sake, for theirs is the kingdom of heaven.* So martyrdom is a virtuous act.

REPLY: As has been stated, the function of virtue is to preserve a man in the good proposed by reason. Reason's good has truth held as its proper

* Reprinted with kind permission of English Province of the Dominican Order from *Summa Theologiae.* IIa IIae Q. 124 in Vol. 42 (London, Eyre and Spottiswode and New York, McGraw-Hill).

objective and justice as its proper effect, as emerges from earlier discussion. Now it is essential to the nature of martyrdom that a man stands steadfastly in truth and justice against the assaults of persecutors. Clearly, then, martyrdom is an act of virtue.

Hence: 1. Some have claimed that the use of free will was miraculously precocious in the case of the Holy Innocents, so that they endured martyrdom voluntarily. But as this is not proved on the authority of scripture, it is better to say that the tiny victims won by God's grace that glory of martyrdom which others win by their own will. For the shedding of blood for Christ's sake is a substitute for Baptism. Just as when infants are baptized, Christ's merit works through baptismal grace to win for them eternal glory, so when they are killed for Christ his merit effectively achieves for them the glory of martyrdom. So Augustine remarks, as though addressing them, *A man will doubt the crown you won in suffering for Christ only if he also disbelieves that the baptism of Christ is effective in infants. You did not reach the age to believe in Christ who was to suffer. But you were able to endure suffering in your bodies for Christ who was to suffer.*

2. As Augustine states in the passage quoted there is a possibility that *divine authority has persuaded the Church, by manifestations worthy of credence, to honour the memory of those holy women.*

3. The Law gives directions for acts of virtue. Now it was earlier remarked that certain commands of the divine law have been given to ensure willingness of mind, so that a man may be ready to do this or that should the occasion present itself. Consequently certain things are connected with an act of virtue as implying a willingness, namely that given the situation he is prepared to act in accord with reason. This seems especially noteworthy in the case of martyrdom, which is the right endurance of sufferings unjustly inflicted. Now people ought not to provide each other with opportunity for unjust action, but if someone does treat us unjustly, we ought to endure this in a balanced way.

article 2. is martyrdom an act of courage?

THE SECOND POINT: 1. Martyrdom does not seem to be an act of courage. For 'martyr' in Greek means a *witness*. Now according to *Acts* it is to faith in Christ that men witness. *You will be witnesses to me in Jerusalem ...* And Maximus says in a sermon, *The mother of martyrdom is the Catholic faith, which famous champions have attested with their blood. So* martyrdom is an act of faith rather than of courage.

2. Moreover, a praiseworthy act is chiefly associated with the virtue which gives one a bent to that act, which is demonstrated by it, and without which the act is worthless. Now the chief incentive to martyrdom is the virtue of charity – hence the statement in a sermon of Maximus, *The charity of Christ prevailed in his martyrs.* Further, in the act of martyrdom

it is charity which is chiefly demonstrated, according to the Gospel, *Greater love has no man than this, that a man should lay down his life for his friends*. Besides, without charity martyrdom is valueless, as St Paul says, *If I deliver my body for burning, but have not charity, it avails me nothing.* Martyrdom is therefore an act of charity rather than courage.

3. Moreover, Augustine says in a sermon about St Cyprian, *It is easy to reverence and venerate a martyr, but a big task to imitate his faith and endurance.* But in every act of virtue it is the virtue governing the act which is chiefly praised. So martyrdom is an act of endurance rather than courage.

ON THE OTHER HAND, Cyprian writes in his letter *To Martyrs and Confessors, Blessed martyrs, with what praises shall I proclaim you? Soldiers most courageous, what words can I find to praise your bodily strength?* Now a man wins praise for the virtue governing the act he performs. So martyrdom is an act of courage.

REPLY: From our earlier statements it is clear that the role of courage is to strengthen a man in the good of virtue, in the face of danger, especially danger of death and chiefly death in warfare. Now obviously in martyrdom a man is firmly established in the good proposed by virtue, when he does not abandon faith and justice because of immediate danger of death with which persecutors threaten him in what amounts to a personal battle. Hence Cyprian says, *The crowd of bystanders witnessed the divine conflict; they saw that Christ's servants stood in battle with voices of free men, minds undefiled and divine strength.* So it is clear that martyrdom is an act of courage; this is why the Church reads in a lesson about the martyrs, *They were made courageous in war.*

Hence: 1. In an act of courage there are two things to consider. The first is the good, the proper end of courage, in which the brave man stands fast. The other is steadfastness itself, by which a man refuses to yield to hostile forces deterring him from that good; this steadfastness constitutes the essence of courage. Now courage in civil affairs establishes a man's spirit in human justice, to preserve which he endures mortal danger; and in the same way the courage which is a gift of grace strengthens the human mind in the good *of God's justice, which is won through faith in Christ Jesus*, as Paul says. So faith in relation to martyrdom is a final good in which a man is made resolute, whereas courage is related to it as the disposition which brings about the act itself.

2. Charity does prompt the act of martyrdom as its first and most important moving force by being the virtue commanding it, but courage does so as the directly engaged moving force, being the virtue which brings out the act. Charity therefore is the directing virtue, and courage the eliciting virtue in the act of martyrdom; and so it manifests both virtues. But like any act of virtue it gets its meritorious nature from charity; so without charity it is of no value.

3. As was stated, endurance is the more important of the two acts of courage. To this and not to aggression, which is courage's secondary action, martyrdom is linked. The patience of the martyrs is praised along with courage, because it ministers to courage in its primary act, namely endurance.

article 3. is martyrdom an act of the highest perfection?

THE THIRD POINT: 1. It seems that martyrdom is not an act of the highest perfection. For apparently what relates to perfection in life is governed by counsel, not by precept, because it is not necessary for salvation. But martyrdom does appear to be necessary for salvation, for St Paul says, *We believe in our hearts to achieve justification, but we confess with our lips to gain salvation.* And in *John* we read, *We ought to lay down our lives for our brothers.* So martyrdom does not relate to perfection.

2. Moreover, to give one's life to God in obedience seems an act of greater perfection than to give one's life to God in martyrdom. So Gregory says that *obedience is preferred to all sacrificial victims. So* martyrdom is not an act of the highest perfection.

3. Moreover, it appears to be a better thing to be of service to others than to maintain oneself in virtue, for *the good of the race is higher than the good of the individual* as Aristotle says. But the man who endures martyrdom is of service to himself alone, whereas a teacher benefits many. So the act of teaching and guiding one's subjects is more perfect than the act of martyrdom.

ON THE OTHER HAND, Augustine places martyrdom before virginity, which is a mark of perfection. Therefore martyrdom appears to be a supreme mark of perfection.

REPLY: We can discuss any virtuous act in two ways. First, we can look at what kind of act it is in relationship to the virtue which most closely elicits it. In this sense martyrdom, the dutiful endurance of death, cannot be the most perfect of virtuous acts. For endurance of death is praiseworthy, not in itself but only as it is directed towards some good found in an act of virtue, for example faith, and love of God. Hence such an act of virtue is better than martyrdom, since it is the end in view.

Secondly, a virtuous act can be considered in relation to the primary impulse, that love which is charity. It is this above all which makes an act relevant to perfection in life. For as St Paul says, *charity is the bond of perfection.* Now of all acts of virtue martyrdom exhibits most completely the perfection of charity. For a man's love for a thing is demonstrated by the degree to which, for its sake, he puts aside the more cherished object and chooses to suffer the more hateful. Now obviously, of all blessings of life a man loves life itself most, and on the other hand hates death most, especially when accompanied by the pains of physical torture – from fear of these even brute animals *are deterred from the greatest pleasures,* as Augustine says. In this sense it is clear that of all human actions martyrdom is the most perfect in kind, being the mark of the greatest love. As St John says, *Greater love has no man than this, that a man should lay down his life for his friends.*

Hence: 1. There is no act of perfection subject to counsel which does not come under precept in some circumstances as necessary for salvation; for example, as Augustine states, a man is bound by the necessity of preserving continence because his wife is absent or ill. Therefore it in no way lessens the perfection of martyrdom if in some circumstance it is necessary for salvation. For there are situations in which the endurance of martyrdom is not necessary for salvation, for example, when we read that holy martyrs on numerous occasions sought martyrdom voluntarily, out of zeal of faith and love of their brethren. The precepts quoted are to be interpreted as referring to willingness of spirit.

2. Martyrdom embraces the highest possible form of obedience – namely, being obedient unto death, just as we read of Christ that *he became obedient unto death.* So it is clear that martyrdom is intrinsically more perfect than just any form of obedience.

3. The argument is based on martyrdom considered in the act's specific character, which does not make it excel all other virtuous acts, any more than courage excels all other virtues.

article 4. *is death essential to the idea of martyrdom?*

THE FOURTH POINT: 1. Death does not seem essential to the idea of martyrdom, for Jerome says, *I should be right to claim that the Mother of God was both virgin and martyr, though she ended her days peacefully.* And Gregory says, *Even though there may be no occasion of persecution, peace has its own martyrdom. For even if we do not actually place our necks beneath the steel, we inwardly slay our carnal desires with the sword of the spirit.* So martyrdom can exist without the suffering of death.

2. Moreover, we read that certain women held their lives in praiseworthy contempt in order to preserve their physical virginity. It seems that in such cases physical integrity of those who are chaste is preferable to life on earth. But there are occasions on which persons are robbed of that physical virginity, or an attempt is made to rob them of it, because they confess the Christian faith. This is clearly the case with Agnes and Lucy. So it appears that the term martyrdom should be used rather for a woman's loss of her physical virginity for belief in Christ, than for the further loss of other bodily life. This is why Lucy said, *If you cause me to be violated against my will, my chastity will be crowned twice over.*

3. Moreover, martyrdom is an act of courage. But courage means refusing to fear not only death, but also other adversities, as Augustine

says. Now there are many other adversities besides death which men can endure for belief in Christ: for example, prison, exile, seizure of property, as is clear in *Hebrews*. For this reason the martyrdom of pope St Marcellus is revered, though he died in prison. So it is not necessary to martyrdom to bear the pain of death.

4. Moreover, martyrdom is a meritorious act, as has been noted. But there can be no meritorious act after death, so it must be performed before death. So death is not essential to the idea of martyrdom.

ON THE OTHER HAND, Maximus says that *the martyr who would have suffered defeat by living without faith, prevails by dying for the faith.*

REPLY: As has been noted, the term 'martyr' means a witness to the Christian faith, by which we hold things visible of little account compared to things invisible, as we read in *Hebrews*. Therefore it is a necessary feature of martyrdom that a man should bear witness to his faith, showing in his action that he holds cheap all the things of this world in order to attain the invisible blessings which are to come. Now as long as physical life remains, a man has not yet shown in action a complete indifference to temporal things. For men usually despise both kin and all possessions, and even endure physical pain, to preserve their lives. Hence Satan objected against Job, *a man will give skin for skin, and all that he has, to save his life*, that is, his bodily life. Therefore the perfect idea of martyrdom requires one to endure death for Christ's sake.

Hence: 1. The authorities cited here, and others of the same kind, speak of martyrdom figuratively.

2. If a woman loses her physical virginity, or is condemned to lose it, because of her Christian faith, it is not clear to other people whether she suffers this for love of the Christian faith or because she puts little stock in chastity. Accordingly insufficient evidence is provided for human judgment by this action. So the deed does not strictly connote martyrdom. But in the judgment of God *who sees into men's hearts*, this act can be credited for reward, as Lucy said.

3. As has been noted earlier, courage is concerned chiefly with the dangers of death, but with other dangers in consequence. Therefore endurance of prison, exile, or loss of wealth does not in itself strictly connote martyrdom, except in so far as death follows these.

4. The merit of martyrdom does not come after death but lies in the voluntary endurance of death, in so far as one willingly endures his execution. It sometimes happens, however, that a man survives for a long time after being mortally wounded for Christ, or after other sufferings which continue until death and are endured at the hands of persecutors for belief in Christ. In this situation there is a meritorious act of martyrdom, even while he is actually enduring sufferings of this nature.

article 5. is faith the sole reason for martyrdom?

THE FIFTH POINT: 1. Faith appears to be the sole reason for martyrdom. For it is said, *None of you should suffer as if he were a murderer or thief* or other such, *but if he suffers as a Christian he should not be ashamed, but should glorify God in Christ's name.* Now a man is called a Christian because he has faith in Christ. Therefore only faith in Christ grants the glory of martyrdom to those who suffer.

2. Moreover, 'martyr' means witness. But witness can be given only to the truth. However, no man is called martyr for witnessing to any kind of truth, but only for witnessing to divine truth. Otherwise, if a man died in support of a truth of geometry or other speculative science, he would be a martyr, which is clearly absurd. Faith alone is then a reason for martyrdom.

3. Moreover, those deeds of virtue which are ordered to the common good seem better than all others, because *the good of the race is better than the good of the individual*, as Aristotle says. If then any other good were a reason for martyrdom, quite clearly those who die in defence of the state would be martyrs. But this the practice of the Church does not uphold, for no celebration of martyrdom is kept for soldiers who die in a just war. Faith only, therefore, appears to be a reason for martyrdom.

ON THE OTHER HAND, there is the statement, *Blessed are they who suffer persecution for justice's sake.* and this has reference to martyrdom, as the *Gloss* on this passage states. Now the other virtues, as well as faith, are associated with justice, so they also can be a cause of martyrdom.

REPLY: As was stated earlier, 'martyrs' means witnesses, because they bear witness to the truth by bodily sufferings which extend even to death, not to any truth, but to *the truth involved in our duty to God* which was made known to us through Christ. So 'martyrs of Christ' means witnesses to him. This kind of truth is the truth of faith, and accordingly the reason for each and every martyrdom is the truth of faith.

But this truth involves not merely inner belief, but also outward profession. Such a profession is achieved not merely by declaration of one's belief, but also through the actions by which a man shows that he possesses faith, in St James's words, *I will show you my faith by my deeds.* Hence too St Paul's judgment on certain persons. *They profess to know God. but they deny him by their deeds.* Hence all virtuous actions, in so far as they are related to God, are professions of the faith by which we know that God demands such works from us, and rewards us for them. In this sense such actions can be a cause of martyrdom, and this is why the martyrdom of St John the Baptist is observed in the Church, for he endured death not because he was required to deny his faith, but because he censured adultery.

Hence: 1. A Christian means one who belongs to Christ. Now a person is said to belong to Christ not simply because he believes in him, but also because he undertakes virtuous deeds in the Spirit of Christ, as St Paul says, *If a man does not possess the Spirit of Christ, he does not belong to him.* Further, in order to imitate Christ, he dies to sin, in St Paul's words, *Those who belong to Christ have crucified their flesh with its vices and evil desires.* Therefore not only the man who suffers for verbal confession of faith suffers as a Christian, but also the man who suffers in striving to perform any good act, or to avoid any evil one for Christ's sake, since all these actions are profession of one's faith.

2. The truth of other branches of knowledge is not connected with the worship of God; so it is not called the truth *unto reverence for him.* This is why profession of such truth cannot be a direct cause of martyrdom. Yet because, as we have seen, every lie is a sin no matter what truth is at stake, the refusal to lie can be a cause of martyrdom, for lying is contrary to the divine law.

3. The good of the community is pre-eminent amongst human goods. But divine good, the proper reason for martyrdom, is superior to any human good. Yet since a human good can become divine, for instance when directed to God, any human good can become a reason for martyrdom, inasmuch as it is directed to God.

Appendix 2

Broadening the Classical Concept of Martyrdom*

Karl Raher SJ

The aim of this article is to plead for a certain broadening of the traditional concept of martyrdom.

As it is used in the Church today, this traditional concept is well known. We are not concerned here with the question how it has developed in the course of the Church's history, what its relationship is to the biblical concept of martyrdom, or once again what the connection is between this New Testament concept and various related concepts and ideas such as proclamation, prophecy, confession, and death. Here we presuppose the concept of martyrdom that is traditional in the Church today: what is meant by this concept of dogmatic and fundamental theology is the free, tolerant acceptance of death for the sake of the faith, except in the course of an active struggle as in the case of soldiers. Faith includes Christian moral teaching, as, for example, is clearly shown by the fact that the Church honours as a martyr St Maria Goretti, who was stabbed to death in 1902 by a young man belonging to a neighbouring family because she vigorously resisted his advances Faith can involve the entirety of the Christian confession of faith or merely one single truth of Christian teaching on faith and morals, though of course this one single truth is always understood within the context of the entirety of the Christian message. Death *in odium fidei* must be consciously accepted, so that a distinction must be drawn between martyrdom and baptism of blood. What is specific about this concept is that as far as the Church is concerned today it excludes death in an active struggle. Our question therefore is whether this kind of exclusion of a death suffered in active struggle for the Christian faith and its moral demands (including those affecting society as a whole) must necessarily and always be linked with the concept of martyrdom. This question is of considerable weight for the life of individual Christians and of the Church, because the recognition of martyrdom with regard to a Christian

*Reprinted with kind permission of *Concilium*, Nijmegen, Netherlands where this article was published, under the title: 'Dimensions of Martyrdom: A Plea for the Broadening of a Classical Concept' in No. 163, pp. 9–11 (March 1983). Following this article, further articles were published in *Concilium* (January 2003) by Jose Ignacio Gonzales Faus on 'Witnesses to Love Killed by Hatred of Love' and by Felix Wilfred on 'Martyrdom in Religious Traditions'.

engaged in an active struggle or fight would mean a significant official recommendation by the Church of this kind of active struggle as an example worthy of imitation by other Christians.

To begin with it is obvious that concepts like the one we are dealing with here have a history and may legitimately vary. All that is involved is the question whether in this case tolerating and enduring death for the sake of the faith and enduring death in an active struggle for the faith (or for this or that of its demands) cannot be included under the single concept of martyrdom: both types of death share a wide-ranging and profound content in common, and bracketing the two in this kind of single concept would not deny a lasting difference between them. There are many concepts that bring two realities together because they in fact resemble each other without thereby denying or necessarily obscuring differences between them. (The concept 'sin' is used within the Church jointly for our inherited corruption and for the state of sin for which we are personally responsible, without any intention of denying a radical distinction between these two states of affairs.) It is of course correct that patiently enduring death for the sake of faith has a special relationship to the death of Jesus, who precisely by the death he endured has become the faithful and reliable witness *par excellence*. But this undeniable distinction between these two kinds of death does not exclude their being brought together under the single concept and term of martyrdom.

Much needs to be considered in order to see this and to bring out the inner and essential similarity between these two kinds of death alongside all the differences between them. First of all, the death Jesus 'passively endured' was the consequence of the struggle he waged against those in his day who wielded religious and political power. He died because he fought: his death must not be seen in isolation from his life. Putting this argument the other way around, someone who dies while fighting actively for the demands of his or her Christian convictions (which of course in certain circumstances can include the demands made on society as a whole) can also be said patiently to endure his or her death. It is not a death directly sought in itself. It includes a passive element, just as the death of a martyr in the usual sense includes an active element, since by his or her active witness and life this kind of martyr has conjured up the situation in which he or she can only escape death by denying his or her faith. The question may of course remain of how active struggle is to be more closely defined and marked off from similar activities so that death in this kind of active struggle can and should be treated as martyrdom. It is not everyone who dies on the Christian or more narrowly Catholic side in a religious war who should be described as a martyr. In practice in religious wars of this kind too many secular motives are included, and the question remains open whether everyone fighting in such wars was really prepared for his or her death and really accepted it. But, for example, why should not someone like Bishop Romero, who died while fighting for justice in society, a struggle he waged out of the depths of his conviction as a

Christian – why should he not be a martyr? Certainly he was prepared for his death.

We should not simply conceive of passively tolerating one's death only in the manner we are used to in the case of early Christian martyrs brought before a court and sentenced to death. There are quite different ways in which the passive but intentionally accepted toleration of death can occur. Contemporary persecutors of Christians do not give their victims any opportunity to confess their faith in the style of the earliest Christian centuries and to accept a death to which they are sentenced by a court. But nevertheless their death in these more anonymous forms of contemporary persecution of Christians can still be foreseen and accepted just as in the case of the old-style martyr. And indeed it can be foreseen and accepted as the consequence of an active struggle for justice and other Christian realities and values. What is in fact strange is that the Church has canonised Maximilian Kolbe as a confessor and not as a martyr.* An unprejudiced approach would pay more attention to how he behaved in the concentration camp and at his death than to his earlier life and would see him as a martyr of selfless Christian love.

In any case the distinctions between a death for the sake of the faith in active struggle for this faith and death for the sake of the faith in passive endurance are too fleeting and too difficult to define for one to have to go to the trouble of maintaining a precise conceptual and verbal apartheid between these two kinds of death. Underlying both is ultimately the same explicit and decided acceptance of death for the same Christian reasons. In both cases death is the acceptance of the death of Christ, an acceptance which as the supreme act of love and fortitude puts the believer totally at God's disposal, which represents the most radical unity in action of love and of enduring the ultimate helplessness in the face of man's incomprehensible yet effective rejection of God's self-revealing love. In both cases death appears as quite simply the perfect and public manifestation of the real essence of Christian death. Even when death is suffered in the struggle for Christian belief it is the witness of faith based on absolute determination springing from the grace of God, a determination that seeks to integrate the whole of existence up to and beyond death, in the midst of the most profound inward and outward powerlessness that the person concerned accepts with patience. This applies, too, to death in battle because, just like the passive martyr in the traditional sense, this fighter experiences and endures the power of evil and his own powerlessness in the experience of his outward failure.

In this plea for a certain broadening of the traditional concept of martyrdom we can appeal to Thomas Aquinas. Thomas says that someone is martyr through a death that is clearly related to Christ if he is defending society (*res publica*) against the attacks of its enemies who are trying to damage the

---

* Editor's note: since this article appeared Maximilian Kolbe has been elevated to the status of martyr. (See above, Chapter Four, p. 80.)

Christian faith and if in this defence he suffers death (In IV *Sent. dist.* 49 q. 5 a. 3 quaest. 2 ad 11). Damage to the Christian faith as is opposed by this kind of defender of society can of course be concerned with a single dimension of Christian belief, because otherwise even the passive toleration of death for the sake of a single demand of Christian faith or morals could not be termed martyrdom. In this way in his commentary on the Sentences Thomas is defending a more comprehensive concept of martyrdom such as is proposed here.

A legitimate 'political theology', a theology of liberation, should concern itself with this enlargement of the concept. It has a very down-to-earth practical significance for a Christianity and a Church that mean to be aware of their responsibility for justice and peace in the world.

Appendix 3

Non-Violent Options for Conflict Resolution in Islam

Harfiyah Haleem

Righting Wrongs: *Jihad* of the Tongue

The preaching of the Qur'an by the Prophet Muhammad (pbuh) could be classified as *jihad* of the tongue and pen to right wrongs in the world, as were the teachings of earlier prophets. Following this precedent, Muslims are told in the Qur'an that there should be 'a group of you inviting to what is good and forbidding what is bad' (3:10). The Prophet Muhammad (pbuh) said:

> There was never a Prophet sent before me by Allah to his nation who had not among his people (his) disciples and companions who followed his ways and obeyed his command. Then there came after them their successors who said that which they did not practise, and practised that which they were not commanded to do. He who strove against them with his hand was a believer, he who strove against them with his tongue was a believer, and he who strove against them with his heart was a believer, and beyond that there was no faith, not even as much as a mustard seed. (Hadith: Muslim)

The first caliphs of the Prophet understood that they were in power to serve the people, and were only ordinary human beings who could make mistakes. They urged the Muslims to correct them if they did wrong, and so they did. Later rulers were not so modest, but it remains the duty of the Muslims to correct them, as they must correct their imam in the prayer if he makes a mistake.

> The Messenger of Allah (pbuh) said: In the near future there will be Amirs and you will like their good deeds and dislike their bad deeds. One who sees through their bad deeds (and tries to prevent their repetition by his hand or through his speech), is absolved from blame, but one who hates their bad deeds (in the heart of his heart, being unable to prevent their recurrence by his hand or his tongue), is (also) safe (so far as God's wrath is concerned). But one who approves of their bad deeds and imitates them is spiritually ruined. People asked (the Prophet): Shouldn't we fight against them? He replied: No, as long as they say their prayers. (Hadith: Muslim)

151

The Prophet (peace be upon him) said: The best fighting (jihad) in the path of Allah is (to speak) a word of justice to an oppressive ruler. (Abu Dawud)

However, there are ways and ways of doing this. In some books of Islamic guidance, such as *The Reliance of the Traveller*,[1] a whole series of gradually escalating forms of admonition are set out, which explain the use of tact, and caution that any ultimate use of force must be with the permission of the authorities.

Jaw, Jaw – Not War, War

Talking to people to avoid potential conflicts occupies an important place in Islamic teachings. The Qur'an describes Muslims as people who decide their affairs by mutual consultation. The Prophet is also encouraged to be gentle with his people and to consult them before making decisions. Discussions with non-Muslims should be equally amicable and rational if at all possible:

[Believers], argue only in the best way with the People of the Book, except with those of them who act unjustly. Say, 'We believe in what was revealed to us and in what was revealed to you; our God and your God are one [and the same]; we are devoted to Him.' (29:46)

[Prophet], call people to the way of your Lord with wisdom and beautiful teaching. Argue with them in the most courteous way, for your Lord knows best who has strayed from His way and who is rightly guided. (16:125)

Even in the classical writings on Islamic law, it was seen as compulsory that an invitation to Islam should precede any attack on unbelievers. Their reaction to this call would then determine the course of action necessary. In some cases the reaction was swift and violent, in others it resulted in dialogue and the exchange of deputations and teachers, resulting either in conversion of the people to Islam or to a permanent treaty of friendship, with reciprocal obligations, like the one made by the Prophet with the Christians of Najran. Even time-limited treaties could be renewed as desirable.

Within the Islamic state, minorities who did not embrace Islam could come to an arrangement whereby they could enjoy the state's protection and welfare benefits in relation to a small tax that exempted them from military service and payment of *zakah* (Islamic welfare due).

Non-Muslims, even from hostile states actively at war with the Muslims, could be given state protection for up to a year to travel in Muslim lands for peaceful purposes, so long as they respected Islam and the Muslims and did not commit any punishable offence.

Propaganda

Where kindness and reason did not work, teasing and harsher criticism might be required. Some hadith also mention the use of satire as a weapon in the armoury of non-violent campaigning:

> Satirize the (non-believing amongst the) Quraysh, for (satire) is more grievous to them than the hurt of an arrow . . . (Hadith: Muslim)

Satirical poems in particular were a popular traditional Arab form of propaganda. The Prophet Muhammad (pbuh) understood the power of propaganda and, in some instances, punished hostile propagandists more harshly than those who fought against him physically. The Qur'an strongly condemns liars in matters of religion, saying:

> Who does greater wrong than someone who fabricates a lie against God or denies His revelation? Those who do such wrong will not prosper. (6:21)

Keeping out of Pointless Quarrels

The Qur'an urges people to avoid petty disputes, especially over religious matters in which they have little knowledge.

> Hold fast to God's rope all together; do not split into factions. Remember God's favour to you: you were enemies and then He brought your hearts together and you became brothers by His grace; you were about to fall into a pit of Fire and He saved you from it – in this way God makes His revelations clear to you so that you may be rightly guided . . . (3:103)

> Obey God and His Messenger, and do not quarrel with one another, or you may lose heart and your spirit may desert you. Be steadfast: God is with the steadfast. (8:46)

> Yet still there are some who, with no knowledge, argue about God, who follow every devilish rebel fated to lead astray those who take his side and guide them to the suffering of the blazing flame. (22:3–4)

Another form of pointless quarrelling the Prophet condemned was *asabiyyah*, mistranslated here as party-spirit, but sometimes also as nationalism, or tribalism:

> I questioned Allah's Messenger (pbuh) as follows, 'Messenger of Allah, does a man's love of his people indicate party-spirit (*asabiyyah*)?'
> He replied, 'No, but when a man helps his people in wrongdoing it indicates party-spirit.' (Hadith: Ahmed and Ibn Majah)

It is actually a form of *shirk* (associating partners with God) when a person puts love of his people before the command of Allah, and so does wrong in its name. *Asabiyyah* could equally well apply to party politics.

Peacemaking and Arbitration

When a serious quarrel does develop, the role of the Muslim, as of the Christian, should preferably be that of peacemaker. Jesus, in the Sermon on the Mount, said: 'Blessed are the peacemakers, for they shall attain peace.' The Qur'an, too, urges Muslims to make peace between quarrelling parties:

> If two groups of the believers fight, you [believers] should try to reconcile them; if one of them is [clearly] oppressing the other, fight the oppressors until they submit to God's command, then make a just and even-handed reconciliation between the two of them: God loves those who are even-handed. The believers are brothers, so make peace between your two brothers and be mindful of God, so that you may be given mercy. (49:9–10)

> There is no good in most of their secret talk, only in commanding charity, or good, or reconciliation between people. To anyone who does these things, seeking to please God, We shall give a rich reward ... (4:114)

In particular, the Prophet Muhammad (pbuh) is commanded to call the 'People of the Book' – Christians and Jews – to reconcile their differences with the Muslims and come together.

> Say, 'People of the Book, let us arrive at a statement that is common to us all: we worship God alone, we ascribe no partner to Him, and none of us takes others beside God as lords.' If they turn away, say, 'Witness our devotion to Him.' (3:64)

But, since not all will wish to do this, Muhammad (pbuh) is told:

> We sent to you [Muhammad] the Scripture with the truth, confirming the Scriptures that came before it, and with final authority over them: so judge between them according to what God has sent down. Do not follow their whims, which deviate from the truth that has come to you. We have assigned a law and a path to each of you. If God had so willed, He would have made you one community, but He wanted to test you through that which He has given you, so race to do good: you will all return to God and He will make clear to you the matters you differed about. (5:48)

The Prophet Muhammad tried constantly to bring people together and reconcile their views. He was a practised arbitrator and peacemaker from an early age when he arbitrated between the rival Meccan clans as to who would reinstate the sacred black stone in the wall of the Ka'bah (the sacred house of worship in Mecca) during its rebuilding. His skills as a peacemaker were the chief reason why he was invited to migrate to Yathrib, where the various local Arab and Jewish tribes were always in dispute and fighting. There he made an agreement with all the resident tribes that they would form one community with the Muslims who had migrated there. Although sometimes obliged to use force against hostile tribes, the Prophet, through his magnanimity towards his friends and enemies alike, lived to see Arabia united for the first time under his leadership:

> It was He who strengthened you with His help, and with the believers, and brought their hearts together in friendship. Even if you had given away everything in the earth you could not have done this, but God brought them together: God is mighty and wise. (8:62–63)

Repel Evil With What is Better

A key principle in Islam, as in Christianity, is to 'repel evil with what is better'. This is mentioned several times in the Qur'an, and earlier by Jesus. Where Jesus said, 'You have heard it said, "an eye for an eye and a tooth for a tooth", but I say unto you, "love your enemy"', the Qur'an says:

> In the Torah We prescribed for them a life for a life, an eye for an eye, a nose for a nose, an ear for an ear, a tooth for a tooth, an equal wound for a wound: if anyone forgoes this out of charity, it will serve as atonement for his bad deeds. Those who do not judge according to what God has revealed are doing grave wrong. (5:45)

> If you [people] have to respond to an attack, make your response proportionate, but it is best to stand fast. (16:126)

> Good and evil cannot be equal. [Prophet], repel evil with what is better and your enemy will become as close as an old and valued friend . . . (41:34)

But it then goes on to say:

> . . . but only those who are steadfast in patience, only those who are blessed with great righteousness, will attain to such goodness. If a prompting from Satan should stir you, seek refuge with God: He is the All Hearing and the All Knowing. (41:35–36)

This last warning is one of several in the Qur'an where believers are taught not to follow their desires, so that they can do justice impartially (see 5:48; 4:13 above). In addition to the Qur'anic advice to 'seek refuge in Allah' to combat such 'whispers from the devil' the Prophet Muhammad (pbuh) also urged his followers to restrain their anger, and taught a practical method of doing so, by sitting down, then lying down.

There are many noble examples of repelling evil with good in Muslim history, starting, of course, with the practice of the Prophet himself (pbuh). After he was stoned in Ta'if when seeking protection, he prayed for forgiveness for the perpetrators, and after the Meccans finally succumbed and many finally accepted Islam, he forgave nearly all his enemies and plied them with gifts to reconcile them, to the extent that the Muslims were jealous, and he had to ask them whether they would rather have him (the Prophet) or the money. Later examples include the Caliph Umar, who refused to pray in the Christian church when he conquered Jerusalem, on the grounds that it might set a precedent for the Muslims to lay claim to it as a mosque; and Salah-ad-Din (Saladin), who was renowned as the most magnanimous of foes by the Crusaders, and sent snow, for example, to cool the fever of King Richard I, his enemy.

Peaceful Demonstrations

During the early period of persecution in Mecca the first attempt to persuade the Meccans by a peaceful 'demonstration' took place. The Muslims marched unarmed to the Ka'bah in Mecca, where their way was blocked by guards and they were stoned. The situation was saved by the Prophet's uncle, Hamza, a respected and feared man of action, who publicly announced his support for the Prophet and challenged members of the hostile crowd to fight him, at which point they began to disperse.

The second, more successful 'demonstration' came later, when the Muslims had migrated to Medina. After three battles against aggressive armies from Mecca, the Prophet had a dream about taking a pilgrimage to Mecca. Accordingly, the Muslims, virtually unarmed, went towards Mecca in their pilgrim garb, with their sacrificial animals. The Meccans sent troops to provoke them but they just stood their ground, and this led to the treaty of Hudaybiyah, which enabled Islam to spread peacefully to the remaining people of Mecca, including its leaders who had been the Prophet's worst enemies.

There is a whole chapter of the Qur'an devoted to this event, the title of which is *al-Fat-h* ('the victory/opening'). The root for this Islamic word is *fataha* ('to open'); it is not, in the Qur'an, applied to any military victory, only to this peaceful one and to the capitulation of Mecca, both of which resulted in the opening of people's hearts. In Surat *al-Fat-h* the word *fat-h* appears three times (48:1, 18, 27), and so does the word *sakina* ('calm', 'tranquillity'). Allah sent down His *sakina* on the hearts of the believers, making them calm in the face of provocation on the part of the unbelievers. This is the essence of pacifism and non-violence, in which a positive force of spiritual peace, faith, moral resolve and conviction, even love, sent directly from God, has the power to counteract and overcome fear, emotional turmoil and hostility.

Modern Islamic Non-violent Campaigns

The Shi'i tradition, mainly to be found in Iran nowadays, but also in Pakistan, Iraq, Lebanon and Eastern Arabia, enshrined, amongst other things, a quietist strain of resistance to oppression, since the early Shi'as rarely achieved political autonomy, despite many violent struggles. One of the first imams, al-Hassan, agreed to abdicate rather than cause dissent in the community and another, Ja'afar al-Sadiq, preferred scholarship and spiritual leadership to fighting, although other descendants of the Prophet Muhammad (pbuh), like al-Hussein and Imam Zayd, and later the Fatimid dynasty, engaged in open rebellion and warfare.

More recently, much of the Iranian revolution was carried out by peaceful means, although there were some groups, more or less influenced by communist propaganda and subversion, or the CIA, who were willing to commit terrorist acts and assassinations. The Muslim brotherhood in Egypt and in other places nowadays prefers peaceful means of influencing and organizing people to campaign for Islamic values and behaviour. Islamists have gained power peacefully in Malaysia and Turkey, by democratic means, and in Algeria, they were about to do the same until the elections were annulled by the government.

Conscientious Objection

Conscientious objection, too, has an integral place in Islam, from the very start, since 'There is no obedience to any creature in disobedience to the Creator.' Muslims are *not allowed* to obey a command from anyone that causes them to do an act forbidden by God.

> The Prophet (pbuh) sent an army and appointed a certain man as their commander. The man made a fire and then said (to the soldiers), 'Enter it.' Some of them intended to enter it while some others said, 'We have run away from it [i.e. embraced Islam to save ourselves from the "Fire"].' They mentioned that to the Prophet (pbuh) and he said about the people who had intended to enter the fire, 'If they had entered it, they would have remained in it till the Day of Resurrection.' Then he said to others, 'No obedience for evil deeds, obedience is required only in what is good.' (Hadith: Bukhari)

During the first civil war between Muslims, a group of people refused to fight on either side on the grounds that the war was wrong. They were called the *Qa'ada*.[2] The Qur'an forbids Muslims to fight those who refused to fight against them and against their own people (4:90), so long as they 'withdraw from you but fight you not, and send you (guarantees of) peace'.

That there have not been many celebrated instances of this phenomenon in Islamic history may reflect the fact that most of the fighting done by Muslims was in self-defence and/or was fully endorsed by those involved. There is no 'conscription' in the Qur'an. The Prophet is instructed only to 'urge on the believers' (4:64). The Qur'an – and the Hadith at greater length – urge the Muslim fighters (those who are defending themselves or the oppressed) in the strongest way, by showing the just cause, showing the bad conduct of the enemy and promising great rewards in the afterlife for those who make such sacrifices.[3] The exhortations in the Qur'an to Muslims to fight 'in the cause of God' (for example, 4:95) also bear witness that not everyone actually did so. Even when some Muslims 'turned back' at the Battle of Uhud, in a premature bid to take booty, so causing the Muslims to lose the battle, the Qur'an endorses the 'lenient' attitude of the Prophet (pbuh) towards them (3:159).

Notes

1   Ibn Naqib al-Misri, *The Reliance of the Traveller*, trans. Nuh Ha Mim Keller (Evanston, Sunna Books, 1994).
2   See, for example, 3:169–72; 9:120–21 and many hadiths in the chapters on *jihad* in many collections of hadiths.
3   *Encyclopaedia of Islam*.

Index